Early Years
Management in
Practice

Early Years
Management in
Practice

Maureen Daly

Elisabeth Byers

Wendy Taylor

www.heinemann.co.uk
✓ Free online support
✓ Useful weblinks
✓ 24 hour online ordering

01865 888058

Heinemann

Inspiring generations

Heinemann Educational Publishers
Halley Court, Jordan Hill, Oxford OX2 8EJ
Part of Harcourt Education

Heinemann is the registered trademark of
Harcourt Education Limited

Text © Elisabeth Byers, Maureen Daly, Wendy Taylor 2004
First published 2004

09 08 07 06
10 9 8 7 6 5 4

British Library Cataloguing in Publication Data is available from the British Library on
request.

10-digit ISBN 0 435401 40 8
13-digit ISBN 978 0 435401 40 5

Designed by Artistix
Typeset by TechType, Abingdon, Oxon

Original illustrations © Harcourt Education Limited, 2004

Illustrated by TechType, Abingdon, Oxon

Cover design by Wooden Ark Studio

Printed in the UK by Scotprint

Cover photo: © Corbis

Acknowledgements
Every effort has been made to contact copyright holders of material reproduced in this book.
Any omissions will be rectified in subsequent printings if notice is given to the publishers.

Websites
Please note that the websites suggested in this book were up to date at the time of writing. It
is essential for tutors to preview each site before using it to ensure that the URL is still
accurate and the content is appropriate. We suggest that tutors bookmark useful sites and
consider enabling students to access them through the school or college intranet.

The authors

Elisabeth Byers qualified as a nursery nurse and then started her career in the United States, where she worked in a kindergarten and in a hospital for sick children as a volunteer. She returned to the UK to work in a school, when she worked with nursery, reception and year 1 children, and became involved in managing an out-of-school club. In addition to this she worked as supply cover for day care centres, when she worked with 0–5-year-olds. She has been teaching at Oaklands College in Hertfordshire since 1998 on a range of early years courses, including those leading to the CCE, DCE, NVQ and Foundation Degree qualifications. As Coordinator for Early Years Placements she is responsible for managing the placement process for each student.

Maureen Daly spent over 20 years working in a variety of early years settings and also managed an early years establishment. She has been a lecturer in early years in colleges of further education, teaching on a variety of courses in childcare and education at all levels. Since 2001 she has worked at Oaklands College, where she has been Curriculum Leader in Care and Early Years, Programme Leader for the Sector Endorsed Foundation Degree in Childhood Studies and Coordinator of the Centre of Vocational Excellence. For the last three years she has also been an External Moderator for awarding body CACHE.

Wendy Taylor has been involved in childcare and education since 1977. She originally trained as an early years teacher at the University of East Anglia. She moved into pre-school work after the birth of her children, and eventually managed her own setting. She has worked at Oaklands College for 10 years, training classroom assistants, nursery nurses, nannies, childminders, babysitters and pre-school workers. She is Coordinator of the CACHE Diploma in Childcare and Education and a Teaching and Learning Leader. She has also assessed settings for the Herts Quality Standards Accreditation Scheme.

Contents

Acknowledgements

The authors would like to thank their colleagues and friends for their ongoing interest and encouragement. They would like to particularly thank Fiona Marks, the Nursery Manager at Oaklands College, for her willingness to participate in this project and her never-ending patience. The authors also gratefully acknowledge the help received from Mary James at Heinemann and Ralph Footring, freelance editor.

Elisabeth Byers would like personally to thank her son, Joseph, who was beginning to think that play was no longer important at home, and his grandparents for the extra hours of babysitting they did during the writing of this book.

Maureen Daly would like to thank her wonderful children, Emma, James, David, Katy and Sophie, for their patience. She also thanks Joy McEwen, Maura Pigram and her sister, Cathy North, and lastly Lucia Federici, Nursery Owner and Foundation Degree Student, for all their support.

Wendy Taylor thanks all the people living in her house – Kevin, Leza and Adam, Natty and Fly (the dogs) – for their love, support and obvious enjoyment of take-away meals. She also thanks Beryl, Stan, Lynda, David, Matthew, James, Emma and Claire for their childcare wisdom, and proof-reading.

The author and publisher would like to thank the following individuals and organisations for permission to reproduce photographs:

Alamy Images UK – pages 151, 223, 253; Corbis – page 171; Getty Images – page 183; Harcourt Education Ltd/Gareth Boden – pages 19, 37, 75, 76 108; Harcourt Education Ltd/Haddon Davies – pages 3, 33, 98, 114 122, 130; Harcourt Education Ltd/Bea Ray – page 159; Harcourt Education Ltd/Gerald Sunderland – page 49

Introduction

'Childcare can make a positive difference to children, parents and communities – helping to tackle child poverty, improve children's achievements at school, enable parents to choose work as a route out of poverty, improve health and reduce crime.' (Department for Education and Skills and Department for Work and Pensions, 2002)

The government's review of childcare in 2002 emphasised the importance of providing children with quality facilities and highlighted the effect such provision has on children and communities. It acknowledged that, in the long term, high quality childcare enhances a child's life by improving opportunities and achievements, and counteracting the effects of poverty and crime. The early years are an exceptionally important phase of the child's life, in that they determine the person's achievements in later life. The review also concluded that it would be very beneficial if services such as early education, childcare, health and family support could be provided 'under one roof'.

The review generated a public expectation of further investment, expansion of new and existing provision, more emphasis on health and family support, and a strengthened role for local authorities in ensuring delivery. There has also been a subtle change in the expectations of the performance of childcare and education workers. The importance of their role has been publicly acknowledged and the significance of training high quality staff to meet demands has been discussed.

There is an emphasis on the expansion of provision for the education of children in their early years, while still maintaining high quality practice. On 31 March 2003, there were 99,300 registered childcare providers in England; 68,200 of these were childminders and 31,100 day care providers. By March 2006 the intention is to raise 250,000 new full- or part-time childcare places with start-up grants for childminders, nurseries and after-school activities to encourage new providers to set up business. Through the SureStart programme (started in 1998) childcare will be more affordable, as £325 million will be made available per year within the Working Tax Credit and more information will be made available to parents through local children's information services.

The world of early years education and childcare is therefore changing, and in the current climate early years professionals are at the forefront of the government agenda. It could be argued that never before have early years professionals had such a high profile. It is essential therefore that all childcare workers and managers have as much knowledge as possible to carry forward the latest strategies and plans for the care and education of children. An early years manager in particular needs to have the vision, knowledge and experience to lead the team and to stay informed about current thinking and expectations.

This book aims to clarify some of the issues that concern new managers and to provide an in-depth knowledge of the current framework for early years services. It considers some of the expectations and responsibilities associated with the manager's role. Frequently asked questions that are investigated within the book include:

- What do I need to do to start up a nursery?
- How do I prepare for an Ofsted inspection?
- How do I recruit and select staff?
- What knowledge do I need to meet current learning requirements?
- How do I manage relationships with the parents/carers?
- How do I ensure the children are treated fairly and kindly within the setting?
- How should I manage the staff team?
- How do I ensure we are a really effective team?
- What other things will I be expected to know?

You will probably ask yourself these and many more questions. The confidence you have as a manager will depend upon the reasons why you became one (or are seeking to become one) in the first place. These could include any of the following:

- You were an experienced childcare and education worker who was qualified to level 3, and you had the opportunity to cover for a manager while she or he was absent and then the post became vacant.
- You were a deputy manager with post-qualifying experience (level 3 qualification and at least 2 years' experience, as required by Ofsted).
- You wanted to move away from working solely with the children and become involved in the running of the setting.
- You were inspired by another manager (a role model).
- You felt that you had been poorly managed and that, given the opportunity, you could do a better job!
- You were interested in the status and better salary.
- You set up your own early years setting and thus became a manager.
- You had been on an advanced course and felt you had the knowledge to take on a new role.

Whatever your reasons for becoming a manager, you will no doubt be eager to build on your skills and further your knowledge in order to do an effective job and enhance the experience being offered to the children in your care.

Many experienced managers have never actually attended any formal management training and more recently appointed managers may not have had the opportunity to do so. The Early Years Development and Childcare Partnerships in all areas (see below) are a good source of training opportunities for staff in early years settings and occasionally run courses for managers which are specific and designed to support managers with certain aspects of the work. The local further education college or training agency will also provide training opportunities for people working at this level, but management may be just one element of a course that also explores other areas of early childhood studies. There is also the option of doing a generic management course, designed for people managing in all walks of life; this has limitations, as such courses will not be designed to meet the specific needs of an early years manager.

If you are a student on an advanced course in childcare or a foundation degree in childhood studies, you will also be able to use this book as a study guide for many of the subjects you will be exploring in your course, not only those directly looking at management.

The authors have used their own experience to produce a book for current or potential managers in early years settings. We have summarised the core issues for childcare practice and linked these issues to generic management practice. We wanted to recognise the reader's existing experiences while drawing attention to new and developing theories as well as long-standing and tested theories. The aim is to give you practical ideas on how to manage while ensuring you have opportunities to reflect on your current practice and review it in light of theorists who have based their findings on research.

We have also highlighted the statutory requirements for early years settings. To varying degrees the four nations comprising the UK have their own legislation. That relating to England is generally presented by way of explication, and readers are advised to check what applies in their own area. The 4 Nations Child Policy Network (4NCPN) (www.childpolicy.org.uk) provides information about policy, consultations and legislation that relate to children across the UK. The 4NCPN is a partnership between:

- the National Children's Bureau (www.ncb.org.uk);
- Children in Northern Ireland (www.ci-ni.org.uk);
- Children in Scotland (www.childreninscotland.org.uk);
- Children in Wales (www.childreninwales.org.uk).

This policy network is a valuable source of information for early years managers.

To make the book 'researcher-friendly' the following features have been included:

- case studies – scenarios and examples from practice, with questions to encourage you to reflect on your current practice;
- figures and tables – to highlight examples, summarise theories and demonstrate models of working;
- 'think it over' boxes – opportunities to look back at what you have read and collect your thoughts (these would also be useful as subjects for a seminar or discussion within a taught class or to provide a focus for team meetings or in-house training);
- good practice checklists;
- top tips;
- 'find it out' ideas for further research;
- at the end of every chapter questions to check your learning, consolidate your ideas and reflect on practice;
- lists of references and further reading;
- a selection of useful websites, including those of the principal organisations, within each chapter.

The early years curriculum has changed significantly over the last few years and workers must have very up-to-date knowledge of the legislation governing the education of the children they are working with. The foundation stage curriculum provides staff with a clear framework from which to plan activities and fits naturally between *Birth to Three Matters* (Department for Education and Skills, 2002) for younger children and the national curriculum. Managers must ensure that the children in their care benefit from a carefully planned, inclusive environment that reflects national expectations and meets their developmental needs. This means having experience and working knowledge of child development and the ability to encourage staff to reflect upon their practice and provide a stimulating, exciting and challenging environment in which children want to learn. There is also a need for managers to understand the ways in which children learn, and this will require knowledge of the work of theorists such as Jean Piaget and Lev Vygotsky.

The quality of the provision will depend greatly on the ability of the team to plan successfully and to use observational techniques to evaluate its success. Many early years professionals find the cycle of planning, implementing and evaluating daunting. Indeed, it can be a confusing aspect of the job. Many people also find it difficult to document the process. Difficulties can arise when the team is not clear about the terminology used and time needs to be given to working together to decide on the following points:

- What do we mean by 'the curriculum'?
- How do we plan to cover all aspects of the foundation stage?

- What are the differences between long-term, medium-term and short-term planning?
- What forms can be used to record the plans for each session?
- How can play be incorporated?
- How can individual educational plans be incorporated?
- How will the child's progress be monitored and assessed?
- What records will be kept?

All these issues are discussed within the book, as it is necessary for managers to have a clear understanding of these points in order to lead and guide their team.

As part of the present guidelines for high quality learning and care, the manager is required to ensure that there is an effective and productive partnership with parents. Parents are the most important people in children's lives. They are children's first educators and generally know their child best of all. It is therefore not surprising that research has shown that high quality relationships between the setting and parents and carers have a positive effect on children and their long-term learning. Through high quality relationships, settings are able to help parents to increase their understanding and knowledge of their child's development and education, as well as enable early years practitioners to build a profile of each child. This valuable knowledge of each child informs the selection and planning of appropriate activities and experiences. High quality partnerships with parents and carers are too important to be left to chance and should be carefully planned and managed.

Managers are also accountable for ensuring that they maintain high quality provision. Quality encompasses all areas of the setting, not just those linked directly with children. The environment, staffing, resources, finances and relationships with parents and carers all affect the standard of provision. The level of quality and availability in each of these areas can differ greatly between settings; therefore it could be argued that there cannot be a universal measure of quality. However, there are guidelines and quality indicators drawn from good practice and National Standards that enable you to develop the best possible practice for young children and their families.

The management of an early years setting is not an easy task. It is fraught with everyday hurdles and potential difficulties that even the most experienced manager will find a challenge. For most, this challenge is a worthwhile one and managers gain a great deal of job satisfaction in running a setting, even on the difficult days! To be an effective manager you need to have a cohesive team. Managers cannot do it alone and they need to ensure that they are working with their team to create the right kind of atmosphere for cohesiveness. In any early years setting the quality of management and team working will have a profound effect on the service offered to children, parents and carers. It is essential in the current climate of accountability that the manager is aware of the importance of creating a vision within the setting, and that the staff team are committed to it and share the same ethos and set of goals and standards.

To do this, managers have both to learn leadership skills and to create their own style of management. The book explores the notion of leadership and clarifies the skills a manager needs to lead a team effectively. How you set about learning such skills will depend upon your previous experiences and on the expectations of the post. There is a plethora of research and theory on how the manager's role is best implemented. The role of a manager is to manage the day-to-day workings of the setting but it is also to inspire and motivate the staff team to provide high quality care for young children. An effective manager will work with the team and ensure that they are all involved in the development of good practice. In this way the individual team members will take ownership of what is going on in their setting and feel valued as a result. It is also necessary for the manager to be able to encourage evaluation as part of the process of building a team, as this can be a very useful tool in implementing further changes. Evaluation and review are good practice and will need to be evidenced for the purpose of inspection by Ofsted.

Managers of early years settings must be open to new ideas and prepared to initiate change within their setting. The Green Paper *Every Child Matters* (Department for Education and Skills, 2003) highlights the need for inter-agency collaboration and early intervention. This call for professionals to work together will mean that today's early years manager will need a broad and in-depth knowledge of their setting and the services available to the children and their families. The National Childcare Strategy aims to improve the quality of childcare and make it more affordable for families. Local Early Years Development and Childcare Partnerships are working closely with providers to ensure that this happens. Early years managers have a very important role to play in the national picture and in supporting this drive to make each child 'matter'.

Throughout the text, frequent mention is made of the Early Years Development and Childcare Partnerships. These represent one of the major recent developments in the early years field. It is the responsibility of the local authorities to convene these Partnerships and to include in their membership all local groups with an interest in childcare. The Partnerships are responsible for the strategic overview of childcare in their area and there are 150 of them across the UK. They are responsible for:

- building up new services in disadvantaged areas (this is a priority);
- supporting all professional and voluntary services in the provision of a more unified service for families;

- consultation and planning;
- allocation of funds at a local level to establish new and develop existing services;
- promoting training opportunities within the early years sector (this is as part of the national recruitment targets for increasing the numbers of workers in early years).

As an early years manager it is vital that you build strong links with your local Early Years Development and Childcare Partnership. It will be a very useful source of information on further training and funding. The Partnerships often provide fully or partly funded training and will offer advice on how to put together a training programme for your staff. They will usually have strong links with the Jobcentres, the Pre-school Learning Alliance and the National Childminding Association.

The general public are well informed about what they should expect in terms of good quality childcare. Parents and carers are more aware of their right to be involved in the care and education of their children and will want to know that the setting will provide a flexible and accessible service which involves them if they wish and which respects them as the child's first educator. The setting will need a strong ethos to convince parents, carers and children that this is a place worth coming to and that children are treated with respect and kindness. The diverse needs of individual children and their families will need to be paramount, within an inclusive ethos.

Historically, children were not valued as part of our society. In the UK this is changing and there is now legislation that protects children as vulnerable members of our society.

Early years managers are constantly striving to make current provision better, by evaluating and reviewing the following:

- the ethos of the setting – a mission statement and supportive atmosphere are required;
- kindness to children – all of the setting's policies should reflect the need for kindness towards and respect for individual children and their families;
- values and attitudes – these underpin working practices and staff should be given the opportunity to reflect upon them;
- skills of managers – all managers need good communication and leadership skills;
- qualities of teams – good working practices can be used not only internally but in working with wider teams and the community when necessary;
- parental input – a basic requirement of the Children Act 1989 and a prerequisite for a child to settle in;

- children's self-esteem – research has shown that giving children this good start will ensure that they have a better chance to become well rounded and confident adults;
- the development and personal growth of staff – so that they can feel valued and confident in their role as professionals.

This book explores all these issues in more detail. You will be asked to reflect on your own ideas and ways of working, and relate them to theories relating to early years management, care and education. The purpose of this is that you broaden your theoretical knowledge and reflect on your present and future practice. Happy reading and researching!

A note on terminology

First, the 'manager' is the person in day-to-day charge of the setting. The manager is generally but need not be the 'registered person' (the one whose name appears on the certificate of registration for the setting). For example, in the case of privately owned nurseries a manager is often recruited by an owner (the registered person) who does not wish to perform the management role in the day-to-day running of the setting. A 'nominated person' is required to act as the point of contact for the Office for Standards in Education – referred to as Ofsted throughout the text.

The term 'setting' is generally used in the text to refer to any sort of organisation that provides early years care and education, such as nurseries and pre-schools.

The terms 'parent', 'carer' and 'family' collectively refer to anyone who is responsible for the child, whether on a long- or short-term basis. Sometimes these responsible adults are the child's biological parents but they could be other adults who are involved in caring for and bringing up the children. Children's primary carers may be:

- grandparents;
- childminders;
- older siblings;
- foster carers;
- guardians;
- step-parents;
- members of the extended family.

In this book 'parents and carers' is used to refer in short-hand to the child's primary carers.

Elisabeth Byers
Maureen Daly
Wendy Taylor
May 2004

References

Department for Education and Skills (2002) *Birth to Three Matters. A Framework to Support Children in their Earliest Years.* London: DfES. An introduction to the framework is available at www.surestart.gov.uk/_doc/0-ACA52E.pdf. Copies can be ordered from DfES Publications, Nottingham, telephone 0845 602 2260.

Department for Education and Skills (2003) *Every Child Matters*, Cm 5860. London: DfES. Available at www.dfes.gov.uk/everychildmatters/downloads.cfm.

Department for Education and Skills and Department for Work and Pensions (2002) SureStart leaflet. Available at www.surestart.gov.uk/.

1 Management and Leadership

There has been an immense amount of material written about management and leadership over the last 50 years. There is clear evidence of the relationship between how staff are managed and how they perform. The deeper the commitment of the staff to their organisations, the better their performance will be. In the early years sector you need to ascertain how you can use this relationship between management and staff to provide the best quality of care for young children.

This chapter looks at the nature of leadership and management. It covers the following areas:

1.1 What does a manager do?

1.2 The need for leadership.

1.3 Leadership and management theories.

1.4 What makes an effective early years manager and leader?

1.1 What does a manager do?

> 'A leader shapes and shares a vision which gives point to the work of others.' (Handy, 1992)

> 'The manager must be able to build and lead the staff team and cope with day-to-day management issues. The manager must also act as the public face of the nursery.' (Jameson and Watson, 1998, p. 67)

You will have done some managing in your everyday life, perhaps by organising an evening out, journey or holiday with others. You will no doubt have had conversations with your tutor about your 'time management skills' and ways of improving them. You will also have had widely different experiences of being managed by others and will be aware of the difference a manager can make to your working life. It may seem difficult to define precisely what a manager is or does, but the manager should be the linchpin to the smooth running of an organisation.

The manager can be perceived in the following ways:

- the person who makes the decisions;
- the person who is ultimately responsible;
- the person everyone goes to with their problems;
- someone who passes on information given to him or her by a higher authority;
- a person who controls and organises the people in the team;
- someone who has to come up with ideas and set examples for the people in the team.

In order to understand what a manager does, it may be helpful first to consider your own experiences to ascertain why you might react in the way you do to instructions or requests from a manager. It could be that you have had a poor experience in the past that has left you feeling that you cannot trust managers, or you may have had good experiences of being managed and feel open to a manager's ideas and plans. You may have had a managerial or coordination role within an early years setting and therefore have some empathy for the manager's role and responsibilities. Look at the case study 'The swan story'.

Case study — The swan story

As a manager of an early years setting there are times when you feel overwhelmed with new guidelines and government initiatives, endless book-keeping and forms to fill in. The last inspection action plan and the preparation for the next inspection are all firmly lodged in the back of your mind during every working day. The parents want answers, the staff want clarity and the children want your attention (which is usually the easiest to provide). This is all on-going and is in addition to the day-to-day trials of resource shortages, leaking taps, letters to go out to parents, visitors to take around, and so on. While all these challenges are whirling about in your mind, you need to remain calm, consistent and always in charge of what is happening.

A close colleague once compared me, as manager, to a swan. 'Ah!' I said, 'Do you mean beautiful and regal?' 'No,' she replied, 'gliding along the water looking calm and collected while underneath the water your little feet are flapping and moving furiously to keep you afloat!' I think I might have preferred 'beautiful and regal' but I think she was probably right: in order to meet the expectations of the children, parents and staff you must appear in control and professional at all times. To do this is difficult as, underneath that exterior, you are working furiously to keep things going. This was some years ago, but I have read other versions of the 'Swan story' in early years management, which have assured me that I was not the only manager to feel like that!

- What has been your experience of being managed so far?
- Have you experienced different styles of management?
- List some of the things your managers did. Do you feel these tasks were necessary?
- If you could change anything about the way your manager worked, what would you change?

Most managers of early years settings are keen to show them off to visitors.

After looking at the case study you will probably have come up with a variety of ways in which you feel you have been managed. You may also have had some thoughts on how these particular managers could have been more effective or supportive. The management of early years settings requires particular skills and knowledge. An early years manager will be required to do the following:

- ensure a good quality service;
- lead and support the staff team;

- provide adequate resources to ensure the smooth running of the setting;
- work in partnership with parents and carers;
- liaise with external agencies;
- ensure that relevant policies, procedures and records are maintained;
- provide a safe, secure and stimulating environment for the children.

Later chapters look at many of these aspects of the role of the manager in more detail, but by way of introduction each of these aspects is briefly discussed below.

Ensure a good quality service

Managers need to be in tune with the needs of people using the setting. They need to ensure that the wishes of the parents, carers and children can be met, and that the setting is a place where parents and carers will want to leave their children and where, indeed, the children will be happy to stay. Without knowing the expectations of the 'customers' (prospective as well as current) the setting will find it very difficult to provide a quality service. The quality of the provision can be measured only against the views of the customers, which requires an evaluation of their needs.

Managers also need to ensure that the setting is meeting various legislative requirements (see Chapters 8 and 9) as well as the requirements of the regulatory body Ofsted (the Office for Standards in Education). Ofsted provides guidance on how to meet the National Standards – a set of outcomes which providers of early years care and education should aim to achieve, and which are detailed in Chapter 2.

In addition to the requirements of the Ofsted inspection process, many settings will also choose to work towards other quality management awards (see also Chapter 7). One such quality management system is that developed by Investors in People (IIP), discussed below. Although such systems and awards may not be specifically designed for early years settings, they can be used as a standard of quality in any business and consequently are used by many nurseries, schools and day care establishments. Parents and carers will also recognise this as the setting's commitment to quality.

The Investors in People approach to ensuring a quality service

The IIP standard is well recognised and IIP offers advice and guidance to its members. The guidance it produces on leadership and management can be a useful tool for managers. Investors in People (2003, p. 5) has stated that: 'Good management and leadership are pivotal to investment, productivity, service and performance – and the need for better leadership and management can only increase.' This increasing need led IIP to produce a leadership and management model as part of its family of support models. IIP has stated that:

> 'In a climate of relentless change, pressure and responsibility, where managers are under constant scrutiny, almost all organisations feel the need for guidance on leadership and management issues ... this is as important to the small entrepreneur as to the leader of 1000 people.' (Investors in People, 2003)

To help organisations improve their leadership and management, IIP has designed a model based on four basic principles – the 'tried and tested four principle framework of the Investors in People standard, which thousands of organisations have used to improve their performances through their people':

- commitment;
- action;
- planning;
- evaluation.

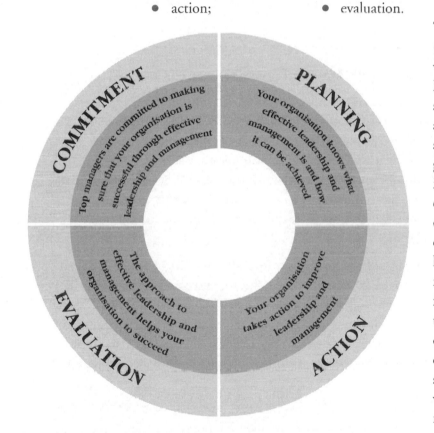

The model (Figure 1.1) (Investors in People, 2003), which is based on the 'real-life good practices of successful organisations', applies well to early years settings. IIP says that getting management wrong in a smaller organisation can have very serious consequences. It deliberately does not define leadership and management, because IIP feels that this is impossible to do, as the terms mean different things to each organisation. It also suggests that this could be why so few of the 2000 management theory books published each year can come up with a definition.

Figure 1.1. Investors in People model.

- What is Investors in People?
- What are its main aims?
- When did it form?
- You can find out more from its website, www.investorsinpeople.org.uk.
- You may also want to look into the work of the Penn Green Research, Development and Training Base and Leadership Centre (see www.pengreen.org).

Lead and support the staff team

It will be the responsibility of the manager to lead, motivate and support the members of the team. The staff will need nurturing and support for further professional development, as well as support in performing their own role within the setting. This particular area is considered further under section 1.2, 'The need for leadership', and also in Chapter 7, 'Developing a team'.

Provide adequate resources to ensure the smooth running of the setting

The principal resource of an early years setting is its staff – be they childcare workers, teachers, unqualified care assistants, students on placement, kitchen staff, caretakers, gardeners, contracted workers or agency staff. Proper use of this resource will involve the manager in timetabling work rotas for part-time and full-time staff, recruitment and selection of staff, professional development and statutory training in, for example, first aid and food hygiene, the appraisal and mentoring of staff, and leading staff meetings (see Chapter 6).

The manager will need to look at priorities for resources. These will depend upon the type of setting. Ofsted requires health and safety to be a priority and this is always checked during inspections. The manager may not be the budget holder but will have responsibility for ensuring that new equipment is purchased as and when necessary. The staff will need to understand how to use the equipment for the benefit of the children and this could require special training.

Not all resources are financial. For example, the manager should work with the staff to make use of all the space available to them. It is also important to maximise the use of staff time as a resource, and to match the staff to the needs of the children. It is the manager's job to ensure that there are the correct staff ratios, as set out in Chapter 2.

Thus, as part of the process of drawing up budgets for resources, the manager will look at the following:

- that there are sufficient qualified staff to meet the Ofsted requirements;
- replenishing and replacing resources;
- health and safety requirements;
- training and staff development;
- plans for improvements to the service.

Think it over

- What systems have you seen in place or used yourself for managing resources?
- How effective were these systems?

Work in partnership with parents and carers

Partnership with parents and carers is of paramount importance in providing a quality service for children. The manager will probably be one of the first points of contact with prospective parents and carers (i.e. customers). Above of all, the manager must make parents and carers feel welcome, and appear professional yet friendly. Managers need to have the skill to inform prospective customers about the ethos of the setting while making them feel that their child's needs are going to be met. This very important aspect of management in early years settings is dealt with in detail in Chapter 5.

Liaise with external agencies

The manager of any early years setting will need to liaise with a variety of external agencies and professionals: social services, the local Early Years Development and Childcare Partnership, schools, training establishments, health visitors, general practitioners, speech and language therapists, physiotherapists, psychologists, family therapists and numerous others. This liaison could be for a number of reasons – emergencies, training needs, supporting a family in crisis, child protection issues, special needs advice or supporting children settling into school. In meeting with other professionals, the manager must remain professionally focused on the needs of individual children, families and staff, while maintaining confidentiality and meeting legal and statutory requirements (see below and Chapter 8).

Ensure that relevant policies, procedures and records are maintained

One of the National Standards (Standard 14, Documentation) specifically relates to the records early years settings must keep, and for each of the other 13 Standards there are policies and procedures which need to be in place in the setting. There are 30 such policies and procedures required by the National Standards and another 11 are recommended by Ofsted to provide evidence of compliance with the standards (see Chapter 2).

Provide a safe, secure, and stimulating environment for the children

The manager's role is to ensure that the children in the setting feel safe and secure and that their developmental needs are being met. This will include overseeing the planning of activities and short-, medium- and long-term plans for the curriculum (more details of this are given in Chapter 3). Each child's progress must be monitored by members of staff and the manager should support the staff team to do this.

General facets of a manager's job

At the start of section 1.1, a list of the ways in which managers could be perceived was presented. When staff are asked what they would ideally like their managers to be able to do, they usually come up with similar ideas. These are set out in Table 1.1. Of course, these are ideals: in reality, performing all of these facets does present quite a challenge for a manager, who may have received very little training for the job or have little experience. Many of the skills needed to perform in this way will develop over time and with experience.

Table 1.1. Facets of the manager's job

Leader	Fixer	Administrator
Is the person in charge	Ensures everything works	Understands all the paperwork
Is the most experienced person	Negotiates for the staff and among the staff	Makes sure all the staff timetables are done
Is able to earn respect and not simply expect it	Finds the resources	Disseminates information
Speaks for the team	Ensures the setting has a good reputation	Deals with all outside agencies and demands
Has a strong sense of conviction and a clear vision	Understands people's personal problems	Organises and plans effectively
Has charisma	Asks for opinions	Writes good, workable policies

Leader

It is clear that although many managers will be respected for their expertise, for their commitment to their work and for their ability to be the person in charge, they may never be charismatic. While some will be charismatic leaders with strong personalities, and lead their teams with relentless enthusiasm and gusto, others will be quietly assertive and lead from the rear of the team, gently pushing them forward when they are ready. Both management styles can be effective in early years settings. (This is discussed in greater detail below.)

Fixer

It is unlikely that one person can fix everything! What the team will expect is that the manager is resourceful and is not easily deterred by things going wrong. A manager may often feel that he or she is 'a jack of all trades and master of none'! In disputes between staff the manager will need to remain impartial.

Administrator

Good managers need to ensure that they are up to date with current issues in early years settings; this is part of good practice. The administrative tasks can often be onerous and the manager can feel isolated in having the sole responsibility for them. This is why it is important to involve members of the team in 'interpreting' paperwork. While working to the team's strengths, managers also need to be aware of their own strengths and weaknesses. This may mean they either employ someone to support them with the things they find more challenging or they enlist the support of one of the more senior members of staff in these duties.

For example, Ofsted inspectors are very keen that the staff are involved in the writing of policies as well as in their implementation. Policy writing is not a job solely for the manager: if the staff are to understand and be committed to policies they need to be involved from the outset in their development, even if the manager does the final write-up and has the last word.

The doctor analogy

Handy and Aitken (1986) compared the manager's role to that of a GP. The manager, like the GP, is the first recipient of problems. Just as a GP would, the manager decides first whether there is indeed a problem, and if so what sort of problem it is, before proceeding to act (Figure 1.2).

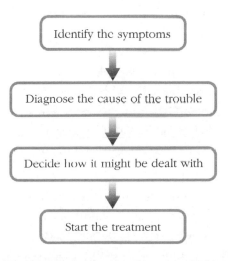

Figure 1.2. Stages in solving a problem.

This is an interesting analogy, as often the manager will feel that, owing to a lack of experience or knowledge, he or she may want to ask someone more senior for a second opinion. Of course, if you take the analogy one step further, it is evident that the manager (the GP) may make the wrong diagnosis or put in place the wrong strategy to deal with the problem. The manager will require an in-depth knowledge in order to make a good 'diagnosis'.

Think it over

- Can you relate the doctor analogy to a manager you know?
- If you are in a management role, do you recognise this as a way in which you work?
- Can you think of any other analogies that can be made with the management role?

1.2 The need for leadership

There are many practical aspects, then, to being a manager – certain tasks must be done and responsibilities met because otherwise the setting may well fall apart. But there also seems to be a need for a manager to have leadership qualities as well. Managers in early years settings have traditionally been reluctant to identify with the concept of leadership as part of their professional role (Rodd, 1998). Although many early years managers have been willing to organise, plan and take ultimate responsibility for their setting, there has not always been an awareness of the need to provide strong leadership in working towards a common vision or set of agreed goals.

Vision and influence

Leadership is about vision and influence. Rodd (1998) says that 'Leaders are able to balance the concern for work, task, quality and productivity with concern for people, relationships, satisfaction and morale.' She also goes on to describe a list of key elements in effective leadership (Figure 1.3).

It could be argued that leadership skills are especially important in early years settings because teams require more than being managed,

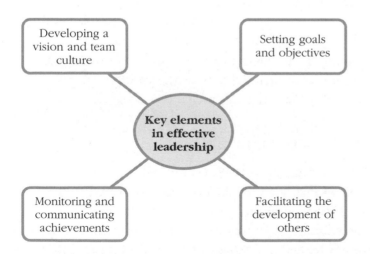

Figure 1.3. Key elements in effective leadership.

as their motivation is in the main different to that of workers in more commercial organisations. Early years workers are motivated in the main by a commitment to working with children and their families. Early years services require innovative managers who are able to carry forward a set of values and principles, because staff will need guidance in finding the way forward, especially in the ever-changing early years climate.

The manager as leader

There have been many inspirational leaders throughout history: Napoleon Bonaparte, Nelson Mandela, Martin Luther King, Margaret Thatcher, to name but a few. You may not have agreed with some of these leaders' views or politics but you cannot refute their *very* strong leadership qualities. It could also be argued that leaders, however visionary, are not always necessarily good and efficient managers! They are very often successful in leading people towards a common goal but perhaps not so successful in the day-to-day running of an organisation.

Good leaders of organisations tend to lead by example, by being a role model for their staff. They inspire trust and work in consultation with their teams, even when challenging the status quo. They have a long-term view and are open to new ideas and projects. A good leader will ensure that the staff are offered opportunities for further professional development and training, for example. Leaders can also be very persuasive, as they are often passionate about their work; this passion can be infectious and motivate others around them.

Case study — The model manager

I always try to model my own management on a manager I had some years ago. She was an excellent role model for all the people in her team, her own performance in her job was exemplary, she was an excellent teacher and she had integrity. When there was a decision to be made or a challenge to take on, she would gather us all together and ask, 'How shall we go about this?' She appeared to manage the day-to-day, mundane things adequately, but these things did not seem a problem as we all worked together. She utilised individual strengths to meet any targets set. We felt she knew us all and that she was interested in us as individuals. We felt valued. I worked really hard for the team because she ensured that we realised our full potential.

- Do you think that the manager in this case was a leader or a manager or both?
- What would you say were her strengths and weaknesses?

It may appear at this stage that 'managing', on its own, implies a lack of skills and that leaders are better to work for. This of course may not always be the case. Some efficient managers may make staff feel secure in their roles, for example.

To be a 'leader' suggests that one must have followers. Leadership has been studied by looking at effective leaders such as the ones mentioned at the start of this section, to attempt to define what makes a leader, but this approach has produced disappointing results. Most people in their first management role draw on their personal experience of being managed. So, if you have been managed poorly you will have probably decided to manage your staff in a very different way. Managers who are willing to continue learning and are aware of their strengths and weaknesses are more likely to adapt their approach to meet the needs of their team and the organisation.

The distinction between managers and leaders is that one manages (copes) while the other leads (points the way):

- The manager looks after the day-to-day running of the organisation or establishment, which involves planning, organising, coordinating and being ultimately responsible.
- The leader leads the team to an ultimate goal or set of targets, will have a vision for the future and a picture of how he or she would like the organisation to move forward. The leader can be an inspirational character, even charismatic.

There could be an assumption that all managers are leaders and that those chosen to manage are people who were 'born to lead' – that is, who have a natural aptitude for the job. To a degree, this is true, as managers today cannot simply expect total, unquestioning compliance from their teams. People in the team are the organisation's most valuable asset and can make the difference between success and failure. Nonetheless, good management is important to the people in the team, as they can be reassured by a manager who can plan, coordinate and control what is going on in the setting.

Case study — The kind manager

The manager of our centre was extremely kind. She was a very likeable person. The systems she put in place were well organised and efficient but I did not feel I was consulted about them. She always seemed to have a million reasons as to why we had to follow these ways of practising, telling us that it was 'because of the inspection' or 'social services state that…'. It appeared that decisions had been made and then directives were passed on to us. Sometimes I felt that it would be pointless bringing things to her, as new ideas appeared to make her feel uneasy.

- In your view does it appear there was anything lacking in this person's management skills?
- How would you compare this manager to the one in the case study 'The model manager', above?
- Which person would you prefer to have as a manager?

The way in which managers perform their role will of course vary according to personality. For this reason it is useful to analyse the experiences you have had of managing and being managed. This in turn might suggest to you some of the strategies and skills that are necessary for the management of early years settings. To this end, consider the statements below. These are drawn from *Good Practice in Childcare. 14: Teamworking* (Department for Education and Employment, 2000). Read each statement and see whether it applies. If you already have experience as a manager, this exercise may help you to see how you lead your staff and whether or not you allow them to help with decision-making. If you are not presently in a management role you could base your responses on a past or present line manager! It should give you some ideas of contrasting approaches to management and leadership.

- I trust my staff.
- The carrot is more effective than the stick.
- I see myself as part of a team.
- The success of my team will reflect well on me.
- My key role is to give the team a direction and support them in heading towards it.
- I expect my staff to put forward ideas without prompting and to contribute in decision-making.
- I need to monitor my staff closely.
- Following the appropriate rules is essential for discipline.
- I need to distance myself from staff to keep rules clear.
- My successes will reflect well on my staff.
- My role is to give my team clear, specific objectives and to monitor achievement of them.
- Leaders have to take key decisions on their own.

Think it over

Consider the series of statements relating to management style.

- Which points match the management strategies used within your organisation?
- Does this indicate that the manager has 'power'? If so, is the manager aware of the power he or she has?
- If you are a team member, how do these strategies make you feel?

You probably have seen a variety of these strategies in use and you may even have employed some of them. The role of the manager is to lead the team and guide and support them without abusing power. A manager who feels he or she is above the staff and uses discipline as a method of control can create problems, as this encourages a 'them and us' culture, which is likely to be negative. The manager who does not feel threatened and is confident in her or his own ability can lead the team effectively while being very much a member of the team.

Many people become managers in early years settings because they want to progress in their career but when they begin in a management role they realise that it actually requires a very different set of skills and that they are no longer able to do the 'hands-on' work with the children that they previously found so rewarding. Much of their time will be filled with paperwork and administrative duties. Also, the manager is required to take ultimate responsibility and so may often feel that he or she has to be a 'Jack of all trades'. The case study 'The childminder who became the boss' relates to a manager who has found herself in just this position.

Case study — The childminder who became the boss

Ellie owns a private day nursery. The nursery offers sessional care and the building has been purpose-built. Ellie was a qualified nursery nurse, but when she had her own children she decided to do some childminding in order to keep her practical expertise up to date. As a childminder she became more and more popular with parents. She then decided to take on some staff so that she could take on more children; this she continued to do in her own home. Very soon her home was being 'taken over' by the children and so she decided to move and start a purpose-built nursery in the same locality. Ellie maintains that it was never her intention to become a manager or a 'boss' and that she still feels more comfortable working with the children, even though she rarely has the time to do so. She has a strong vision for her nursery and a set of values and principles she is able to justify to potential parents. Ellie has a management structure within the nursery that promotes and values the staff who use their initiative. She tries hard when introducing new ideas to discuss them fully with the staff and get them on board. Although some of the practice is not exactly as she would like it to be, she is working slowly to train and educate her staff and give them opportunities to learn more.

- Would you say Ellie was fairly typical of today's early years manager?
- Would you say that Ellie is more a manager or a leader? Give some reasons for your choice.

1.3 Leadership and management theories

Many researchers have looked at what constitutes a good manager and leader. They have tried to identify characteristics which could enable employers to select and train effective leaders, but no clear characteristics have been found. It is apparent, however, that to be a leader a person requires a certain kind of interpersonal behaviour and that strong leaders are often people who inspire confidence in others and support team members or colleagues to achieve their full potential. Leadership involves getting the very best from people. Leadership in early years settings is promoted by the common goal or ethos of meeting the needs of children.

Before the chapter moves on to consider what it is that makes an effective early years manager and leader, it is important to look at the various ways in which management and leadership have been interpreted. There have been many theories concerning managers and leaders. A selection is presented in Table 1.2. You can use this table as a point of reference for research. It gives only a small sample of the plethora of information on management theory.

Table 1.2. Some notable management theories and theorists

Name	Work	Comments
Fayol (1841–1925)	Henri Fayol was a French mining engineer. He spent his life with one company and became its managing director. It is said that he invented management, by distinguishing it as a separate activity. He identified 14 principles of management and initiated a theoretical analysis appropriate to a wide range of organisations. He suggested that all activities to which industrial undertakings give rise are divided into six groups. He said that 'without principles there is darkness and chaos'.	Fayol is the earliest known proponent of a theoretical analysis of managerial activities – an analysis which has withstood years of critical discussion. His ideas, along with others, are collectively called classical management theory. They are somewhat limited to industrial management and therefore do not represent a coherent body of thought.
Herzberg (1959)	Frederick Herzberg was research director of a psychological consulting firm. He worked on industrial mental health and focused on areas such as the individual, attitudes and motivation to work, which led to his theories of 'hygiene' and motivation. The hygiene factors were essentially environmental and he labelled those dissatisfiers. He argued that removing the dissatisfiers did not motivate people to work harder or make them happier. The five principal motivation factors (satisfiers) were: achievement; recognition; whether work is meaningful; responsibility; and advancement. After a number of studies within a cross section of industry he came to the conclusion that pay was not a motivator – just the most important hygiene factor.	Herzberg's ideas were well received at the time and led to considerable work on 'job enrichment' so that jobs contained more motivators.

Name	Work	Comments
McGregor (1960)	According to Douglas McGregor, 'theory X' bosses believe their employees dislike work and try to avoid it; they assume people have to be bullied into work. 'Theory Y' bosses feel that people do like work and value it as part of their lives. McGregor said that the employees behaved in the way their bosses expected them to, and so if they had a theory Y boss they would enjoy and value their work.	Some of the problems with this theory could be that it makes assumptions about the employees. For example, would all people be influenced by their boss in this way? The two types of boss could be seen as extremes, whereas in real life a blend of the two types is more likely.
Likert (1961)	Rensis Likert's 'Michigan studies' theorised about high-producing and low-producing managers. The research indicated that high-producing managers tended to build their success around interlocking and tightly knit groups of employees who had been motivated by a range of forces, such as money, security, ego and creativity ('self-actualisation'). Likert looked at four systems of management.	Some of this work is still valid today, as it looks at the essential elements of teams and the motivation of teams.
Peters (1989)	Tom Peters wrote an international bestseller, *Thriving on Chaos*. He looked at innovative ways of dealing with change in the world of management, and targeted five key areas – responsiveness, innovation, people power, leadership and systems.	Peters challenged many of the traditional theories on management, and could even be said to be revolutionary, but is nonetheless highly respected.
Jeffers (1991)	Susan Jeffers wrote about the challenges of life. She held that the motivators were no longer the same as they were – quality of life and a better sense of balance between job, family, friends and contribution to society were taking precedence.	Society may well be moving towards this but the bottom line of money and status still applies to many of the workforce.
Senge (1994)	Peter Senge suggested that managers should works towards: 'organisations where people continually expand their capacity to create results they truly desire, where new and expansive patterns of thinking are nurtured, where collective aspirations are set free, and where people are continually learning to see the whole together'.	These theories are currently very popular with early years researchers in leadership and management, and are being utilised to train and develop managers and leaders in early years centres of excellence.

Management theorists over the years have looked at the key concepts of organisations – such as culture, motivation, leadership, power, group working – and discussed ways of helping managers to find solutions to familiar problems experienced in all organisations. It is useful to look in some detail at a range of theories because, at this level of study, you will need to understand how organisations work and how this links directly to leadership and management styles.

Handy's 'have a go'

Handy (1992) stated that there had formerly been three general categories of theory on leadership – trait, style and contingency theories.

- *Trait theories.* By 1950 there had been over 100 studies of the personality traits of managers and leaders. These had found that they had in common the following: intelligence; initiative; self-assurance; and, in more recent studies, 'the helicopter factor' (the person had the ability to 'rise above' a situation and see it in its relation to the overall environment). However, possession of all of these traits became an impossible ideal. These theories were also criticised on the grounds that they seemed to imply that there were elite groups of people who could become managers and leaders because they had inherited these characteristics.
- *Style theories.* These theories predicted that employees would work harder for a person who adopted a certain style of leadership, but it was found that style alone was not an answer to effective leadership. Nonetheless, it was shown that a supportive style of leadership led to more contentment and greater involvement on the part of employees. This would not necessarily generate higher productivity but it would be a good basis on which to build. It became evident that the effectiveness of a workforce came from more than leadership style alone, and this led to the development of 'contingency theories'.
- *Contingency theories.* These concentrated on the relationship between the manager and the employee, but also took into account the task, the work group and the position of the leader within that group. Thus, for example, employees would be most effective in situations where the leader was well liked and the task to be done was clearly defined.

Handy looked at all these theories but concluded that the only way to train people to become effective leaders and managers was by simply 'letting them have a go', provided they were given good support. Handy advocated the use of mentors to support new managers.

Peters' tools for effective leadership

Tom Peters has written a number of successful books about the world of management and the ways in which managers can be most successful. He maintains that leaders require three 'tools' for effective leadership:

- establishing direction;
- channelling interest, by living the vision – that is, motivating staff to love change and be inspired by the positive development which takes place as a consequence of change;
- practising 'visible management', for the purpose of preaching the message and enhancing the leader's understanding of the context – this is done by the manager being visible and being aware of all that happens 'on the shop floor'.

Peters sees the principal challenges as empowering other people and cherishing those who are at the front line. He says that it is important to create a sense of 'urgency as part of loving change'. He also says that managers need to 'become the vision's most itinerant preacher ... to work with everyone to develop and instil such a philosophy'. Although some may argue that Tom Peters is extreme in his expectations, a manager in an early years setting may find some of his strategies useful (see Peters, 1989).

Theory into practice

Theories help to identify characteristics or traits of successful managers and teams – they do not always have the definitive answer to how you should lead and manage.

Think it over

- How can the information and advice of management specialists be used in your present role?
- If you were researching management theory for an assignment or work-based project, what would you look at in more detail because it directly related to your work practices?
- Has this look at management theory made you feel any differently about the skills and abilities needed to be an effective manager or leader?

1.4 What makes an effective early years manager and leader?

Bogue (1997), cited by Rodd (1998, p. 15), said that 'leaders are organisers of time, talent and task'. This explains in one short statement all the functions of a leader or manager – the manager will have to complete the tasks on hand, in timely fashion, by making the best use of the talent, skills and attributes of the people in the team.

Effective management

Having looked above at some management and leadership theories, it is possible to draw some conclusions as to what makes an effective early years manager. These ideas concern not only effective management but also ensuring that the *team* is successful. There are several ways in which an early years manager can ensure maximum effectiveness:

- *Defining a mission.* This will be a vision for the future, a statement which encapsulates the values and principles of the setting. This vision will need to be communicated to the team regularly and to service users. A good manager will have a long-term plan in mind.
- *Having good communication skills.* A manager needs to be able to communicate, and so must be a 'people person', with good listening and speaking skills.
- *Creating an atmosphere.* The manager should create a setting with a 'family atmosphere', in which trust and confidence can be nurtured.
- *Respecting confidentiality.* All managers need to prioritise confidentiality, as this will inspire trust in children, parents and carers, and staff.
- *Being prepared to delegate.* A manager who is interested in the development of the team will delegate duties and responsibilities to other team members, and put their expertise to good use. This need not make the manager feel threatened; on the contrary, it will support him or her in the role, knowing that experienced staff are able to share some of the burden of responsibility. It will also build the self-esteem of team members and confirm that they are both trusted and valued.
- *Representing the views of the team.* A good leader will ensure that the setting reflects the views of all members of the team, and will be ready to listen to new ideas and to discuss old ones.
- *Finding out what motivates the team.* Managers need to know what makes the team tick, what interests them, what their personal goals and ideals are.
- *Providing support to team members.* Support can be offered in many different ways, for example in the form of a 'listening ear', taking on new ideas, offering staff opportunities for training, and networking with other professionals.

A manager can be effective by providing a listening ear.

- *Being a good role model.* A leader needs to be someone people are prepared to follow and they will follow only someone in whom they have confidence.
- *Being prepared to take risks.* Sometimes being a manager and leader means taking calculated risks for the good of the setting and the team.
- *Thinking strategically.* The manager should have a plan which the team can work to. Implementation of the plan should be monitored and the results evaluated. All the team need to show commitment to and understanding of the plan. This is strategic thinking.
- *Encouraging a 'can do' culture.* This will involve inspiring confidence in the team and making them feel valued and useful – then all team members will feel more confident to take on new challenges.
- *Sharing success.* A good manager does not take personal credit for success; it is important to involve the team so that they have the opportunity to celebrate their contribution, no matter how small.
- *Ensuring optimum use of resources.* The manager will need to make sure that all resources (including human resources) are made the best use of.
- *Possessing a sense of humour.* A sense of humour is very important – a team will respect a manager who can see the funny side of things and enable a release of tension.

An effective leader needs to put all of the above into place, but this takes time and cannot be rushed. People expect their leaders to have integrity and to be credible; this can be achieved only by ensuring that you keep promises and by doing what you say you will do. To be trusted, the manager will need to be prepared to tell the truth and to show humility, which involves admitting when he or she has got things wrong. This will require self-evaluation and looking at your own strengths and weaknesses before you take on such a responsibility. The people you manage need to know where they stand and this means it is not always possible for the manager to be 'one of the team'. Moreover, if the manager forms too close a relationship with particular members of the group, this can cause jealousies and sometimes conflict.

The qualities of an effective manager

The list presented above suggests many of the practical steps a manager can take to ensure his or her effectiveness. In addition, effective managers do require certain qualities, but what are they? Can they be learnt or are some of us 'born to lead'? Handy (1992), and Jameson and Watson (1998), quoted earlier in this chapter, looked at some specific qualities a person might need in order to be an effective manager. Figure 1.4 presents this collection of qualities; it represents, of course, a wish-list – we are only human, after all! Many practitioners will have experienced working with

Figure 1.4. The ideal attributes and qualities of an effective manager in early years settings. Can you think of any others? Perhaps you feel some of these qualities would conflict with being efficient. If so, which ones?

managers with some (if not all) of these qualities. Why are these qualities so important then?

Experience

A manager who has had a good deal of experience in early years work will of course demand greater respect than someone who has little or no experience, because there is a natural assumption that experience indicates knowledge. This, however, is not always the case. Some very successful early years managers have had experience in other walks of life that can be useful in the early years setting. It is important that the manager has a wide knowledge and expertise which makes him or her a good role model for the staff.

Energy

Energy is an essential quality of an effective manager. The role requires measured amounts of energy to get through each day – to deal with the mundane details and responsibilities. Moreover, the manager will need to draw on energy and personal enthusiasm to keep the staff on track and working towards common goals, especially at particularly stressful times, such as Ofsted inspections!

Sensitivity

A sensitive approach is required in dealing with the formative years of a child's development. The manager will need to be sensitive to the ever-changing needs of the children and their parents and carers. The latter may need sensitive handling when they encounter temporary challenges, and confidentiality and trust are paramount. A good manager will also be sensitive to the needs of the staff and their personal and professional development. To balance a sensitive approach with sound, trustworthy management is a challenge for the most experienced and effective manager and requires practice!

Understanding

Understanding on the part of the manager is required when dealing with staff and service users. A good manager will be understanding but will also need to remain professional. For example, it is important not to become too involved in the problems of a particular member of staff, as other staff need to feel that they are being treated fairly, and that there is no favouritism. A manager may need to be understanding of challenges faced by particular staff at especially stressful times; this must be recorded and discussed in appraisal. If managers decide that, for instance, a member of staff is able to reduce working hours temporarily during a family crisis then this will need to be documented and a time for review agreed. In the main, the same will apply when dealing with parents, carers and children – it is important to meet individual needs without generating a negative effect on others.

Courage to take risks

The manager will need to be courageous in determining the way forward for the early years setting. This will, on occasion, mean taking some risks in order to achieve goals. It may be necessary for the manager to argue his or her case with members of staff, parents and carers or even Ofsted. In relation to Ofsted, for example, if one of the National Standards (see Chapter 2) requires that the setting provides water play, the manager may provide evidence that this is met through the children washing dolls or other toys, instead of the normal water play activity in a water tray. The manager will require a sense of conviction and confidence to do this, and the courage to take the risk that it will not be accepted by Ofsted as water play.

Determination

In order to run a setting efficiently and effectively, the manager will need determination and continuing commitment.

Awareness of own limitations and strengths

A manager who knows his or her limitations can draw on other team members for support in those particular areas. A manager does not need to be the leader in *all* aspects of the running of the setting. The recognition and realisation of the qualities and skills of other members of staff will be seen as a sign of strength on the part of the manager.

Vision and conviction

A good manager with a strong team will need a real vision and a sense of conviction to carry it forward. But this will need to be joined with the ability to see the 'other point of view', while keeping an open dialogue with staff, parents, carers and children.

Reflective practitioner

A reflective practitioner is one who reviews and evaluates his or her work. This is especially important for those who work with children. If the staff in the team are to be expected to carry out evaluation and reflection, then the manager should also demonstrate the ability to do this, as a role model. The work of managing a setting in any case benefits from a reflective approach. The theme of reflective practice is taken up in Chapter 2.

Accountable

Managers take on many responsibilities as part of their role. The manager is accountable to the staff team, parents and carers and children to ensure that the setting is managed well. If the manager is also the 'registered person' (see Table 2.1) then she or he will also be accountable to Ofsted in meeting the requirements of the National Standards within the setting (see Chapter 2).

There is also presently an accountability framework enforced by Ofsted, which covers responsibility for dealing with issues such as child protection. The protection of children is a high priority for all childcare practitioners, especially in view of the report by Lord Laming (2003) on the death of Victoria Climbié and the 2003 Green Paper *Every Child Matters* (Department for Education and Skills, 2003). Managers are required by Ofsted to have a named person for child protection and they should be aware of the importance of that role. Indeed, in many cases managers will be the named person. All child protection concerns must be brought to the attention of the named person, so that he or she can refer them if necessary to the proper authority. The named person may be called on to give evidence in court or be involved in case conferences held by social services.

The manager needs to have a good working knowledge of the legislation surrounding these issues. The Green Paper and the accountability framework are addressed in Chapter 9.

Conclusion

This chapter has looked at what is meant by management and has considered the manager's role and some of its functions. It has also considered the need for leadership skills within early years settings. Some of the plethora of theories linked to leadership and management have been reviewed. You will have had the opportunity to reflect upon your own management skills. The last part of the chapter looked briefly at what it takes to be an effective manager. This will be explored in more detail in Chapter 2.

Check your understanding

1 What is meant by 'management'?
2 Which principles does Investors in People suggest can be used to improve the manager's performance?
3 What are the main functions of management?
4 What are the main differences between managing and leading?
5 Who are some of the most influential theorists on management and leadership?
6 Which theory do you think best applies to early years settings?
7 What will a manager need to do to ensure a team works effectively?
8 What do you feel are the personal qualities needed to be a manager and leader in an early years setting?
9 What additional responsibilities might there be for those who manage staff working with children?

References and further reading

Bogue, R. J. (ed.) (1997) *Health Network Innovations: How 20 Communities Are Improving Their Systems Through Collaboration.* Chicago: American Hospital Publisher.

Department for Education and Employment (2000) *Good Practice in Childcare. 14: Teamworking* (prepared by Churchill Associates on behalf of the DfEE). London: DfEE. Available at www.surestart.gov.uk/_doc/0-65FABF.pdf.

Department for Education and Skills (2003) *Every Child Matters*, Cm 5860. London: DfES. Available at www.dfes.gov.uk/everychildmatters/downloads.cfm.

Handy, C. (1992) *Understanding Organisations* (Penguin Business Library). Harmondsworth: Penguin.

Handy, C. and Aitken, R. (1986) *Understanding Schools as Organisations*. London: Penguin.

Herzberg, F., Mausner, B. and Snyderman, B. (1959) *The Motivation to Work*. New York: Wilcy.

Investors in People (2003) *Leadership and Management. The Investors in People Guide to Supporting the Development of Your Leaders and Managers*. London: IIP.

Jameson, H. and Watson, M. (1998) *Starting and Running a Nursery*. Cheltenham: Nelson Thornes.

Jeffers, S. (1991) *Feel the Fear and Do It Anyway*. London: Random House.

Likert, R. (1961) *New Patterns of Management*. New York: McGraw-Hill.

Lord Laming (2003) *The Victoria Climbié Inquiry. Report of an Inquiry*. Available at www.victoria-climbie-inquiry.org.uk/finreport/finreport.htm.

McGregor, D. (1960) *The Human Side of Enterprise*. New York: McGraw-Hill.

Peters, T. (1989) *Thriving on Chaos*. London: Macmillan.

Rodd, J. (1998) *Leadership in Early Childhood. The Pathway to Professionalism*. Buckingham: Open University Press.

Senge, P., *et al.* (1994) *The Fifth Discipline Fieldbook: Strategies for Building a Learning Organisation*. London: Nicholas Brealey.

Smith, A. and Langstone, A. (1999) *Managing Staff in Early Years Settings*. London: Routledge.

Whitaker, P. (1998) *Managing Schools*. Oxford: Butterworth Heinemann.

Useful websites

Investors in People: www.investorsinpeople.co.uk.

Ofsted: www.ofsted.gov.uk.

2 Providing a High Quality Service

Early childhood care and education have become increasingly recognised as playing a vital role in laying the foundation for successful later learning. Research has shown that high quality early childhood care and education can affect subsequent academic achievement and social behaviour. In the last few years the government has been working towards raising standards in both education and care, and so has introduced a range of initiatives and accreditation to improve standards. These have included the National Childcare Strategy (see Chapter 8) and the SureStart initiative (see Chapter 9). The principal instrument for ensuring the quality of provision, however, has been the introduction of the National Standards, and this chapter begins by detailing these.

All of these initiatives aim to increase the quality of services for children and their families. The National Standards provide us with a framework of quality; however, if quality is viewed through an imposed framework this will give only a partial view of practice. Inspection, rating scales and quality checklists can measure only those areas of practice that can be easily observed, and tend to impose changes to practice externally, rather than change being initiated by practitioners. Therefore this chapter focuses on assessing, evaluating and building quality from the inside. There is no doubt that encouraging practitioners to evaluate their own work closely results in a heightened awareness of high quality practice.

Quality encompasses all areas of the setting, not just those directly linked to the children. These include:

- the physical environment;
- materials and equipment;
- the characteristics of staff–child relationships;
- the qualifications of the staff and staff turnover;

2

- health and hygiene procedures and standards;
- relationships with parents and carers;
- systems of observation and record-keeping;
- systems of planning.

This chapter explores strategies that the early years manager may use in order to enable the team to meet the National Standards, as well as to improve quality, in a way that maintains the setting's own ethos. It also identifies key quality indicators which managers and teams must meet in order to provide the best possible service for children and families. The chapter covers the following areas:

2.1   Meeting the requirements of the National Standards.

2.2   Ensuring quality.

2.3   Quality indicators.

2.4   Maintaining quality.

2.1 Meeting the requirements of the National Standards

The government is committed to promoting the welfare and development of young children and has therefore created a set of National Standards for early years practitioners to follow. These represent a mandatory baseline of quality, below which no provider may fall. Ofsted requires all early years settings to meet the National Standards. During an inspection, Ofsted inspectors will talk to the manager about how the criteria are met and question the staff team to evaluate how the Standards are being implemented. Chapter 8 looks at the registration and inspection of settings.

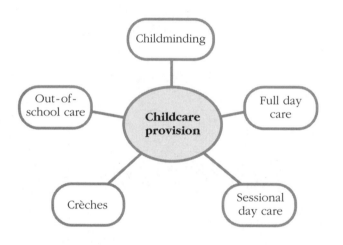

Figure 2.1. Childcare provision is divided into five categories.

For the purposes of the National Standards, childcare provision is divided into five categories (Figure 2.1).

Most providers will know into which of the categories their setting falls and therefore which criteria apply. There will be circumstances, however, where a setting has characteristics of more than one category. In these cases Ofsted will notify the provider which category of childcare is being used for registration, and whether alternative or additional criteria need to be met. Links to all five sets of documents are presented on the website www.childcarelink.gov.uk/standards.asp. This chapter focuses on the National Standards set for full day care (Department for Education and Skills, 2003).

Top Tip

Keep a separate folder for each of the National Standards containing evidence of how each criterion is being met. These folders will need to be kept up to date. As well as being valuable in terms of Ofsted inspections, they can be used for training purposes, for the induction of new staff and childcare students on placement. Folders should be available for all staff to refer to when necessary.

There are 14 National Standards for full day care, each of which is accompanied by a set of supporting criteria that describe how the standard is to be met. This section outlines all 14 Standards and some of the supporting criteria (listed as bullet points), to give an idea of their scope and content; however, this does not imply that these are more important than those that are not discussed here – all of the supporting criteria must be met in order to meet Ofsted requirements. It is important to note that the National Standards do not override the need for providers to meet other regulations. These relate to, for example, health and safety, food hygiene and procedures in the event of fire, some of which are touched on in Chapter 8.

Table 2.1 defines the terms used within the National Standards.

Table 2.1. Definitions of terms used within the National Standards

Day care	Facilities that provide care for children aged under 8 years for a continuous period of 4 hours or more in any day in non-domestic premises.
Registered person	A person deemed qualified to care for children and whose name appears on the certificate of registration. The registered person has overall responsibility for ensuring that the requirements of the National Standards are met.
Manager	The person in day-to-day charge of the setting. A manager must have a level 3 qualification at minimum, as well as relevant experience.
Parents	Any person with parental responsibility for a child.
Early years childcare inspector	A person employed by Ofsted who is responsible for regulating and inspecting day care and childminding provision.

Standard 1. Suitable person

Adults providing day care, looking after children or having unsupervised access to them are suitable to do so.

- The registered person complies with all conditions of registration.
- Criminal record checks are carried out on all staff and volunteers.
- The manager has at least a level 3 qualification (e.g. Diploma in Child Care and Education, Btec National Diploma Childhood Studies, NVQ 3 in Childcare).

Standard 2. Organisation

The registered person meets the required adult:child ratios, ensures that training and qualifications requirements are met, and organises space and resources to meet the children's needs effectively.

- Minimum staffing ratios are: 1:3 for children under 2 years; 1:4 for children aged 2–3 years; 1:8 for children aged 3–7 years.

The registered person ensures that:

- all supervisors hold or are working towards a level 3 qualification appropriate for the care or development of children;
- at least half of all other childcare staff hold an appropriate level 2 qualification (CCE, NVQ 2);
- trainees under 17 years old are supervised at all times and are not counted in the staff ratio.

Top Tip — Standard 2

Provide all members of the team with training in:

- child protection;
- first aid;
- child development;
- food handling;
- behaviour management;
- observation.

Keep copies of all certificates on file.

Standard 3. Care, learning and play

The registered person meets the individual needs of the children and promotes their welfare. The registered person plans and provides activities and play opportunities to develop children's emotional, physical, intellectual and social capabilities.

- Children are encouraged to develop their confidence, independence and self-esteem.
- Resources, activities and play opportunities are carefully selected to allow children to build on their natural curiosity as learners, develop their language and mathematical thinking, use their imagination and develop their social skills.
- The registered person encourages positive relationships with children and their parents to facilitate a good understanding of individual needs and home circumstances.
- All the staff observe and record what children do, and use these observations to inform planning.
- Children are helped to work towards the 'early learning goals' detailed in *Curriculum Guidance for the Foundation Stage* (Qualifications and Curriculum Authority, 2000).

Top Tip — Standard 3

Budget for regular staff training to help staff keep up to date with new initiatives and ideas. Contact the local Early Years Development and Childcare Partnership, which provides regular updating training, often free of charge. Team up with another setting when buying in training to help keep costs down. Make arrangements for your team to visit other settings in order to share good practice.

Standard 4. Physical environment

The premises are safe, secure and suitable for their purpose. They provide adequate space in an appropriate location, are welcoming to children and offer access to facilities for a range of activities which promote the children's development.

- The setting is welcoming and friendly.
- The setting is clean, well lit, ventilated and well maintained.
- Children do not have access to the kitchen unless it is for a supervised activity.

Standard 5. Equipment

Furniture, equipment and toys are provided which are appropriate for their purpose and help to create an accessible and stimulating environment. They are of suitable design and condition, well maintained and conform to safety standards.

- Age-appropriate toys and play materials are available to provide stimulating activities and play opportunities for the children in all areas of play, learning and development.
- Furniture, toys and equipment on the premises are in good repair and conform to the applicable safety standards.

Some recommended suppliers of nursery equipment are listed in Table 2.2.

Table 2.2. Nursery equipment suppliers

Company	Type of equipment supplied	Contact
ASCO	Games, maths equipment, art materials, large physical equipment, nursery consumables	0113 270 7070 www.ascoeducational.co.uk
Community Insight	Early years care and educational books	01793 512 612 www.communityinsight.co.uk
Community Play Things	Furniture, physical equipment, bikes, equipment to promote imaginary play	01580 883 301 ww.communityplaythings.co.uk
Puppets by Post	Large and small puppets	01462 446 040 www.puppetsbypost.com
Story Sacks	Sacks containing a story with props and supporting activities	0161 763 6232 www.storysack.com
The Festival Shop	Books, posters, resources and games that contain positive images of children from a variety of backgrounds	0121 444 0444 www.festivalshop.co.uk

Company	Type of equipment supplied	Contact
County supplies	Games, toys, maths equipment, art materials, large physical equipment and nursery consumables	Local education department
Cost Cutters	Specialist supplier of furniture and ancillary items for early years education	0800 019 4470 www.costcuttersuk.com
Helo Health Engineering Ltd	Range of childcare products including high-chairs, safety seats, furniture, changing units	01284 772 400 www.hel-o.co.uk/
Galt Educational and Pre-school	Tough, hard-wearing toys and equipment	08451 203 005 www.galt-education.co.uk
J & M Toys	Specialist in role-play costumes for 3–8-year-olds	01274 599 314 www.jandmtoys.co.uk
Spacekraft	Range of furniture, toys and equipment for inside and outside play. Sensory equipment	01274 581 007 www.spacekraft.co.uk

Standard 6. Safety

The registered person takes positive steps to promote safety, both within the setting (inside and outside) and on outings, and ensures proper precautions are taken to prevent accidents.

- The registered person carries out and reviews a risk assessment of the premises.
- The premises and outside play area are secure and children are not able to leave them unsupervised. There is an effective system for managing access to the premises, and a record is kept of visitors.
- Children are supervised at all times. A clearly defined procedure is in place in the event of a child being lost (this is mandatory).

Top Tips — Standard 6

- Teach and remind children regularly how to use equipment safely (e.g. a climbing frame).
- When making the outside area safe and secure remember to plan an exit route in the event of an emergency and consider how the emergency services can gain access if needed.
- As part of the induction process for new staff and childcare students, provide them with a map that shows the location of all fire exits, fire extinguishers, and alarms and outside meeting points.

Standard 7. Health

The registered person promotes the health of children and takes positive steps to prevent the spread of infection and appropriate measures when they are ill.

- The premises and equipment are clean.
- The registered person ensures that staff are aware of the importance of good hygiene practice in order to prevent the spread of infection.
- Children are encouraged to learn about personal hygiene through the daily routine.
- A record is maintained of any accidents (this is mandatory).
- There is a policy regarding the exclusion of children who are ill or infectious, which is discussed with parents.

Top Tips — Standard 7

- Let the children practise hand-washing as part of an adult-led activity.

- Have boxes of tissues available in each room for blowing noses.

- Ask parents to sign a consent form for occasional use of oral medicine. For topical medicine (e.g. treatment for eczema) parents can sign an on-going consent form, which is valid until any changes in treatment are required. Parents are responsible for informing the setting of any changes.

- Always tell parents about an accident as soon as possible. Provide details of the injury and treatment received on a form that includes a body map. This form is to be read and signed by parents and taken to hospital if further treatment is required. Keep a copy on file for any future reference.

- In order to minimise confusion, provide parents with a definition of a well child: a well child is not reliant on Calpol, does not have a high temperature, is well enough to participate in all nursery activities, has a normal appetite, is happy and sociable, does not require a greater staff ratio and has normal bowel function.

- There is a 'no smoking' policy.

Children who are in day care are routinely offered a midday meal.

Standard 8. Food and drink

Children are provided with regular drinks and food in adequate quantities for their needs. Food and drink are properly prepared, nutritious and comply with dietary and religious requirements.

- Fresh drinking water is available to children at all times.
- Children who are in day care for the whole day are routinely offered a

midday meal and other snacks and drinks.

- Information is kept and followed regarding any special dietary requirements.

Standard 9. Equal opportunities

The registered person and staff actively promote equality of opportunity and anti-discriminatory practice for all children.

- All staff implement the equal opportunities policy, which is periodically reviewed.
- All children and staff are treated with equal concern.

Standard 10. Special needs

The registered person is aware that some children may have special needs and is proactive in ensuring that appropriate action can be taken when such a child is identified or admitted to the setting. Steps are taken to promote the welfare and development of the children within the setting in partnership with the parents and other relevant parties.

- The registered person has regard to the Department for Education and Skills' (2001) code of practice on special educational needs.
- The registered person has a written statement about special needs, which is consistent with current legal legislation and guidance and includes both special educational needs and disabilities.

Standard 11. Behaviour

Adults caring for children in the provision are able to manage a wide range of children's behaviour in a way that promotes their welfare and development.

- The registered person produces a written statement on behaviour management, which states the methods used to manage children's behaviour. This is followed by all staff and discussed with parents.
- Staff provide an environment that supports good behaviour.

Standard 12. Working in partnership with parents and carers

The registered person and staff work in partnership with parents to meet the needs of the children, both individually and as a group. Information is shared.

- Information is shared with parents. This includes information about the setting, the role of the parents, details of policies, the complaints procedure and activities.

Top Tips — Standard 12

- To help maintain communication and exchange information, provide home–nursery books for each child, which come and go with them each day. Parents, carers and staff can note down any comments they feel are relevant to the care and well-being of the child.
- Ensure parents read and sign copies of policies and procedures before the child starts in the setting. Keep a copy of these documents in individual children's files.
- Ask parents to sign a consent form giving permission to observe and record their child's progress and to share these records where appropriate (e.g. with subsequent settings).

Standard 13. Child protection

The registered person complies with local child protection procedures approved by the Area Child Protection Committee and ensures that all adults working with and looking after children in the setting are able to put the procedures into practice.

- The protection of the child is the registered person's first priority.
- There is a written procedures statement which states staff responsibilities with regard to reporting suspected child abuse or neglect in accordance with local Area Child Protection Committee procedures. It includes procedures to be followed in the event of an allegation being made against a member of staff (this is mandatory).

- The registered person ensures that all staff are aware of possible signs and symptoms of children at risk and are aware of their responsibility both to report concerns to police or social services in accordance with local Area Child Protection Committee procedures, without delay, and to keep concerns confidential.

Standard 14. Documentation

Records, policies and procedures which are required for the efficient and safe management of the setting, and to promote the welfare, care and learning of children, are maintained. Records about individual children are shared with the child's parents.

- Records relating to individual children are retained for a reasonable period of time after the child has left the setting.
- The records are always available to the early years childcare inspector (this is mandatory).

Care of babies and children under 2 years

The National Standards document (Department for Education and Skills, 2003), in its Annex A, also details the requirements for caring for children under 2 years. It covers the following areas:

- organisation;
- physical environment;
- safety;
- partnership with parents.
- care, learning and play;
- equipment;
- food and drink;

Top Tip — Baby care

Either at the end of each cot or above it display details of how the baby likes to be put down to sleep. For example: 'My name is Rory. I like to sleep on my back with a dummy having my face stroked.' This ensures continuity between staff in meeting each baby's needs.

Notification of changes

The early years childcare inspector must be informed of the following at the earliest opportunity:

- any changes in staff and people living on the premises;
- any significant changes in the premises;
- any significant changes to the operational plan;
- allegations of abuse by a member of staff or volunteer, or any abuse which is alleged to have taken place on the premises;
- any other significant events.

Mandatory requirements

The setting will normally show that it is reaching each Standard by meeting the supporting criteria. However, most of the criteria do not have to be followed precisely, as long as Ofsted is satisfied that the Standards are being met. Settings do, however, have to meet the supporting criteria that relate to:

- record-keeping;
- adult:child ratios;
- training and qualifications.

Other mandatory requirements include the following:

- A record is maintained of any accidents.
- There are clearly defined procedures for emergency evacuation of the building.
- The name, address and date of birth of each child who is looked after on the premises are recorded.
- Accessible individual records are kept on the premises containing the names and addresses of the staff.
- Physical punishment, or the threat of it, is not used.
- There is a written statement that includes procedures to be followed in the event of an allegation being made against a member of staff.
- The records are always available to the early years childcare inspector.

(See also 'Notification of changes', above.)

Nursery schools

The team includes a qualified teacher and nursery assistant.

Nursery schools are educational settings that deal almost exclusively with children under 5 years. They are open for the period of the school day, during term time only. The team includes a qualified teacher, who is supported by an early years practitioner qualified to level 3. All the standards of full day care apply to this type of setting, apart from staff ratios. The minimum staff:child ratio is 2:20. If the head teacher is excluded from ratios the minimum is 2:26. In either case there must be a qualified teacher and a qualified nursery assistant.

2.2 Ensuring quality

Moss and Penn (1996) define quality as being both subjective and relative. Quality is fluid, as it is determined by (in the early years setting):

- the professional and personal values and beliefs of those who work directly with the children;
- the environment in which the children learn;
- the resources available to the setting.

Therefore it can be argued that there is no universal measure of quality – only guidelines and indicators (discussed in the next section) for each setting to follow and implement.

In relation to the first point, early years practitioners' values and beliefs will affect their teaching and how children learn. Most early years practitioners recognise that in order for children to develop to their full potential the adults need to interact actively and sensitively with the children, supporting and extending their learning. However, in order for children to develop to their full potential, all adults in the setting need to share the same professional values and beliefs. Regular evaluation, updating and training can help to ensure a common and consistent approach between the adults in the setting.

Quality provision can exist only when early years practitioners work towards incorporating the principles of early years education into all aspects of the setting. Managers also need to carry out regular reviews and assessments of practice, the environment, resources and procedures, and make any necessary changes – this is taken up in section 2.3. This section considers those areas of practice that will principally determine the quality of provision:

- a child-centred approach;
- meeting the needs of children;
- treating children as individuals;
- equal opportunities;
- inclusion;
- enhancing self-esteem;
- play as a vehicle for learning.

A child-centred approach

A child-centred approach aims to incorporate children's interests as the central focus of all aspects of learning and care within the setting. A child-centred approach relies on the adults in the setting interacting with and responding to the children in the following ways:

- They support and extend children's learning sensitively and appropriately.
- They appreciate what children can do for themselves and that this differs between children.
- They enable children to enjoy their childhood.
- They have consideration for the children as individuals.
- They are respectful and caring, and they ensure the welfare and safety of each child without being overprotective.
- They provide an environment that allows children to progress and develop at their own pace to fulfil their potential.
- They plan and implement a range of learning experiences that encourage and support all areas of development.

Think it over

Use the list of ways in which adults should interact with and respond to children to evaluate whether your setting has a child-centred approach. In order to gain an accurate picture, gather evidence for each point. This can be through either observation or discussion with your team.

- Are there any points you are unable to find supporting evidence for?
- Compare your answers with someone from another setting and share any points of good practice.

Meeting the needs of children

Early years settings should offer a range of learning opportunities that meet the diverse needs of children, to enable them to achieve their full potential. All activities and learning experiences should be responsive to and respectful of individual differences and promote acceptance of each person, positive self-esteem and a strong personal identity. The planning of activities and the curriculum (which is dealt with fully in Chapter 3) must therefore take account of the needs of:

- both boys and girls;
- children with special educational needs;
- more able children;
- children with particular needs;
- children from all social, cultural and religious backgrounds.

In order to meet the diverse needs of the children, the *Curriculum Guidance for the Foundation Stage* (Qualifications and Curriculum Authority, 2000) highlights the importance of practitioners doing the following:

- ensuring that careful consideration is given to planning activities that use a wide range of teaching strategies, which reflect the individual learning styles of children and thereby maximise learning experiences;
- planning activities that build on children's interests, prior learning and existing skills;
- implementing a wide range of opportunities to motivate, support and develop children and help them to be involved, concentrate and learn effectively;
- providing a safe and supportive learning environment, free from harassment, in which the contribution of all children is valued and where racial, religious, disability and gender stereotypes are challenged;
- using materials that positively reflect diversity and are free from discrimination and stereotyping;
- planning challenging opportunities for children whose ability and understanding are in advance of their language and communication skills;
- monitoring children's progress, identifying any areas of concern and taking action to provide support, for example by using different approaches, additional adult help or other agencies.

It is the responsibility of the early years manager to ensure that the team is fully aware of these key principles and that they are put into practice. One effective way of achieving this is to allocate responsibility for monitoring individual areas to different team members. Regular feedback during team meetings will ensure that everyone is familiar with each key principle, responsibility for which can be regularly rotated. Copies of statements of these key principles can be included in information packs for new staff and students, with examples of good practice.

Treating children as individuals

Early years practitioners have an essential role to play in helping each child develop to her or his full potential. A profile of each child is built from the first meeting between manager and parents and child, and is added to through observation of the child and discussion with parents throughout the child's time in the setting. These profiles inform the planning of appropriate activities and experiences, which should also take into account the individual interests of each child. It is important to remember that all children develop along a determined continuum but at different rates. A high quality early years setting would ensure that the social, emotional, physical and intellectual aspects of the continuum are incorporated into the planning of appropriate activities. It is vital for early years practitioners to have an in-depth knowledge and understanding not only of child development but also of the likes and dislikes, interests and preferences of each child.

Many early years settings use the key worker system to enable children to develop a strong relationship with an individual adult. Research has demonstrated that this system supports children when they are separated from their primary carers. Experience has shown that early years practitioners can really get to know individual children and families through this system and use any information gained to inform planning.

Equal opportunities

Every early years programme and curriculum must offer all young children high quality experiences that reflect their individual needs and abilities. It is the responsibility of the early years manager to ensure that the team actively promotes equal opportunities in the setting, in all aspects of their work (see Chapter 9). Equality of opportunity cannot be left to chance: it has to be carefully planned so that it becomes fully integrated into every aspect of the setting.

The way young children see themselves and the way others see them is crucial to their development. A child's positive self-image can be achieved only through a policy of equal opportunities that actively sets out to promote anti-bias and anti-discriminatory practice. In order to achieve this, practitioners should:

- actively involve parents and carers in the planning process;
- research unfamiliar topics and issues;
- keep up to date with related research and changes in practice;
- make use of support and information available from specialist organisations.

In addition, the setting should:

- have in place a special needs policy that is regularly reviewed and updated;
- have a designated special educational needs coordinator (SENCO), who is responsible for guiding and supporting colleagues.

Think it over

Equality of opportunity is too important to be left to chance. How does your setting provide equal opportunities for the following groups?

- The children.
- Parents and carers.
- The staff.
- Other adults in the setting.

How does your setting monitor and review practice? Compare your answers with someone from a different setting.

Providing positive role models

Equal opportunities messages are best reinforced by the provision of positive role models. The following are examples of good practice:

- Invite both male and female visitors to the setting.
- Invite people who are generally not well represented in a particular role – for example a female doctor.
- Encourage mothers and fathers, grandmothers and grandfathers to help in the setting.
- Always avoid dividing the children by gender, for example 'Girls line up first' or 'Can I have two strong boys to help me?'
- Represent different cultures in your resources, books, dressing-up clothes, cooking activities and experiences.
- Demonstrate positive attitudes to different races and cultures.
- Encourage people from different ethnic backgrounds to become involved in the setting.
- Respect the restrictions and choices of different cultures and religions.
- Collect items and resources from a range of cultures to be used for display or to stimulate discussion.
- Have a welcome notice in different languages and dual-text books, and refer to them in talks with the children.
- Emphasise the value of cultural diversity through learning about different festivals and celebrations.

In addition to promoting equal opportunities, practitioners are also responsible for modelling a range of behaviours. Children learn a great deal from adults around them. They learn how to communicate appropriately, how to apply social rules and how to interact with others. Early years practitioners model these skills through interaction with children, each other and the parents and carers. Other positive behaviour that can be modelled includes:

- active learning, exploring, problem-solving and questioning;

Figure 2.2. Encourage parents, grandparents and carers to help in the setting.

- respect and courtesy;
- active listening;
- negotiation skills;
- care for the environment;
- social and emotional skills.

Many of these skills can also be encouraged through play, which is discussed below.

Young children learn a great deal from those around them, about themselves and others. Early years practitioners should offer children guidance and support in developing positive attitudes towards all people. In order to achieve this, all adults in the setting need to have an understanding and awareness of what equality of opportunities really involves and how to facilitate it. Inclusive practice helps to provide an environment rich in diversity that enables children to develop interpersonal skills and understand and appreciate differences, and this is considered next.

Inclusion

Inclusion is based on the belief that young children with particular or special needs are more similar to than different from their peers and that all young children benefit from learning together as members of a diverse community. Children with particular needs are more likely to develop positive social skills when they are integrated with their typical peers.

Case study — Children with special needs

During an introductory visit to her new placement, Masuma, a student on a Diploma in Child Care and Education course, sat with Andrew, aged 4, who was struggling with a cutting activity. Masuma thought that he appeared younger than the other children and noticed that he was less able to use the scissors effectively. Masuma offered to help Andrew by holding the picture as he attempted to cut it out. Andrew enjoyed the attention and began to talk about what he was doing. Masuma praised him for working hard and encouraged him to continue to the end. After a short while, a member of the nursery staff interrupted them and suggested that Masuma might enjoy helping a more able child.

- What effect do you think the attitude of the member of the nursery staff might have on this child?
- What message is being given to the student?
- Why do you think the member of staff feels this way?
- As an early years manager how would you deal with this situation?

Enhancing self-esteem

Children appear to develop their level of self-esteem from early experiences; these build up for the child a picture of her or his own ability, competence and social acceptance in a range of activities. Such experiences will be gained in the family and in the early years setting, and can either build a strong foundation from which self-esteem will grow or cause a child to feel incompetent and insecure. It is the role of the early years practitioner to ensure children can develop their self-image through helping children to feel:

- competent and able;
- confident in their physical skills and abilities;
- socially accepted;
- that they belong.

Children who have high self-esteem can recognise that they are not good at everything and may find some things difficult. They understand that they are not less worthy because they struggle with some tasks. They are not inhibited in trying out ideas and are not frightened of making mistakes.

Children who develop low self-esteem are less likely to develop to their full potential, either academically or socially. Children with low self-esteem:

- may dislike themselves and have few feelings of self-worth;
- may appear over-confident, which is a common strategy to cover a fragile self-image;
- may have difficulties in forming and maintaining relationships.

It is the role of the early years practitioner to support children with low self-esteem through consistent praise and encouragement. Such a positive approach can lead children to begin to develop the skills they need to learn and socialise.

Think it over

Children with a poor self-image are less likely to achieve their full potential. How can a setting actively promote a good self-image? Use the following questions to help you to evaluate practice in your setting. Try to think of examples for each question.

- Are children praised regularly, not only for achievement but also for effort?
- Do adults give time and attention to individual children?
- Do adults value the contributions made by children and their families?
- Do children see that their families are welcomed and valued?

Share your findings with someone from another setting. Are there any common approaches to how a good self-image is promoted?

Play as a vehicle for learning

Play is regarded as the primary vehicle for children's development and learning and should be used as an opportunity for children to question, try out, test and explore ideas. A high quality setting values the importance of play as a vehicle for high quality learning. It is a fundamental principle that children learn through play, and high quality play can provide children with the motivation for self-directed learning. In addition, play is essential to a child's healthy growth and development. Through purposeful play, children are able to develop a range of skills at their own individual level and pace (see Figure 2.3).

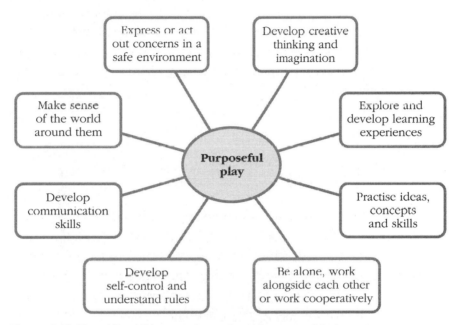

Figure 2.3. The skills children can learn through purposeful play.

The role of the adult in supporting play

The early years manager should ensure that the team understands their important role in both facilitating and supporting all varieties of play. Without well planned, purposeful play opportunities, resources and sensitive support from adults, learning opportunities are not maximised. Sensitive support requires early years practitioners to know:

- how to offer physical support, for example holding a piece of paper being cut out by a child who is struggling with the task;
- when to offer encouragement in order for children to complete tasks by themselves;
- when to ask questions in order to support problem-solving;
- when to make suggestions;
- when their involvement, help or support is not needed.

It could be argued that the most important point is the last one.

Early years practitioners should always resist the temptation to add to or complete children's work, as this takes away the children's ownership of it and minimises the value of the experience. They should also be prepared to have their offers of involvement rejected by children, who have the right to choose to play without adult input.

Think it over

Observe a colleague giving a group of children a creative activity to do.

- What level of adult interaction or support did the children require during the activity?
- Did the children receive uninvited adult support and attention?
- Were opportunities taken to extend the activity and the children's learning?
- What factors may have prevented your colleagues from providing the children with support during the activity?

Share your findings with the group.

2.3 Quality indicators

Quality indicators should be evident in all areas of practice. They are specific areas of practice that can be assessed and, if necessary, improved. They can therefore demonstrate whether or not high standards of learning provision and care are being consistently met in the setting. An important role of the early years manager in assuring quality is regularly to review and evaluate all aspects of the setting. For that evaluation to be effective, it must lead to any necessary changes being made to practice.

Childcare currently has a high profile nationally and is the focus of new policies, accreditations and initiatives that aim to increase the quality of provision for young children. Both the Children Act 1989 and Sir Christopher Ball's *Start Right* report (1994) emphasised the importance of high quality early childhood education. Many of the ideas set out in these have helped to identify a range of quality indicators for early years settings, and these include:

- clear aims and objectives of individually planned activities and experiences;
- an effective management structure;
- an equal opportunities policy;
- positive relationships between all team members and parents and carers;
- high levels of parental involvement in the running of the setting;
- a positive atmosphere in which both children and adults feel valued and confident;

- a developmentally appropriate curriculum which is balanced and reflects the children's interests;
- planning informed by regular observation and assessment of the children;
- an environment that encourages children to be actively involved in their learning, with a strong emphasis on play and talking;
- effective record-keeping of children's progress and learning;
- well trained staff who can understand and respond to the needs of individual children;
- low staff turnover;
- an effective key worker system;
- the implementation of a staff development plan that ensures access to regular support and training;
- a well organised environment, with high quality equipment and resources inside and outside, where health and safety standards are met;
- links developed between the setting and community to promote children's health, care and education;
- regular evaluation and review of practice.

These quality indicators apply to all settings with young children and can be used as a guide for good practice. High quality practice that is developmentally appropriate can be achieved only when all practitioners in the setting share the same professional principles and values. As an early years manager it is important to ensure that all of your team are familiar with the quality indicators so they can be consistently incorporated into practice. Practical ways of achieving this include:

- providing a list of quality indicators in staff induction packs;
- displaying a copy of the list of quality indicators on the staff notice board;
- regularly selecting different points to evaluate during team meetings to assess how well each is being met.

Below, more detailed consideration is given to the use of quality indicators in one of the areas listed above – a well organised environment – to illustrate how practice can be evaluated.

A well organised environment

A well organised environment, with high quality equipment and resources inside and outside, is central to providing a quality learning experience for young children. The range of resources provided by a setting will greatly depend on budget, storage and availability; however, there are some basics that all settings should provide. These are listed in Table 2.3. By evaluating this aspect of the setting you can identify any areas that need to be added to or improved.

Table 2.3. Equipment and resources: basic provision checklist

Type of equipment/resource	Check points
Sand	Wet and dry sand, plus tools and equipment that are changed frequently to maintain interest. Freedom to add other toys (e.g. cars, animals and people) to stimulate imaginative play
Water	Changed daily. Add colour, bubbles, warm water, ice cubes, snow to stimulate and extend learning
Imaginative play area	Changed regularly with the help of the children to encourage role-play and provide a range of learning experiences (e.g. vets, post office, home, café)
Book corner	Frequently changed books as well as a stock of old favourites. Both information and story books available and books made by the children
Art and craft activities	A large range of materials and resources for children to access freely, without the support of an adult. Space for work and models to dry, be displayed and opportunities to return to finish work
Large construction blocks	Placed in a suitable area, which allows the children to be freely creative without disturbing other children at play
Small construction materials	Freely accessible
Table-top activities	'Small world' play, jigsaws, threading beads, etc., available for children to choose from and work with
Music area	Displaying both bought and child-made instruments, which can be freely used (i.e. not just with adult supervision)
Cooking facilities	A regularly provided range of cooking experiences, including a variety of sweet and savoury foods from different cultures. Cooking activities can be used to extend learning experience
Live animals and plants	Those that do not pose a health risk
Investigative area	Regularly changed resources and equipment that are interesting and stimulating
Space and time for physical activity	Including dance, drama, movement
Quiet area/baby sleep-room	For younger children to rest or sleep
Well equipped outside area	With a range of equipment to encourage physical development
Staffroom	Space away from the children where staff can have meetings and take breaks
Toilets	Minimum of one toilet and washbasin with hot and cold water available per 10 children over the age of 2. Separate toilet facilities for adults

Use Table 2.3 to assess the environment in your setting.

- Does it provide all the equipment and resources listed?
- If not, can you say why not?
- How are these areas organised in your setting?
- How might these areas be developed to maximise their potential?

Equipment used by children should be regularly checked for signs of wear or damage.

When evaluating the equipment and resources in your setting it can be helpful to consider the following points:

- Are all resources, equipment and furniture appropriate to the age and developmental stage of the children?
- Are all the resources and equipment easily accessible and attractively presented?
- Is all equipment maintained properly and checked regularly for safety?

Top Tip

List all equipment and resources in an inventory. This will be invaluable in the event of an insurance claim.

In addition to the fundamental basics of equipment, Hertfordshire's Early Years Development and Childcare Partnership (see websites listed at end of chapter) has identified some key principles in relation to the early years environment, many of which are echoed in the National Standards for under-8s day care and childminding (section 2.1):

- All areas both inside and out should be interesting and inviting, with the flexibility to cater for the children's individual stages of learning.
- The atmosphere should be warm, happy and relaxed, with a familiar routine and structure.
- Accommodation should have a good quality light source where children work and play.
- Access should be adult controlled by means of a security system.
- Display areas for children's work and interactive experiences should be offered at a variety of levels.

- Furniture and fittings should be appropriate to the child's age.
- Toys and materials should be stored attractively, and be readily accessible and clearly labelled.
- There should be a carpeted area for floor play and an easily washed floor for messy and creative play.
- The layout should give children the opportunity to mix freely and work individually, in pairs and in groups of varying sizes.
- There should be at least one quiet area.
- There should be separate, defined areas appropriate to various activities.
- The children should have enough clear space to use their energy safely, and in this regard they should be provided with stimulation and challenge.
- The staff need to plan a space for confidential listening and talking to children and parents.

Think it over

Think about the list of key principles for providing a high quality environment.

- How many of these principles are already met by your setting?
- Are there any areas you feel need addressing?
- Do you monitor the layout of your setting and discuss any changes identified as a result of observation?

Organisation of equipment and resources

Careful thought needs to be given to how equipment and resources are presented. Children need space to work individually, in pairs and in groups, according to age and preference. They need the freedom to make choices, select materials and be freely creative. How equipment and resources are presented will greatly affect their use by children. In order to encourage children to use their natural curiosity and freely explore the range of equipment on offer, it needs to be easily accessible and attractive to them.

Many of the resources used in early years settings are consumable, particularly those linked to art and craft activities, for example paint, pencils, paper and glue. As these types of resources do not last long they can easily be neglected. In order to avoid this they need to be taken into account when each term's budget is set. How art consumables are managed is very important, as children who persistently have to work with resources and materials that are worn out or in short supply are unlikely to gain much from the experience. Poor management of these types of resources gives a strong message to children and parents that creative work is not valued.

- How does your setting ensure that there is an adequate supply of consumable art materials and resources?
- How are these materials presented to the children?
- Are the children encouraged to be responsible for the care of consumable items, for example replacing lids on felt pens?

Case study — Renewing resources

Pip and Carol have recently taken over the running of their local playgroup. They have inherited a vast range of equipment and resources, some of which date back to when the playgroup was first established, 15 years ago. Part of their reorganisation strategy involves evaluating which pieces of equipment are no longer required, are out of date or are no longer suitable. They start by observing the children at play and recording which pieces of equipment are used regularly. From their observations they note that few of the children play with the very large range of jigsaws available. The jigsaws are stacked on low shelves in a quiet area of the room. Some are still in their original box while others are stored in plastic boxes with lids.

- Why do you think the children were not choosing to play with the jigsaws?
- Consider how equipment and resources are presented in your setting and whether this has an effect on their use.

Organisation of space

The organisation of space is vitally important and should be focused around children as much as possible. The room arrangement should encourage and support play, not restrict or limit it. A sound knowledge of child development and an understanding of how children play should inform how a room layout is planned.

How the room is organised will have an impact on children and how they behave. You might consider:

- how well the resources are used by children;
- how active children can be;
- how welcoming the setting appears;
- the overall atmosphere;
- the choices children make;
- their relationships with adults and peers;
- their behaviour;
- their ability to play freely.

In the nursery class of an infant school a group of 3- and 4-year-olds regularly play a game which involves loading up trolleys and pushchairs with dolls and blankets and filling up bags and boxes with food and equipment from the home corner. These are then transported around the room where 'camps' or picnics are set up. The room arrangement supports this form of play and allows children unrestricted access to equipment and to move freely about the room without disturbing others. The early years practitioners regularly monitor and review the room arrangement in their team meetings. During a recent meeting it is suggested by Siobhan, a newly qualified early years practitioner, that the room is rearranged to discourage this type of play as it causes too much tidying up at the end of the session.

- What skills are children developing through this type of play?
- Why is it important to allow children to play in this way?
- How can this type of play be supported and extended?
- What can the early years practitioners learn from observing children playing in this way?

An evaluation of the layout and organisation of the environment would cover the following points.

- Does the room look well organised?
- What are the first impressions when newcomers see the setting?
- Does the room look clean, bright and inviting?
- Are the hazardous items clearly labelled, correctly stored and out of children's reach?
- Are resources used by the children clearly labelled, easily accessible and nicely presented?
- Are adult resources well organised, labelled and easily accessible?
- Is there suitable storage for equipment and resources?
- Is the outside environment used as an integral part of the children's learning, and do children have freedom to move between inside and out for part of the session?

Think it over

Consider whether all of the spaces within your setting are used effectively.

- Is there space for children to engage in active learning?
- Do children have space to move around the room without disturbing others?
- Are all areas valuable for young learners?

Draw a floor plan of your setting, remembering to include: access points and emergency exits, toilets, classroom sinks and non-movable items of furniture. Look at each area.

- Could they be organised more effectively?
- Are the resources required for each area stored nearby?

2.4 Maintaining quality

Throughout this chapter ways of achieving a high quality provision have been identified. Equally important as achieving it is maintaining it. Regular reviews of practice enable the manager to ensure that the very best service is provided for children and families in the setting. Therefore, to maintain quality, it is good practice:

- to review policies and procedures regularly;
- to monitor achievement;
- to review practice against quality indicators (section 2.3) and the National Standards (section 2.1);
- to include parents and carers in the assessment and evaluation process;
- to implement change as a result of assessment and review.

The quality of early years provision can be assessed in many ways. Most approaches examine quality by selecting characteristics of the setting, equipment or programme, and measuring them against the National Standards. There is no doubt that this is an important and valuable method of assessment; however, viewing quality through an imposed framework gives only a partial view of practice. Therefore it can be a worthwhile exercise to determine how those who use it experience the provision. Users will include children, parents and carers and the staff.

Reviewing the setting from different users' perspectives

The children's viewpoint

By evaluating the children's experience of the provision you can gain a valuable insight into its effectiveness. This evaluation requires answers to the central question 'What does it feel like to be a child in this environment?' You can use the following points as a guide to answering this question.

- Do the children appear to feel welcomed?
- Do they appear to feel that they belong as an individual or as just one of the group?
- Do they appear to feel accepted, understood and protected by the adults in the setting?
- Do they appear to feel accepted by each other?
- Do the adults in the setting address the children respectfully?
- Are the majority of the activities engaging, absorbing and challenging?
- Are the majority of the planned experiences meaningful?
- Are the activities and experiences age appropriate?
- Do the children enjoy being in the setting?

- Are routines and procedures in place to meet the needs of the children and not for the convenience of the adults?

Each point represents a criterion of quality derived from what is known about the influences on children's long-term growth, development and learning. If the answers to these questions are mostly positive you can assume that the setting is providing a high quality service from the children's point of view. It will be one in which learning experiences are consistently intellectually and socially engaging. Research has shown that infrequent and isolated learning experiences are unlikely to have an affect on long-term development. In order to stimulate and satisfy curiosity, planned activities and experiences need to be frequent, and have clear aims and learning outcomes in order to be most effective. However, these activities and experiences do not have to be exceptionally dynamic or unusual to have an impact. Young children view the world with fresh eyes and it is easy to forget that what may seem mundane for adults is full of possibilities for children.

The parents' and carers' viewpoint

The assessment and evaluation of quality practice will always take into account the viewpoint of parents and carers. You can use the following questions to help evaluate the relationship between parents and carers and the setting.

- Is information about the setting provided before children start?
- Are parents and carers encouraged to stay until their child has settled?
- Are they welcomed each day and are staff available to them?
- Are individual families' levels of involvement respected and understood by staff?
- Are parents and carers actively encouraged to discuss concerns, problems and changes involving the child or family as they occur?
- Does the setting celebrate achievements and milestones as they occur?
- Are experiences and activities shared through 'open' sessions, parents' workshops, outings, social events, publicity and fundraising?
- Are parents and carers invited to come in and talk about their own skills, hobbies and jobs with children or join in sessions to support children?
- Are themes, routines and 'happenings' shared via a notice board or newsletter?

Many of these questions form the foundation of work with parents and carers. However, it is good practice to review and evaluate what is done in order to maintain standards and to ensure that the needs of all the families in the setting are met.

The staff viewpoint

When assessing the quality of the setting, it is always useful for the manager to include an evaluation from the team's viewpoint. High quality environments cannot be created unless they are also good for the adults who work in them. Experience shows that early years practitioners who feel good about themselves and their professional practice are more able to provide challenging experiences for the children in their care. They are more likely to have time, confidence and energy to fulfil all aspects of their responsibilities with children and families.

There are three aspects to the quality of an early years setting from the practitioners' viewpoint:

- relationships with other team members;
- relationships with parents;
- relationships with managers, head teachers and or owners of the setting.

The quality of the relationships between team members will affect the quality of the setting. It is difficult to be consistent and work towards shared aims when team members do not get on. It can be helpful for the manager to carry out a confidential assessment of the team's relationships with each other. An assessment of this aspect of quality would be based on how each team member answered the following question:

- Are your relationships with other team members mostly supportive, cooperative, accepting, trusting, respectful?

The answers can help you to organise your team. However, because skills and responsibilities also need to be taken into account, it is not always possible to separate team members. These answers will also highlight areas for staff development – by equipping individuals with the skills needed to work in teams in a professional manner you are able to work towards providing a more positive working environment.

The development of respectful and supportive relationships between staff and parents and carers from a diverse range of backgrounds requires staff professionalism based on a combination of experience, training and personal values. Parents and carers are more likely to approach staff when staff initiate positive relationships with them. Part of the process of assessing the quality of the setting would involve evaluating the characteristics of the relationship between the staff and the parents. The following question can help team members to evaluate their own relationship with parents.

- Are my relationships with parents mostly respectful and supporting, accepting, non-judgemental and non-biased, and on-going, with frequent contact?

Parents and carers are more likely to feel part of the setting when the staff show that they value them.

Lastly, one potential indirect influence on the quality of provision is the nature of the relationships the team have with those to whom they are accountable. Research has shown that staff treat children in a similar way to how their managers treat them. If a team feels under-valued it can be hard for them to feel enthusiastic and positive about the work they are doing. They may not behave in an unprofessional manner but their lack of enthusiasm will reduce the quality of their work. The following questions can help the early years manager to assess the team's relationships with him or her:

- Do the working conditions encourage the staff to develop their knowledge and skills, and take on more responsibility?
- Are staff usually treated with respect and understanding?

Some thought and consideration will need to be given to how these questions are presented to the team. Staff may feel that it is hard for them to answer these questions honestly and openly; therefore it can be good practice to present such questions on a form that can be completed anonymously.

Reviewing organisational systems and practice

Most early years practitioners recognise the value of regularly evaluating practice and procedures. As group dynamics change with each new intake, so do the needs of children and their families. Evaluation of practice ensures that these needs can be met. Regular review and assessment of organisational systems and practice enable you to identify achievements and areas for development. This enables the service to progress and meet the ever-changing needs of parents and children.

All organisational systems need to be frequently evaluated. Areas to be considered include:

- *The management of all team meetings.* Are there clear agendas?
- *Programme reviews.* Are there regular dates (termly) set for reviewing individual programmes in order to assess whether the needs of the children are being met?
- *Current research and ideas.* Are staff encouraged and given the opportunity to keep up to date with new ideas and current research?
- *Professional development.* Do all members of the team have the opportunity to attend regular training?
- *The management of policies, parental comments and concerns, and staff suggestions.* Are these being appropriately addressed? Are policies and

procedures updated as necessary and always available to all staff and students for reference?

Staff training and professional development

Research has found a correlation between high quality provision and the level of staff training. Early years practitioners in the UK are generally better trained than their counterparts in mainland Europe. Currently all those early years practitioners who are responsible for supervising staff are required to hold a level 3 qualification appropriate for caring for young children. At least half of all other childcare staff need to hold a level 2 qualification (see section 2.1).

High quality work in early years settings is possible only when staff are appropriately trained. Initial training is important but continuous training and professional development are crucial (this is discussed further in Chapter 7). Early years practitioners need to continue to learn, and to be open to new ideas and approaches. As in any profession, early years practitioners can become stale and approach work always in the same way merely because that is how it has always been done. As an early years manager it is your role to ensure that your team receives on-going training. This can include:

- in-house training;
- update training for first aid and other renewable certificates;
- short courses, seminars and talks provided by local networks;
- college courses;
- university courses.

Training and updating should include the following topics, as they are the subject of constant research and development:

- equal opportunities;
- child protection;
- special educational needs;
- managing children's behaviour.

Observation, assessment and record-keeping

In order to help you ensure that your setting is implementing developmentally appropriate practice it is necessary to carry out regular observations of the children in the setting. These observations add to individual profiles built over time and inform planning. It is not possible to plan effectively without knowing exactly where children are starting. Regular observation, assessment and record-keeping are considered to be the basis of good childcare practice.

- *Observation* allows you to maintain and update the profile of each child. It alerts you to any causes for concern and highlights advancement in development. Observation can be either formal or informal. Practitioners make frequent and regular informal observations of children, noting and sharing any significant points. Formal observations are most successful when there is a focus. Through formal observation practitioners are able to build a full picture of individual children's strengths and abilities and those areas that need support. Regular, focused observations are key to developmentally appropriate practice, as they inform all aspects of planning.
- *Assessment* is made of the results of observation and of information shared by parents and carers. Assessment results are used to inform planning and to identify areas in which children may need extending or supporting. Assessment of children's performance enables you to evaluate the effectiveness of educational strategies.
- *Record-keeping* is essential for good practice as it provides evidence for future reference. Records of observations, assessments and planning should always be kept.

A variety of record-keeping strategies are commonly used in early years settings (Figure 2.4).

Figure 2.4. Record-keeping strategies.

High quality provision combines observational evidence with a range of other techniques to provide a rich record of the achievements, interests and needs of children attending the setting. Early years practitioners constantly observe children and make formal records of observations according to a predetermined focus. Individual profiles containing samples of children's work and photographs of experiences can be shared with parents and carers.

Reflective practice

Another key aspect of maintaining quality is to be a reflective practitioner. Effective assessment and record-keeping support the process of reflecting on practice, as they provide evidence of past events. Reflecting on practice enables you to identify areas for improvement or change, and highlights areas of success.

The curriculum content and procedures and routines that are offered to young children must match the content of their thinking, their development and understanding in order to extend their learning and understanding. The reflective practitioner may devise a variety of teaching approaches to support children's learning and needs to know which is most successful. For example, the practitioner may decide to change from a structured approach to one which allows children to select their own activities and wishes to know whether change has been beneficial.

Being a reflective practitioner requires you:

- to think about issues from more than one point of view;
- to review activities and approaches, and to find scope for improvement;
- to be open to new ideas, approaches and changes in practice;
- to acknowledge and recognise the feelings of children, parents and colleagues;
- to be actively involved and enthusiastic.

All early years managers are responsible for encouraging reflective practice within their team. Areas that benefit from reflective practice include:

- planning for children's learning;
- the organisation of developmentally appropriate learning opportunities;
- supporting and extending learning;
- recording children's progress;
- meeting the individual needs of children;
- working in partnership with parents, carers and colleagues.

Case study — Teddy Bears day nursery

Diane is the manager at Teddy Bears day nursery. As part of the regular review of practice, Diane has asked each room supervisor to carry out a series of observations over a week, focusing on procedures and practice in order to identify any areas for development. The supervisor of the toddler room, Sarah, sees that the children frequently become distressed at lunchtime, when they are moved into the dining room to join an older group of children for their lunch. Further investigation shows that it is taking almost 15 minutes to complete hand-washing and that the children are becoming frustrated waiting for this to be completed.

- Why do you think the children are distressed at this time of day?

Time management

Lastly, maintaining a high quality service for the children and families using the setting is a time-consuming process. It is an on-going process of review, evaluation, assessment and reflection, all of which have to be carefully planned and facilitated. Time needs to be managed carefully in order to achieve this. There are two elements to good time management: effectiveness and efficiency, or doing the right jobs and doing each job correctly.

As an early years manager you will find that your team is an essential resource to time management. Team members have a range of skills and abilities that should be utilised. Once these have been identified, related tasks can be delegated and redistributed, allowing you more time for other projects. By giving team members individual roles and responsibilities you are recognising their skills and demonstrating that their contribution to the setting is valued.

Conclusion

High quality early years childcare and education have a significant impact on later academic achievement and social behaviour. Providing a high quality service is not about taking on a whole new approach: it is about recognising and celebrating what you already do well and identifying areas that could be improved. Many, if not most, aspects of practice in your setting will be of a high standard and it is this level that needs to be maintained. It is probably impossible to share a common definition of quality and therefore there is a need to work towards a common understanding of how staff, parents and children define the term.

There is no universal measure of quality, as it is relative and subjective. For example, parents, staff and children will have different views on what they believe is good quality. However, the key aspects of quality provision as outlined in this chapter include:

- regular review and assessment of practice, followed by change in practice where necessary;
- a child-centred approach that is developmentally appropriate and values play as a primary vehicle for development and learning;
- a programme that values and recognises the importance of diversity;
- staff training and professional development;
- reflective practice.

Early years practitioners generally share the same values and principles and work towards a set of nationally recognised quality indicators in order to facilitate developmentally appropriate practice. In practical terms this means that early years programmes take into account the child's level of development – social, cognitive, physical and emotional – and practice is based on child-initiated activities and experiences. Early years practitioners widely accept that social, physical, cognitive and emotional learning is as important as academic learning. Programmes that incorporate these principles create a positive learning environment that is conducive to healthy emotional development and motivates children to learn.

Regular review and changes to practice enable settings to ensure they are consistently meeting the needs of children and that the provision is developmentally appropriate. These changes need to be 'owned' by practitioners rather than imposed through inspection or accreditation frameworks in order to be most effective.

Check your understanding

1 'Quality encompasses all areas of the setting, not just those directly linked to the children.' What areas do you think this statement is referring to?
2 How is quality both subjective and relative?
3 What do you understand by the term 'developmentally appropriate practice'?

References and further reading

Ball, C. (1994) *Start Right. The Importance of Early Learning.* London: Royal Society for the Encouragement of Arts, Manufactures and Commerce.

Department for Education and Skills (2001) *Special Educational Needs. Code of Practice.* London: DfES. Available at www.teachernet.gov.uk/ doc/ 3724/SENCodeOfPractice.pdf.

Department for Education and Skills (2003) *National Standards for Under 8s Day Care and Childminding. Full Day Care*, DfES/0651/2003. London: DfES. Available at www.surestart.gov.uk/_doc/0-ACA52E.PDF. Copies can be ordered from DfES Publications, Nottingham, telephone 0845 602 2260.

Dowling, M. (2000) *Young Children's Personal, Social and Emotional Development.* London: Paul Chapman.

Dury, R., Miller, L. and Campbell, R. (2000) *Looking at Early Years Education and Care.* London: David Fulton.

Early Childhood Education Forum (1998) *Quality in Diversity in Early Learning.* London: NCB.

Moss, P. and Penn, H. (1996) *Transforming Nursery Education.* London: Paul Chapman.

Qualifications and Curriculum Authority (2000) *Curriculum Guidance for the Foundation Stage.* London: QCA. Available at www.qca.org.uk/ages3-14/downloads/cg_foundation_stage.pdf.

Useful websites

Hertfordshire Early Years Development and Childcare Partnership: www.hertsdirect.org/hcc/csf/homelife/younginherts/aboutyoung.

Qualifications and Curriculum Authority: www.qca.org.uk/ages3-14.

SureStart: www.surestart.gov.uk/ensuringquality.

3 Managing the Early Years Curriculum

There have been a lot of changes over the past few years in the way children are viewed and more importance is now attached to the early years stage of development. There is a clear focus on practitioners providing a common framework for children's learning. The idea is that all children in Britain must have access to high quality provision in order to have the same opportunities to learn. The expression of this commonality is seen in the national curriculum for 5–16-year-olds (see www.nc.uk.net/index.html), the *Curriculum Guidance for the Foundation Stage* (for 3–5-year-olds) (Qualifications and Curriculum Authority, 2000) and more recently the *Birth to Three Matters* framework (Department for Education and Skills, 2002).

As an early years manager you will need to focus on interpreting the requirements of national legislation in a way that meets the needs of individual children and those of groups of children. You must consider the practical application of the curriculum and the relationship between planning and the relevant curriculum guidance and legislation. Ofsted inspectors will assess the provision on this basis.

This chapter discusses the key issues involved in the management of the early years curriculum and covers the following areas:

3.1   Defining the curriculum.

3.2   Theories of how children learn and their influence on practice.

3.3   Planning, implementing and evaluating the curriculum.

3.4   Assessment and assessment systems.

3.5   The development of children and the role of play in the curriculum.

3.1 Defining the curriculum

As a leader of an early years team it is necessary that you have a clear vision and understanding of the term 'curriculum' to ensure that you provide your team with a focus for their work. The term can be defined in two ways:

- as a planned overview of activities that have specific learning outcomes;
- as everything that children do, see, hear or feel in their setting.

With regard to the former, national guidance and legislation determine what activities the children should have access to, and should be taught, and the goals that should be met by a predefined stage (see Table 3.1). However, each setting will need to determine the stage of development of its children and the most appropriate way to meet their needs. Your own educational views, the national legislative framework and the strengths of your staff will influence the curriculum that you offer, in the second sense above, which is the focus of this chapter. The curriculum you can offer will also be influenced by the environment within which you are working, as well as commonly held views on how children learn (section 3.2).

Within an early years team, people will hold different views on what a curriculum is and how it should be implemented. It will be necessary to spend time and energy on agreeing the fundamental principles behind an early years curriculum and how these can be implemented in your particular setting in order for all team members to share ownership of it. There may need to be a series of meetings to ensure continuity of approach and opportunity for reflection on the success of the curriculum.

In the UK the curriculum is generally based on a Western approach towards education and reflects the work of theorists such as Piaget (see section 3.2) and modern practitioners, including Margy Whalley (1994) and Bernadette Duffy (1998). The child is seen as the focus of the curriculum and is respected as a person with individual needs, not as a miniature adult.

Meeting curriculum requirements

Modern approaches require that the curriculum is:

- child-centred;
- developmentally appropriate;
- differentiated;
- inclusive.

Child-centred

The starting point for the child is what he or she can do, rather than what he or she cannot do, and progression is encouraged through exploration and experimentation. The curriculum is carefully structured to ensure all areas of learning are explored while ensuring the interest of the child is maintained. This may be referred to as a child-centred curriculum, which will emphasise the child's development and relationships with others. Adults working with children in the early years will need to have a sound understanding of child development and a working knowledge of activities that promote development. To ensure the curriculum is balanced, practitioners will spend considerable time planning, reflecting on and evaluating the curriculum they offer. For the manager this process must be documented in order to meet Ofsted regulations.

Developmentally appropriate

The Western approach towards education acknowledges the need for a developmentally appropriate curriculum that recognises the child's age and stage of development. The curriculum will set out what activities and experiences will consolidate and enhance the child's learning. National curriculum guidance specifies a developmentally appropriate curriculum for children of given ages. The foundation stage, for example, gives clear goals for learning that are appropriate for 3–5-year-olds and includes extension activities.

Differentiated

A differentiated curriculum enables individual children to learn in their own particular way. Children will progress through their educational life at their own pace and in their own style. Some children will learn to read at 4 years old while others will not do so until the age of 6. Counting may be easily mastered by a few children at pre-school but others will not understand how to count with understanding until they are in nursery. A differentiated curriculum recognises this fact and ensures that children have the opportunity to learn at their own pace.

Inclusive

Children who are challenged in their learning through disability or developmental delay will also need to have their learning needs accounted for within the curriculum. Some of these children are currently educated in separate provision; the modern approach is towards inclusive education. The challenge for early years educators is to integrate all children and meet the needs of individuals and the group as a whole. There is also a need to incorporate the wishes of parents and to work alongside learning support assistants (LSAs) to provide the best possible curriculum. This may include the writing of individual educational plans (IEPs) (for children ages 3 years and over) and it is good practice to include all practitioners involved with the child in the planning process.

Table 3.1. Regulatory and legislative framework

	Key features	Assessment	Further information
Birth to Three Matters	Acknowledgement of the importance of this age and stage of development. Holistic approach to the child with the child as the focus. Importance of good quality provision. Child seen in terms of: skilful communicator, competent learner, strong child, healthy child. Each area has four components linked to development and highlights the interrelationship between growth, learning, development and the environment in which children are cared for and educated. The emphasis is on a non-structured curriculum and steering away from distinct curriculum headings.	National guidance rather than regulations. A framework to support practitioners working with children from birth to 3 years. Ofsted will use the framework as guidance for inspection. The importance of observation is noted.	The framework (Department for Education and Skills, 2002) aims to raise the status of staff working with this age range. The framework must be considered in relation to the *National Standards for Under 8s Day Care and Childminding* (Department for Education and Skills, 2003) and the *Curriculum Guidance for the Foundation Stage* (Qualifications and Curriculum Authority, 2000). Principles underlying the framework include the importance of parents and families to the well-being of the child. Recognition is made of the role of other people in the child's life and the relationships with key people. Learning is seen as a shared process. Children need to have the opportunity to make decisions and errors. The role of learning by doing is also acknowledged. The guide comes as a box containing information cards, a poster, a video and a CD-ROM and is available through SureStart. It is distributed free to childminders and day care providers. Contact DfES publications on 0845 602 2260.
Foundation stage	Published in 2000. For ages 3–5 years. Preparation for key stage 1 of the national curriculum. The principles of early years education are outlined.	Early learning goals should be met by most children by the end of the foundation stage.	Copies of the *Curriculum Guidance for the Foundation Stage* and the *Foundation Stage Profile* are available from Qualifications and Curriculum Authority Publications, tel. 01787 884 444, and see www.qca.org.uk/ages3-14/160.html.

The Foundation Stage Profile summarises the child's achievements at the end of the foundation stage. It provides a baseline assessment in preparation for key stage 1 and information for year 1 teachers.

The stepping-stones show the knowledge and understanding that children need in order to achieve the early learning goals. They can be used to record progression through skills and attitudes towards the early learning goals and are not age related.

'Stepping-stones' show what practitioners need to know for each area of learning.

The Foundation Stage Profile encourages on-going observation and assessment of progress. Reports given to parents.

Six areas of learning:

- knowledge and understanding of the world;
- personal, social and emotional development;
- communication, language and literacy;
- mathematical development;
- physical development;
- creative development.

Copies of the national curriculum guidance are available at www.qca.org.uk/ages3-14,5-14/2812.html. Information on the national numeracy and literacy strategies are available at www.standards.dfes.gov.uk/numeracy/ and www.standards.dfes.gov.uk/literacy/

All teachers check progress as a normal part of teaching. Pupils are also assessed against the national curriculum standards of achievement. In England, national tests currently take place at ages 7, 11 and 14.

Schools must also compile yearly reports for parents.

National curriculum

Sets out in broad terms what schools must teach for each subject. Applies only from age 5 to 16. Divided into four stages:

- key stage 1 for children aged 5–7;
- key stage 2 for children aged 7–11;
- key stage 3 for children aged 11–14;
- key stage 4 for children aged 14–16.

Core subjects of English, maths and science are taught alongside physical education, history, geography, music, art and design/technology, information technology and a modern foreign language. Pupils also study religious education and sex education.

3.2 Theories of how children learn and their influence on practice

Children have an innate ability to learn and this should be fostered by the environment around them and the experiences they have. The way in which children learn is therefore important to practitioners. It forms a basis for their work. Understanding how children learn and how to support this learning requires a knowledge of child development, which in turn can be used to implement the curriculum.

Theorists and educators differ in the emphasis they put on the importance of 'nature' and 'nurture'. Biological theorists believe that there are biological or genetic explanations for the way children develop. Learning theorists hold that children develop as they do because they have contact with other people and learn from them. Psychoanalytical theories are in some ways a mixture of biological and learning theories: they describe children as being born with a set of needs that must be met if children are to develop healthily. Whatever your own views on genes versus environment, it is important to recognise the value of early experiences and how to build upon these within the educational setting.

Many have been influential in the development of the curriculum in the UK today. The two who have perhaps been most influential on modern practice are discussed in detail below, as is a recent study that had important findings regarding the way in which children learn. The work of many other theorists is summarised in Table 3.2. Research continues into how children learn. You may wish to spend time looking in more depth at the work of various theorists and educators. You can then use this information to inform your planning. It is good to spend time reflecting on practice and why the curriculum is implemented in certain ways.

Find it out

Choose a theorist or educator from Table 3.2.

Research for yourself the work that he or she did and make notes on the key points.

Reflect on that person's influence on modern-day practice in general.

Discuss with a colleague the influence on your own approach to implementing the curriculum.

Table 3.2. Influential early years theorists and educators

Name	Area of study	Key points and influence on current practice
Chris Athey	Schemas	A schema is 'a pattern of repeatable behaviour into which experiences are assimilated and that are gradually coordinated' (Athey, 1990). Work has contributed to observation skills developed by early years practitioners. Building on Athey's work, Cathy Nutbrown (1994) suggested that children perform best if they have adults who are interested in self-development and who value children's rights and needs. Staff in early years settings are now encouraged to participate in continuous professional development.
Albert Bandura	Social learning theory	Children can learn through imitation of others. The most influential people, for children, are those who are warm and loving towards the child or similar to them. In an experiment with the Bobo doll, children were shown a film in which an adult hits the Bobo doll and shouts at it. Three different endings were recorded, showing the adult rewarded, punished or nothing at all happening. When the children were later given their own Bobo doll they tended to hit the doll if they had seen the adult being rewarded for this behaviour. Conclusions were drawn that children will imitate behaviour they see rewarded, particularly if it is by someone they love. It was felt that children who were smacked or shouted at by adults would reflect this in their own behaviour. This emphasised the importance of positive role models.
John Bowlby	Attachment, separation, grief and loss	Worked on how babies become attached to the mother figure and what happens when they are separated. Young children can experience feelings of loss and grief when they are separated from loved ones. Children need to develop strong bonds with parents or key carers for healthy development. Bowlby's work has influenced how children are settled into a new setting and the assignment of key workers to babies and children. Films by James and Joyce Robertson showed Bowlby's theory in action, in that they illustrated the stages that a child goes through when left by families in hospital. These include protest, despair and detachment in dealing with people. This has led to important work on how to deal with the hospitalisation of children, including the use of play workers, and provision for parents to accompany their child.
Tina Bruce	Early years education and play	Practical application of work of theorists. Reasserts in a modern way the principles of early childhood tradition (Bruce, 1997). Emphasises the holistic nature of children's learning, the value of play and the importance of the adult. Looked to the future by building on the past.

Name	Area of study	Key points and influence on current practice
Jerome Bruner	Learning	Particularly interested in the role of the adult in children's learning. Adult provides the environment and the structure for learning. Scaffolding – the adult works with the child in a structured and supportive way. A skilled adult can enable the child to consolidate previous learning and move forward to the next step. Viewed language as central to children's thinking and learning. Believed a child could be taught any subject as long as it was in an appropriate way. Sequenced cognitive, or intellectual, development into three areas: enactive (learning through doing), iconic (imagining things they have done) and symbolic (e.g. talking, writing, reading). The impact has been to encourage practitioners to think carefully about the way they help children and to be aware that the adult role is significant in encouraging learning.
Friedrich Froebel	Learning	Founder of the kindergarten system in 1840, who devised activities for young children to learn through play. Saw the importance of children having 'real' experiences. Recognised importance of parents as first educators of their children. Considered that children's best thinking is done when they are playing. Saw importance of relationships with other children and adults. Very influential in the way we view children today; for example, considered children learn from the outdoor environment as well as indoors, invented finger rhymes and songs, and encouraged creativity.
Harry and Margaret Harlow	Attachment	Experiments on monkeys. Believed that contact and comfort are critical to emotional and social development. This work has given us greater understanding of this area of development, and the way in which children express emotions and build relationships.
Susan Isaacs	Emotional expression	Valued play as a means through which children can express their feelings. Also saw play as a child's work. Very significant input to the way we view play as a learning tool today. Considered that parents were the most important educators of their children.
Mia Kellmer Pringle	Children's needs	Stressed the importance of intrinsic motivation based on the quality of a child's early social relationships. The social experiences children have had will affect the way they interact with other children in the setting. This has led settings to consider children's ability to make relationships based on previous experiences.
Lawrence Kohlberg	Moral reasoning	Identified six stages of moral reasoning in three levels. Interested in the way children reason and justify their moral judgements. The implication for the early years is in helping children to understand moral issues, or the right thing to do. This could be pertinent when trying to encourage children to share toys and equipment or to see another person's point of view.

Name	Area of study	Key points and influence on current practice
Abraham Maslow	Children's needs	There is a hierarchy of needs through which individuals move. Early years practitioners consider the child's individual needs and consider ways to meet them, and to move the child on to the next stage of the hierarchy.
Margaret McMillan	Nursery schools	Keen for children to learn through first-hand experiences and active learning in order to understand the world. She believed that play helped children to apply and understand their existing knowledge. She pioneered nursery schools as an extension of the home and worked in close partnership with parents.
Maria Montessori	Learning	Designed 'didactic' materials that are structured to encourage children to learn particularly through use of senses. Observations of children led her to believe that children are particularly receptive to certain areas of learning during sensitive periods of development. Also believed that children learn best from self-chosen activity and by doing things independently (i.e. without adult interference). Adults need to be trained to give sensitive support. The learning environment was seen as being particularly important, with child-appropriate equipment and freedom to explore environment. Some of these ideas are continued in mainstream provision today as well as in specific Montessori schools. Many parents see the benefits of the approach and choose to send their children to a Montessori nursery or school.
Christine Pascal and Tony Bertram	Learning	The Effective Early Learning project (Pascal and Bertram, 1997) suggests that the child who is an involved learner is experiencing a quality curriculum. This project has been influential in encouraging practitioners to reflect on their practice as a team and has contributed to the modern approach of continual assessment of the effect of the curriculum. Some emphasis is placed on the quality of interactions between child and adult, child and child.
Ivan Pavlov	Classical conditioning	Experiments on dogs showed that some behaviour was a response to stimuli. Showed humans could learn through associations. Adults can get children to behave in the way that they want them to, by shaping their behaviour.
Michael Rutter	Nature/ nurture debate. Family break-up	Found a correlation between stress in a child's background and the likelihood of that child becoming deviant in later life. Considered learning is 60% nature and 40% nurture. Believed children can experience maternal deprivation within the family setting even when the mother is there. Defined deprivation as: privation, disruption and distortion. There is a growing awareness in today's society of the effects of stress on children and the way this affects their behaviour in group settings.

Name	Area of study	Key points and influence on current practice
B. F. Skinner	Operant conditioning	Known for work on rats! Identified positive and negative reinforcers for behaviour. Behaviour can be manipulated through the use of reinforcements. This has encouraged early years practitioners to use positive reinforcement such as praise or rewards to encourage desirable behaviour.
Rudolf Steiner	Education	True purpose of education should be to allow children to develop. Believed in the importance of the community in sharing the educational experiences of the child. Children should stay with one teacher for as long as possible in order to build strong relationships. They should be encouraged to work together and help each other with activities and experiences. This is a particularly beneficial approach when considering the integration and inclusion of children with special needs.
Barbara Tizard	Attachment	Found that children can make attachments with 'new mothers'. Highlighted importance of key relationships between children and childcare workers.
D. W. Winnicott	Attachment	Showed, for example, how 'comforters' were important to children who were making a transition to a new setting. These were referred to as 'transitional objects' that comforted a child alone in a new situation. The object becomes a symbol of the mother/carer who will return. Winnicott's work has encouraged practitioners to be sensitive to young children's emotional needs.

Jean Piaget (1896—1980)

The key aspect of Piaget's work is the emphasis he put on children developing through stages. He believed that children were born with the ability to think as part of their genetic inheritance. He said that thinking develops in the same way in all human beings and through the same sequence of stages. These are set out in Table 3.3. Each stage was characterised by particular features identified by Piaget through detailed observations of children.

Table 3.3. Piaget's stages of child development

Stage of development	Age of child	Key features
Sensory motor	Birth to 2 years	Reflexive behaviour in first weeks. Absorbs information through the senses as control of movement progresses. Learns from interaction with objects by seeing what they can do. Needs opportunity to explore. No concept of object permanence so that when an object disappears the child thinks it has gone forever. At a later stage the child will demonstrate object permanence by searching for the missing object. This is when peek-a-boo becomes an appropriate game to play.
Pre-operational	2–7 years	The age range of this stage is wide. A child of 2 years will behave very differently to the 7-year-old, but Piaget identified this as the stage at which children are not yet able to think in an operational way. He defined operational thought as the ability to think in an orderly, logical manner. Thought processes are developing but are not yet at the adult stage. Piaget considered that for full operational thought to take place children needed the ability to combine schemas. Schemas are the ideas or mental pictures established by a child through interaction with the environment. Schemas will exist for all aspects of life such as 'crossing the road' or 'picking up a book'. Operational thought allows the child to combine schemas in a sensible way that gives children the means to think imaginatively and to consider 'what may happen' if something else occurs. Egocentric behaviour is continued from the previous stage where the child is unable to see another person's viewpoint. Children are still unable to conceptualise abstractly but they do at this stage have an increasing ability to symbolise (e.g. writing, reading and imaginary play). They have strong respect for rules.
Concrete operations	7–11/12 years	More rational and 'adult-like' in thought processes. Able to think logically, although may still need concrete objects to assist with logical thought. Egocentricity declining. Less influenced by the appearance of objects. Ability to conserve (e.g. mass, number, length, and area).
Formal operations	11/12–16 years	Cognitive structures are more like those of adults. Able to use own ideas to consider problems and to think abstractly. Presence of hypothetical thinking. Children also able to consider different arguments and points of view and to form their own opinions on moral and philosophical issues.

Piaget had a background of scientific discovery, initially in biology. He also developed an interest in psychology while working in laboratories in Zurich in 1919 and in a psychiatric clinic. In 1920 he conducted research for the intelligence test procedures developed by Alfred Binet. It was here that he became interested in the way that children absorbed information and used it to further their understanding. Using scientific interviewing techniques he began to investigate how children reason. His work convinced him that logical thought processes were used by children to solve problems and to give answers to specific questions.

Piaget devised a series of tests to gauge the level of thought the child had reached. One such test involved providing the child with a three-dimensional model of mountains and figures, and asking the child to describe the viewpoint of the different figures. If the child was unable to do so, Piaget deemed that the child was egocentric and therefore unable to see someone else's point of view. Another test involved counters set out in identical rows. The child was asked to agree that the rows were identical in number. The position of the counters in one of the rows was then changed in front of the child. If the child had understanding of conservation, he or she would realise that the number of counters remained the same even though the appearance of the rows had changed. A child who was unable to conserve would consider that the longer row had more counters in it. Similar tests were devised to test conservation of volume and capacity.

Although these tests have been criticised subsequently, they have ensured that early years educators are aware that children may not see things in the same way as an adult. This means that planned activities should consider the level of understanding a child has reached.

Influence on current practice

Despite criticisms of his work, Piaget remains a major contributor to the way we view children and echoes of his theories are seen in the foundation stage curriculum. There is an emphasis on the importance of the environment and the quality of the children's interactions. There is also an acknowledgement that children develop through different stages and therefore the early years curriculum must reflect these individual differences.

The influence that Piaget has had on modern practice can be summarised in the following points:

- Planning activities that are age- and stage-appropriate. It is necessary to consider the level of thought the child is capable of in relation to the stage he or she has reached, for example whether the child will be able to participate in an activity that requires cooperation if she or he is still at the stage of egocentricity.

An example of learning by discovery.

- Planning activities that encourage abstract thought. These should include problem-solving and number work.
- Providing children with concrete materials to solve abstract problems. These could include bricks to help when building train tracks or number bars to help children calculate simple addition sums.
- Providing first-hand, practical experiences. These help children to continue to build mental processes and structures.
- Understanding children as individuals.
- Observing children and responding appropriately to them.
- Careful structuring of the curriculum to reflect the stage of development the child has reached.
- Providing a well planned and organised learning environment that allows children to explore, experiment, plan and make their own decisions (see Chapter 2).

Lev Vygotsky (1896—1934)

Like Piaget, Vygotsky firmly believed in the idea that children were active learners. He emphasised that children learn by exploring their world and by testing their ideas against reality. He believed that children were constantly seeking to expand their knowledge.

Vygotsky differed from Piaget in that he did not see the child as a solitary learner. He determined that a child's social environment was an active force in their development. Children need social interactions with other people who are more skilled than them in order to further their knowledge. These interactions promote cognitive development through instruction and assistance. He proposed the concept of the *zone of proximal development*, defined as the difference between what the child can do alone and the potential for what can be achieved with assistance from a more skilled adult or peer. Vygotsky did not specify how adults and children worked within the zone of proximal development but other researchers have developed this. In particular, Jerome Bruner (1977) termed this assistance *scaffolding*. It is an interactive process in which adults adjust the support they offer to the child until the child has mastery of the skill being taught. The key to effective scaffolding is sensitivity to the child's level of development.

Vygotsky also emphasised the importance of mastery of language and its use as a communication tool. He considered that when children have developed the means to interact with other members of their social group they are able to transform their innate abilities into higher mental functions.

Another interesting aspect of Vygotsky's work concerns pretend play. He noted that children's pretend play tends to function at a level beyond their stage of life. They take on roles, such as parent or car driver, that are appropriate to adult life. Through pretend play children place themselves in the zone of proximal development. They are playing at a level that is beyond their true capabilities. Vygotsky believed that pretend play was important for children to learn about their world.

Influence on current practice

Vygotsky's work has had a major impact on our current educational approach. This is largely due to the emphasis on social development and the need for interaction between the child and more experienced people. For example, it is common practice to encourage paired reading between children of different ages or to enable children of mixed abilities to work together. This method of learning enables children to work beyond their capabilities but within their zone of proximal development.

An example of scaffolding of learning.

Another important influence on modern practice is the emphasis that is put upon the role of the adult in encouraging children to achieve their maximum potential. Practitioners consider carefully how they can sensitively respond to children in order to ensure they master new skills. They aim to enable children to work within their ability and provide scaffolding to facilitate development.

Effective Pre-school and Primary Education 3–11 Project

The project was funded by the Department for Education and Skills (1997–2003) and was the first major longitudinal study in the UK to focus specifically on the effectiveness of early years education. A key conclusion of the study is that the quality of interactions between children and staff is particularly important. It was found that the most effective arrangement was where two individuals work together to solve intellectual problems. This is termed 'sustained shared thinking' and is most beneficial when children interact on a 1:1 basis, either with an adult or with another child. The project supports the principles of the foundation stage and encourages practitioners, and government, to reflect on the issues of quality and the effectiveness of pre-school provision in the UK. Information on the study is available via the website http://ioewebserver.ioe.ac.uk/ioe/cms/get.asp?cid=2773.

Think it over

- List three ways in which you and your team could increase the number of 1:1 interactions with children in your setting.
- How might this benefit the children's intellectual thought?

3.3 Planning, implementing and evaluating the curriculum

Planning the early years curriculum

As a manager of an early years setting you will be responsible for curriculum planning. You may be asking yourself why you need to plan if the children come into the setting very happily, play contentedly during the session and go home smiling. What more could anybody want? However, early years practitioners can be guilty of setting activities that are purposeless in order to occupy children and keep them quiet. In order to provide a quality curriculum, activities must be purposeful and encourage the child to learn, and ultimately to achieve independence.

Good planning is essential for the following reasons:

- It promotes equality of opportunity for all children.
- It ensures that each area of the curriculum is covered and that the associated standards are met.
- It raises professionalism, by encouraging early years practitioners to reflect on practice.
- It enables practitioners to build upon what the children already know and can do.
- It helps to encourage a positive attitude to learning and prevent early failure.
- It helps parents and practitioners to work together on common themes.

- It ensures that the content of sessions is relevant and appropriate to children's needs.
- It ensures that each activity within every session is purposeful and provides opportunities for learning, both indoors and outside.

It is essential that the planning of the curriculum is led by the manager, who has an overview of the setting and is ultimately responsible for curriculum management. It is possible, however, to delegate responsibilities to colleagues and in fact the whole team should be involved in the process. This empowers staff and gives them ownership of the curriculum.

Case study — Planning at the Wendy House playgroup

Kezi has recently taken over the leadership of the Wendy House playgroup. The group had previously been run by Beryl, and the majority of the staff have worked at the playgroup for a long time. They are an established and experienced team who work well together. There had been no written curriculum plans – the group concentrated in the past on providing play activities for the children, and these were chosen each morning by the staff. Kezi has worked in other playgroups and has a Diploma in Childcare and Education. She is very aware of the importance of planning in relation to the foundation stage curriculum and feels that there ought to be a more systematic approach to the activities offered to the children.

- Why is it important for the team to work together on the planning?
- What do they need to think about?

The planning cycle

Planning of the curriculum should be an on-going process that is based upon your knowledge of the children in your care. You need to match this knowledge to your understanding of child development and the way that children learn. The framework is provided by *Birth to Three Matters*, the guidance for the foundation stage, and the national curriculum (Table 3.1).

Planning takes the form of a cycle. This is illustrated in Figure 3.1. The planning cycle begins with the needs of the child. These needs will be established through observations of the child's skills and abilities in the different areas of the curriculum. Parents' knowledge should also be considered and that of previous workers. For example, a child starting in a year 1 class will already have a foundation stage profile. This will give the new staff information about that child to guide their planning. They will continue to make observations to build up their own knowledge and opinions of the child's capabilities based upon the profile.

At the planning stage, early years practitioners will need to discuss and decide upon suitable activities to consolidate and enhance learning. Initial

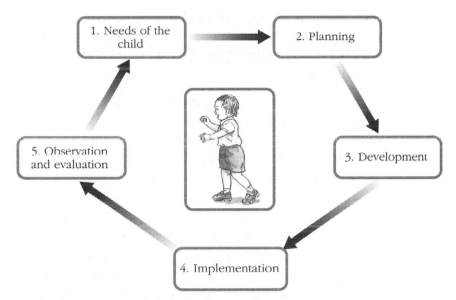

Figure 3.1. The planning cycle.

ideas will be developed to ensure all aspects of the curriculum are being met. During the implementation of the plan, children will be observed and the activities evaluated. Staff will then need the time and opportunity to discuss individuals and groups of children and their responses to the chosen activities. It is necessary to evaluate and reflect upon the success of the plan in order to continue the planning cycle in a productive way. If staff do not take time to assess the suitability of the activities and to consider the learning that has taken place for individuals and groups, the children may become 'stuck' and not show the progression they are capable of.

Activities offered should have breadth and be balanced to match the children's abilities. They should be relevant to young children and varied in order to maintain interest. Although the three elements of the early years curriculum (see Table 3.1) set the framework of what children must know, the implementation and interpretation are down to individual settings.

The key worker system

Early years practitioners often use group working and the key worker system to ensure that children are meeting their potential. The key worker has a small group, usually of about 10 children, to focus upon in observations and assessments. Differentiation of the curriculum, whereby practitioners adapt activities to enable children to consolidate and develop their learning, helps to ensure that individual needs are met (see also 'Individual education plans', below).

How do you approach planning?

There is not a definitive approach to planning. Some people prefer to document planning by using charts, others by writing a piece of continuous prose. It does not really matter how you write your plans down as long as the resulting plan is accessible to all team members and benefits the children.

The main priority in any approach to planning is to ensure that you develop a clear overview of the child's time in the setting, whether that is for a year or for four or six terms. It is necessary to plan in order to promote the use of activities to support the children's learning. The planning must be carefully documented to show how the learning needs of the children are met and extended. Each setting will devise its own workable plans over a period of time to fit individual circumstances and groups of children. Expectations held by Ofsted will also play a part in the creation of these plans and examples of good practice (for the 3–5-year-old range) can be found in the document *Planning for Learning in the Foundation Stage* (Qualifications and Curriculum Authority, 2001). This document also cites the importance of observation and assessment in the planning cycle.

Most people use long-, medium- and short-term plans. These are discussed below, and an example of each is given for a group of 3–4-year-old pre-school children. These examples are intended only to form the basis of discussion for settings and to illustrate possible approaches – they should not be viewed as models.

When considering the form that plans will take and the content of the curriculum, you must incorporate the individual needs of children as well as the group as a whole. Children with particular needs should be included in the overall plans, as well as having IEPs. Managers must give thought to the inclusion of children in their setting and also to the best ways in which to use extra help, such as learning support assistants.

Long-term plans

Staff teams use long-term plans to provide an overview of the planned activities. These provide an overview of the learning opportunities that will be offered and help to keep the curriculum varied and challenging. They often follow a thematic approach initially, as young children enjoy the focus of a theme for their learning and staff find that an appropriate subject can motivate children. It is also possible to use themes as a basis for implementing the guidance set out in *Birth to Three Matters*, for the younger child, but the emphasis for planning is different to that for the more formalised curriculum for older children. It is generally recognised that planning for the younger age group may be less intensive, but should cover all aspects of the child's development (physical, intellectual, emotional and social) and needs. There is more emphasis on individualised, personalised development, with children progressing at their own rate.

Table 3.4. Example of a long-term plan for 3–4-year-olds

Month	Topic
September	Ourselves
October	Babies
November	Fireworks and sound
December	Christmas preparations and traditions
January	Books
February	Cars
March	Homes
April	Gardens
May	Animals and 'mini-beasts'
June	Rainbows
July	Summer

When using a thematic approach to learning it is important to remember that a theme is a starting point. The reactions of the children and their interests may well take you in unexpected directions.

Table 3.4 presents an example of a long-term plan for 3–4-year-old children. For children of this age the themes will need to be short and related to their immediate experiences. As children grow older they can sustain interest over a longer period and reflect on previous knowledge.

When looking at this plan you may feel that it does not reflect sufficient breadth and balance of learning experience or identify the learning that should take place over the year. In this case you will wish to add more detail at this stage of your planning, and include different themes, such as celebrations, that would enable children to develop awareness and enjoyment of other cultures and festivities. You may also wish to extend this plan to 2 years if the children are in the setting for that time. Some settings prefer to use areas of learning as a basis for their long-term plan and to include an indication of when to teach aspects of learning, and how regularly and frequently. Other settings prefer to spend longer than 1 month on each theme. Your choice will depend on a consensus of opinion among the staff and knowledge of the developmental stages of the children.

Medium-term plans

These provide a framework for the themes identified in the long-term plan for all subjects or learning areas. They should highlight what resources will be needed and what trips or visitors have been planned. Medium-term plans are often used to bridge the gap between the broad outline of the

Table 3.5. Sample parts of a medium-term plan for 3–4-year-olds, for the month of May, as set out in the long-term plan: animals and 'mini-beasts'

Area of learning	Stepping-stones	Stepping-stones extension	Activities to support and encourage learning	Activity extension	Resources needed	Role of practitioner
Personal, social and emotional development	Show curiosity	Show increasing independence in selecting and carrying out activities	Introduction of snails to the group	Children to consider where the snails normally live and to investigate the garden to see where they might be living	Plastic tank to house the snails with suitable greenery and stones to provide a natural habitat	Interact with the children, supporting their interest and allowing them to make mistakes
	Have a positive approach to new experiences		Children asked to observe the snails initially and encouraged to talk about them		Access to a garden area, on a wet day ideally. Children to wear wellies. Hand-washing facilities	Observe the children and use for planning
	Have a strong exploratory impulse		Children able to hold the snails and look at them closely			
	Listen to others one-to-one or in small groups	Begin to use more complex sentences	Small-group discussion about animals we know	One-to-one discussions with adults or peers	Photographs	Talk with and listen to children, responding to what they say
	Listen to stories	Use a wider range of words to express or elaborate ideas	Stories connected to animals		Display	Provide new vocabulary

Area of learning	Stepping-stones	Stepping-stones extension	Activities to support and encourage learning	Activity extension	Resources needed	Role of practitioner
	Engage in activities requiring hand–eye coordination		Farm animals to play with		Vet's equipment (e.g. cotton wool, leads, a dog bed, blankets)	Help children expand what they say
			Soft toys in imaginative area, set up as a vet's		Soft toys	
			Picture lotto – can you match the animals?		Stories and games	
			Pairs – baby and mother			
			Display – photos of different animals			
Knowledge and understanding of the world	Show curiosity and interest by facial expression, movement or sound	Comment and ask questions about where they live and the natural world	Collect different mini-beasts and observe them	Children to find out where animals live. Where do cats go to sleep? Where does a bear doze?	Access to garden	Arouse awareness of features of the environment
	Show an interest in why things happen and how things work		Look at how animals move – for example, what does a snail use to move (provide a plastic sheet so children can see underneath)		Containers for insects etc. (e.g. a wormery)	Talk about and show an interest in children's experiences
	Remember and talk about significant things that have happened to them		Discussion about pets, explore how pets make you feel and what you can do with pets		Pictures and books showing different animals	Help children find out information through books and pictures

long-term plan and the detail of the short-term plan. At this stage you could also include a rationale for the use of each type of resource area in the setting and for each routine, such as tidying away. You could also make the aims and objectives of the activities clear, and link these to individual learning outcomes for the children. This would be based on your own knowledge of the children in the setting.

Table 3.5 presents an example extract of a medium-term plan for pre-school children. This medium-term plan is closely linked to the areas of learning outlined in the *Curriculum Guidance for the Foundation Stage* (Qualifications and Curriculum Authority, 2000) (it sets out by way of example only three of the six areas of learning and would be extended to incorporate mathematical, physical and creative development).

These areas are not a curriculum in themselves but establish a basis for planning. They help to lay strong foundations for future learning. Some children will exceed the goals by the end of the reception year at school; others will be working towards them, particularly children who have special educational needs and those learning English as an additional language. The *Curriculum Guidance* highlights the stepping-stones of progress that children cross as they progress to reach each goal. It gives early years practitioners a clear idea of the learning that needs to take place.

Short-term plans

The long- and medium-term plans provide the basis for the short-term plans, with a focus on the stepping-stones. They are developed using on-going observations and informal assessment of the children. Short-term plans usually cover one week at most and are necessary for the team to know the focus of the sessions and their own responsibilities within the week. The plan should be used as a guide and not followed rigidly, as you will need to use your observations of children to adjust your plan in accordance with their needs and interests. Also, it is sometimes important to capitalise on unplanned events.

Managers and teams will want to devise their own particular form of plan, but Table 3.6 offers an example of one variety, derived from the long-term and medium-term plans set out in Tables 3.4 and 3.5. It is based on one week within the theme 'Animals and mini-beasts' and is intended to be implemented in a pre-school setting that has a set routine during the session. This routine is based on providing learning through play and children are given a large amount of free choice. There are key times when children work in small groups with their key worker, and as a large group for story and rhymes. Many of the activities are repeated during the week to consolidate learning and to give children the time to practise skills.

This example does not include detail of the learning intentions for individuals, so you may wish to use this plan as a basis for discussion in

Table 3.6. Short-term plan: week of activities

Day	Personal, social and emotional	Communication, language and literacy	Mathematical development	Knowledge and understanding of the world	Physical development	Creative development
Monday	Snails introduced to the class. Key worker groups to ensure all children can see and have opportunity to observe	Imaginary play area changed to vet's. Ensure all children have access if desired. Opportunity for one-to-one discussion. Discussion with key worker about snails	Looking at the shape of a snail shell. Can you find any similar shapes?	Looking at snails with magnifiers	Making animals out of dough and clay	What does a snail look like? Making snails out of dough or clay
Tuesday	Snails available in the room, with free access for children. Magnifiers available	Imaginary play area changed to vet's. Ensure all children have access if desired. Put up display of mini-beasts to generate discussion	Number rhymes in whole-group time	Putting snails on a plastic sheet – how do they move?	Jigsaw puzzles with theme of animals	Drawing pictures of snails using different materials – chalk, paint, charcoal
Wednesday	Opportunity to handle snails again and discuss where they might live	Imaginary play area changed to vet's. Ensure all children have access if desired. Discussion about where snails live	Counting the snails	Books and pictures available showing different homes for animals	Small animals in the sand – can you make a home for them?	Materials available for children to make homes for a snail out of a shoebox

Day	Personal, social and emotional	Communication, language and literacy	Mathematical development	Knowledge and understanding of the world	Physical development	Creative development
Thursday	Encourage children to think independently when making shoebox homes	Imaginary play area changed to vet's. Ensure all children have access if desired. Looking at the homes children have made. Asking open questions	Number rhymes	Discovering snail trails by putting snails on black paper	Outside activity – equipment to crawl over and under	Materials available for children to make home for a snail out of a shoebox
Friday	Encourage children to explore the garden for other mini-beasts	Imaginary play area changed to vet's. Ensure all children have access if desired	Finding other mini-beasts. Comparing their shape and size	Finding other mini-beasts. Where do they live? What do they eat?	Provide children with boxes and equipment to make their own obstacle course	Look at other mini-beasts. Talk about how they feel to the touch

your own setting as to how you would incorporate these. Many settings also highlight which activities will be child initiated or adult directed and how the children will be organised. A short-term plan can also be extended to include opportunities for observations, vocabulary to be focused on and opportunity for informal assessments of individual or groups of children.

You could put the short-term plan on display, so that staff and parents can share it, which may entail reproduction in other languages in order to ensure equality of opportunity.

It is necessary to give staff time to observe the children and reflect upon the success of the week's sessions, and to discuss whether stepping-stones have been reached. Assessment and evaluation will enable practitioners to consider how to plan for the next week, bearing in mind the learning taking place and the interest shown by the children.

Individual education plans

Individual education plans (IEPs) are for children with a particular need. They are necessary when a child is identified as making little progress and when he or she is not responding to targeted teaching activities. The child may be working significantly below the level of classmates or have emotional or behavioural difficulties (Tassoni, 2003). IEPs will draw upon the experience of the whole team, particularly any staff with SENCO (special educational needs coordinator) responsibility, the parents and carers, and the child.

Case study — Tasnim

Tasnim has recently started at a day nursery. She is 3 years old and is currently in the Grasshoppers room, for children aged 2–3 years. Tasnim is exhibiting behaviour consistent with developmental delay and learning difficulties. Her developmental stage is comparable with a child of 18 months. Consider how you and your team will ensure Tasnim's needs are met in a developmentally appropriate way.

- What will you need to think about in terms of planning?

- How will you evidence this?

A child with learning difficulties will benefit from play with materials that are at an appropriate developmental level and from some time spent playing with children of a similar developmental age. It is important, though, to ensure that you do not limit your expectations of children and that you plan the steps that will encourage progression. Managers will need to give careful consideration to the opportunities provided for repetition and practice, and how to take small steps towards the learning of new skills.

Top Tip — Planning documents

It is a good idea to keep copies of all plans, perhaps in a file, where copies of IEPs and notes on differentiation and evaluation can be slotted in beside the planning documents.

Implementing the early years curriculum

When implementing the early years curriculum, it is helpful to consider:

- the fundamentals of good practice;
- the need for creativity and free choice.

The fundamentals of good practice

The way that you decide to implement the curriculum is to a certain extent influenced by your ideals and personal philosophy of education. This will be based upon your understanding of child development and how children learn. It will also be influenced by your own attitudes to learning and experiences.

Case study — Leza's maths

Leza is training for a diploma at her local college. She is currently in her first term. She began her school placement 2 weeks ago and is working in a large class of 5–6-year-olds. The children and staff at the school welcomed her from the beginning and she has quickly found her way around the school and has begun to interact with the children and staff. She has taken part in playground duties, found the toilets and even read stories to small groups of children. Leza's placement supervisor, Adam, is pleased with her progress but is concerned about her attitude towards the curriculum. She has a very negative attitude towards mathematics as a result of her own experiences at secondary school. This is proving to be difficult in the classroom. When Leza is asked to help small groups of children with their number work she avoids doing so and clearly lacks confidence. Adam is worried that this will influence the children's approach to their work and he is anxious to encourage Leza to feel more confident.

- Decide how you could tackle the problem.
- Consider situations where your attitudes might interfere with children's learning.
- Analyse your own attitudes. Are there areas of learning where your approach encourages children or has a negative effect?

If you are honest about your influence on children's attitudes towards learning you can improve their opportunities. A practitioner who is enthusiastic about art activities can communicate this to the children and will see a similar enthusiasm reflected in the children's achievements. The staff member who loves to read stories will be the person who is surrounded by entranced children. The challenge for the manager is to recognise the strengths and weaknesses of staff members and to create a quality curriculum that meets the children's needs. It is important that this is a commonly agreed curriculum, based on discussion and reflective practice by all staff members.

The Rumbold report (Department for Education and Science, 1990) stated that 'how children are encouraged to learn – is as important as, and inseparable from, the content – what they learn' and Siraj-Blatchford (1998, p. 10) says that 'educators should guard against pressures, which might lead them to over-concentration on formal teaching and upon the attainment of a specific set of targets'.

In today's world of continuous assessment of children, you must not lose sight of the importance of *how* children learn and the pleasure that they get from knowledge. Who can forget the excitement and achievement of a child learning to ride a bicycle for the first time, or the pride of the child who makes their parents a cup of tea and brings it to them in bed?

The *Start Right* report (Ball, 1994, pp. 51–53) set out the fundamental principles of good practice that underpin early learning:

- Early childhood is the foundation on which children build the rest of their lives. But it is not just a preparation for adolescence and adulthood; it has an importance in itself.
- Children develop at different rates, and in different ways – emotionally, morally, socially, physically and spiritually. All are important; each is interwoven with others.
- All children have abilities, which can and should be identified and promoted.
- Young children learn from everything that happens to them and around them; they do not separate their learning into different subjects or disciplines.
- Children learn most effectively through actions, rather than from instruction.
- Children learn best when they are actively involved and interested.
- Children who are confident in themselves and their own ability have a head-start in learning.
- Children need time and space to produce work of quality and depth.
- What children can do (rather than what they cannot do) is the starting point in their learning.
- Play and conversation are the main ways in which young children learn about themselves, other people and the world around them.
- Children who are encouraged to think for themselves are more likely to act independently.
- The relationships which children have with other children and with adults are of central importance to their development.

Work with a colleague. Select two of Ball's principles and reflect on the influence they have on the curriculum.

- How can you put these principles into practice?

- Compare your answers with someone else's. Are there contrasting views? Can you reconcile any differences of opinion?

Allowing for creativity and free choice

An interesting argument emerges when considering the implementation of the modern curriculum, and that concerns the place for creativity. Duffy (1998) states that creativity involves:

- the ability to see things in fresh ways;
- learning from past experiences and relating this learning to new situations;
- thinking along unorthodox lines and breaking barriers;
- using non-traditional approaches to solving problems;
- going further than the information given;
- creating something unique or original.

Suggestions have been made that the current curriculum offered to children, in particular key stage 2 of the national curriculum, is not giving children enough breadth and is stifling creativity. The Qualifications and Curriculum Authority (QCA) is currently running a 3-year project to investigate how to promote pupils' creativity in the national curriculum subjects and religious education. At the completion of the study it will produce a pack of materials for teachers to test and evaluate. The QCA proposes four characteristics of creativity:

- thinking or behaving imaginatively;
- purposeful imaginative activity;
- generating something original;
- outcomes that are of value in relation to objectives.

It also states that creative thinking can advance pupils' learning by taking thinking forward. It can enhance all-round development and raise educational standards by boosting self-confidence and self-esteem.

Whatever your views on the place of creativity in the curriculum you must create exciting learning environments which inspire children to question, reason, solve problems and create. Adults can support and extend the learning and creative process. They can help children to communicate their thoughts, feelings and ideas. Some activities naturally allow more creativity than others, such as art, music and drama. With thought, other areas of the curriculum also lend themselves to a creative approach. Young children who are set the task of designing a new imaginative play area will respond with creative ideas. A group of children who have collected snails from the garden can be encouraged to design and make a suitable home for them. This activity will encourage problem solving, leadership and innovative ideas.

The child's self-confidence is important to the learning process. A child's sense of self-worth is strongly influenced by the response to their activities of parents, carers, siblings, key workers and peers. This is particularly relevant to the creative process. When anyone creates something – be it a drawing, a model or a cake – that person is at his or her most vulnerable. It is like baring the soul. Imagine the child who has spent all morning creating a model village from the Lego bricks, only to have it destroyed by the adult who is 'tidying up'. Figure 3.2 illustrates how early years practitioners can show that they value children's creative work.

Think it over

- How comfortable do you feel with your own creativity?
- Can you remember a time when someone responded to your work with ridicule?
- What effect did this have on you?

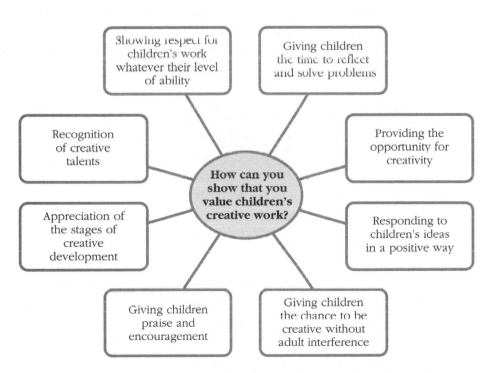

Figure 3.2. Ways in which you can show children that you value their creative work.

Despite the importance to children of their self-belief many adults often try to 'take over' their work. They tell them what to draw and how to draw it. They give them 'cut-outs' and tell them to fill them in with tissue paper. They provide resources to make a clown and a template, and so a class of 34 children all produce identical clowns.

As the manager of an early years setting you will need to consider how to encourage creativity.

Case study — Use of cut-outs

A table was set out for a group of five 4-year-old children to make hedgehog models. There was one marker pen and five hedgehogs cut out on the table. The children were instructed individually by the adult to draw one eye on their hedgehog, to give the impression of a side view. The adult ensured they completed the task.

- Was this activity developmentally appropriate?
- What did the children learn?
- Was creativity encouraged?
- How could you encourage the adult to present this in a more meaningful way?

Too often practitioners are concerned with the end product and fail to realise that the process of learning is what is really important. Sylva (2000) found that children who were exposed to a balanced curriculum benefited most from their experiences. Balance in the curriculum was defined as being between free and guided choices. Benefits across the curriculum included:

- higher academic skills in reading and writing;
- a high level of pretend play;
- a low level of anxiety on entering school;
- a high level of informal conversation;
- a positive effect on children's perception of their own social acceptance and competence.

It is therefore important to give time and thought to the amount of free choice children are given within the delivery of the curriculum. The manager and staff do need to provide some sort of focus, of course, but children need the opportunity to make decisions and solve problems for themselves. They need to learn by doing and, if necessary, from their own mistakes. When adults learn to drive they have to experience doing a three-point turn or reversing round a corner. They have to learn practically, not by being told the theory of how to do it. Adults also need time to reflect on their efforts and to practise. How many times have you heard an adult say to a child 'but I have already shown you how to do that'?

There are two key issues for the manager and team.

- How much free choice should children have in their learning?
- How influential should the adult be in guiding the child?

Careful thought must be given to the quality and form of adult interaction. High levels of adult–child interaction can optimise learning. A high level of contribution from both the child and the adult can lead to open and interactive learning. The education tends to be of a high quality, with the child achieving maximum potential. In contrast, where the child has autonomy and the adult contribution is low, the quality of education tends to be lower, with the child achieving less success. However, where the adult approach is didactic, with little value placed on the child's contribution, opportunities for learning are often lost.

Research by Schweinhart and Weikart (1997) into the High/Scope pre-school curriculum produced some astonishing findings regarding the approach to learning that values the contribution of children in making choices and contributing to their education. Their study showed that children exposed to this approach benefited in the long term through more confidence and pro-social behaviour. Conclusions were drawn that this play-based programme of learning enabled children to learn to direct and control their own behaviour. The social skills they developed were also useful later on, and the children grew up to lead more fulfilled lives. They were more likely to be married, in well paid employment and less likely to commit a crime.

Pascal and Bertram (1997) have confirmed the importance of adult interaction in learning. Their work looked at three aspects of the interaction between children and adults: sensitivity, stimulation and autonomy.

- *Sensitivity.* The sensitivity of the adult to the feelings and emotional well-being of the child – includes elements of sincerity, empathy, responsiveness and affection.
- *Stimulation.* The way in which an adult intervenes in the learning process and the content of such interventions.
- *Autonomy.* The degrees of freedom that the adult gives the child to experiment, make judgements, choose activities and express ideas. It also encompasses how the adult handles conflict, rules and behavioural issues.

To put this into the context of the learning environment, you need to consider the amount of interaction that takes place and the quality of that interaction. Some interactions with children can be meaningless. By close observation you can determine the interaction that enhances learning and improves the learning experience for the child.

Consider the three aspects of the interaction between children and adults: sensitivity, stimulation and autonomy.

- How could a practitioner put these into practice?
- How can the child be more involved in the learning process?

Evaluating the early years curriculum

Evaluation of the curriculum is part of the planning cycle described earlier in this chapter. It is essential to reflect upon the implementation of the curriculum and to use your conclusions to inform future planning. You must ensure that you are meeting the needs of all the children and that you are creating a learning environment in which adults and children work positively together.

How to evaluate the curriculum

Despite the importance of evaluating and reflecting on practice, often, for one reason or another, this is an area that is neglected. At the end of a session, practitioners are often too tired, or too busy preparing for the next session, to record their thoughts.

It is imperative to work together as a team to devise practical methods of recording and assessing each session, either during the session or at an appropriate time afterwards. It is interesting to note that the Pen Green Early Excellence Centre at Corby sets aside Wednesday afternoon as a planning and assessment session, which all staff attend. During this time parents and carers run sessions for the children.

Good practice checklist — Areas to consider when evaluating a session

- ☐ What learning took place?
- ☐ Were the children's needs met?
- ☐ How effective was the adult's interaction?
- ☐ Were all children able to participate?
- ☐ Was there a good use of time, space and resources?
- ☐ What was significant about what was observed?
- ☐ Does anything that was observed need recording?
- ☐ What changes can be made?
- ☐ How can the evaluation inform future planning?

It may be necessary to change and adapt curriculum plans in the light of evaluation. As a manager you must be aware of the difficulties practitioners may experience in undergoing change.

3.4 Assessment and assessment systems

Why assess children?

It is essential that each child is given the opportunity to achieve success, to show what he or she knows, understands and can do. Assessment can be used to help children recognise the standards they are aiming for. It can inform parents about their child's progress and the next steps they need to take. It also provides feedback to the practitioner about children and enables planning to be more effective. It provides the setting with information to evaluate the staff's work. However, formal assessment is not required until the end of the foundation stage.

Vicky Hutchin in her book *Tracking Significant Achievement in the Early Years* (2000) suggests that a tracking record of significant achievements is beneficial to children and practitioners. This prevents recording becoming a burdensome task yet allows progress to be identified and celebrated. In particular, Hutchin (p. 21) believes that a tracking record is able to show, at a glance:

- whether there are any children who appear to have shown no significant achievement, and therefore need to be focused on;
- whether there are any children who have shown significant achievement in, say, reading, but not in writing, and therefore need to be observed;
- whether none of the children has shown any significant achievement in, say, knowledge and understanding of the world, which indicates a need for the practitioner to rethink the curriculum on offer;
- whether any bright children appear to have made no significant progress, which would indicate that they need to be given more challenging, open-ended tasks.

Hutchin also highlights the need to pass on to the next practitioner information that is relevant and can be read quickly and easily.

Case study — Observation and assessment

A group of four children aged 3–4 years had been involved in a practical activity relating to the topic of the month, 'Animals and mini-beasts'. The children had been looking at snails in a plastic tank and observing how they moved across the surface of a plastic sheet. The children have now been asked to search in the garden to see if they can find any more snails. The objective of the activity is to encourage the children to show curiosity and have a positive approach to new activities. Marco is immediately interested in the activity and scuttles around the garden looking under bushes and up trees for snails. He responds positively to the task and soon has a collection of three snails. He takes them inside and starts showing them to other children in the classroom. Leroy is very interested in Marco's snails and goes outside to see if he can find any for himself. When he gets outside he sees that Robert has found one. He snatches it from Robert and runs to show it to Marco. In the meantime Robert gives up looking for snails and joins Eleanor and Sean on the slide.

- What is significant about this observation?
- How would you present this information?

The system for assessment

A new system has recently replaced the baseline assessment previously used by early years practitioners. The *Foundation Stage Profile* (Qualifications and Curriculum Authority, 2003) sets out how to record and summarise the progress and learning needs of young children, based upon the information gathered by practitioners through observations and knowledge of the child. The profile is used during the final year of the foundation stage and is based on practitioners' own assessments of children's progress, and needs, based on the early learning goals.

The six early learning goals of the foundation stage curriculum (see Qualifications and Curriculum Authority, 2000) were not intended to be used as assessment criteria. Rather, the foundation stage profile takes these goals and presents them as a set of 13 assessment scales, each of which has nine points. There are three or four assessment scales for the first three early learning areas, and one scale for each of the other three. The 13 assessment scales are therefore:

Personal, social and emotional development
- Dispositions and attitudes
- Social development
- Emotional development

Communication, language and literacy
- Language for communication and thinking
- Linking sounds and letters
- Reading
- Writing

Mathematical development
- Numbers as labels and for counting
- Calculating
- Shape, space and measures

Knowledge and understanding of the world

Physical development

Creative development

The profile booklet is designed to be completed as an on-going task, to give a cumulative system of assessment. Parents, children and other settings are encouraged to contribute to the booklet, in order to have a full picture of the child. Professor Tina Bruce of the University of North London (2003) has said that: 'The foundation stage profile recognises the importance of parents as partners, including those with children with special education needs and disabilities, in the assessment process.' Parents have unique knowledge of their children. The summarisation of young children's achievements at the end of the foundation stage provides important information for parents and also for year 1 teachers.

The practicalities of assessment

For any setting using the foundation stage profile, thought will need to be given to the practicalities of observing children. Some members of staff may need training in the different observation techniques and methods of evaluating results. All staff will need to consider how to make well planned observations, using a flexible approach.

The success of the assessment scheme will depend on:

- the quality and continuity of practitioners' assessments;
- the standardisation of assessments;
- the practicality and ease of administering the scheme;
- the credibility of the scheme;
- the willingness of staff to undertake the assessments;
- the importance attached to the assessment at the next setting.

If staff within the setting are to participate in the assessment scheme, they must have sufficient training and experience to be able to recognise the achievements of individual children. They will need to have realistic expectations of the children, based upon sound knowledge of child development. Time will need to be set aside for the completion of assessments and to discuss progress. It may be necessary to discuss the standardisation of assessments with other settings.

It is important that the assessment scheme is practical and easy to use. There is never enough time when working with children. The use of assessments must not detract from the overall learning experience. There is no point in the practitioner walking around the classroom with a clipboard waiting to record Michelle's speech when she is too busy to talk to him!

Staff must perceive the assessment as valuable to the child and the learning process. They must not have the feeling that they are simply filling in boxes that no one will ever look at. Relevant information about individual progress and achievements must be readily accessible to parents and colleagues. There will also need to be respect between settings in order to ensure that notice is taken of assessments made by the previous setting. It is simply a waste of time and energy for nurseries to redo the assessments made by the previous pre-school setting because they do not value the professionalism of these colleagues.

The credibility of the assessment scheme is therefore essential. The foundation stage profile is drawn from the work of respected early education specialists and practitioners. This has ensured that the assessment criteria are based upon sound understanding of children's development.

Think it over

- How would you encourage your staff to participate in the assessment process?
- How would you ensure the standardisation of assessment?
- What are the difficulties of sharing assessment data with parents?

3.5 The development of children and the role of play in the curriculum

Early years practitioners have fought long and hard to establish the importance of play as a learning tool for young children (see also 'Play as a vehicle for learning', in Chapter 2). Too many people, parents and politicians in particular, under-value the role of play in the curriculum. Many playgroups have changed their name to pre-schools in order to raise the public perception of their work. Indeed, the Pre-school Playgroup Association is now the Pre-school Learning Alliance.

Fortunately, the *Curriculum Guidance for the Foundation Stage* (Qualifications and Curriculum Authority, 2000) includes an acknowledgement of the benefits

Children involved in play that is not adult led may act out aspects of their own lives and the lives of those around them.

of a well planned play environment. Play is identified as a key way for children to learn with enjoyment and challenge. With a planned and challenging environment and adults supporting children's learning, play can be used as a suitable vehicle for the foundation stage. Adults will need to ensure that play is challenging, and play needs to be planned if it is to be educational, but there must be a balance between child and adult input. An ill-equipped environment with little thought given to play is not likely to produce high quality 'learning through play'. Similarly, children need time and opportunity to get involved in play that is not adult led. They will use this time to act out aspects of their own lives and of those around them, to help them make sense of their experiences. They will have opportunity to practise skills and refine their abilities. They will also have the chance to interact and communicate with peers. When children are truly stimulated by play they show great depths of concentration.

Think it over

Consider an early years setting in which you have worked.

- Did the children use play as a learning tool?
- Did the setting stimulate high quality play in a challenging and inspiring environment?
- Were the children excited by their play?
- Did the children spend time and effort in one area of play?
- Did the children concentrate and become involved through their play?
- Were there areas of play that were ignored by the children?
- Were all areas of play accessible to all children?
- How much do you know about how children play and the value of play to learning?

It is useful to observe children playing. It can be very revealing about the amount of learning that is actually taking place. For example, two children of different ages spending a whole summer engaged in making tents and wigwams of different types and structures would develop tremendous skills of negotiation and team working. Other aspects of learning can be developed by the adult providing different materials and equipment or by participating in the fun. It is very important that play is enjoyable for children and always has that element of fun.

If all the elements of quality play are in place then, as the *Curriculum Guidance for the Foundation Stage* (Qualifications and Curriculum Authority, 2000) states, children can:

- make sense of the world through role-play;
- practise skills and learn ideas;
- learn how to control impulses and understand the need for rules;
- be alone, be alongside others or cooperate as they talk or rehearse their feelings;

- take risks and make mistakes;
- think creatively and imaginatively;
- communicate with others as they investigate or solve problems;
- express fears or relive anxious experiences in controlled and safe situations.

Jean Piaget (see section 3.2) highlighted the importance of children learning through play and showed that play changes with the child's stage of development. At the sensory motor stage, play gives an opportunity for the child to engage in experiences that activate the senses, particularly sight and touch. It also gives the opportunity for language to develop and for skills to be practised and repeated. Children may be engaged in playing with other children at this stage but the expectation is that children will play alone. At the later pre-operational stage there is more likelihood of children participating in symbolic play and using language to reflect on their own experiences. Games begin to have simple rules and there is more play with other children.

An early years manager needs to think carefully about the value of play as a vehicle for learning, and to consider the emphasis that staff in the setting place upon it. It is also necessary to consider the quality of the play that is offered. Do children have the opportunity to develop their play and contribute ideas to it? Is play stimulating for them? Do they spend time concentrating and communicating with others in their play? You should not underestimate the value that play has in encouraging and enhancing children's learning.

Conclusion

In this chapter the key features of the statutory and advisory curriculum structures – *Birth to Three Matters*, the foundation stage and the national curriculum – have been outlined. The planning, implementation and evaluation of the curriculum for the under 8s have been considered in some detail, alongside the assessment of children's learning and the influence of researchers and theorists. Play as a vehicle for learning has also been discussed. It is vital that the manager and staff have sufficient time to think about what the setting offers and that they continually adjust and improve the curriculum.

Check your understanding

1 What is your understanding of the term 'curriculum'?
2 What is your overall vision for the education you offer children?
3 How would you communicate this to staff?
4 How would you ensure that all the children have equal access to the educational opportunities offered?
5 How could you assess the learning that is taking place?
6 How could you use this assessment to inform your planning?
7 How much emphasis would you put on the value of play as a vehicle for learning?
8 How would you communicate to colleagues and parents and carers the value of play?

References and further reading

Athey, C. (1990) *Extending Thought in Young Children*. London: Paul Chapman.

Ball, C. (1994) *Start Right: The Importance of Early Learning*. London: RSA.

Barnes, P. (ed.) (1995) *Personal, Social and Emotional Development of Children*. Oxford: Blackwell.

Bee, H. (1992) *The Developing Child*. New York: Harper Collins

Bruce, T. (1997) *Early Childhood Education* (2nd edition). London: Hodder and Stoughton.

Bruce, T. (2001) *Learning Through Play: Babies, Toddlers and the Foundation Years*. London: Hodder and Stoughton.

Bruce, T. (2003) Quoted in *OnQ*, issue 13, p. 7. London: QCA. Available at www.qca.org.uk/ages3-14/downloads/fs_p7OnQ.pdf.

Bruner, J. (1977) *The Process of Education* (2nd edition). Cambridge, MA: Harvard University Press.

Bruner, J. (1990) *Acts of Meaning*. Cambridge, MA: Harvard University Press.

Davenport, G. C. (1988) *An Introduction to Child Development*. London: Collins Educational.

Department for Education and Science (1990) *Starting with Quality: The Report of the Committee of Inquiry into the Quality of Educational Experience Offered to 3 and 4 Year Olds*. London: HMSO (the Rumbold report).

Department for Education and Skills (2002) *Birth to Three Matters. A Framework to Support Children in Their Earliest Years*. London: DfES. An introduction to the framework is available at www.surestart.gov.uk/_doc/0-75E2C9.pdf. See also www.surestart.gov.uk/ensuringquality/birthtothreematters/.

Department for Education and Skills (2003) *National Standards for Under 8s Day Care and Childminding. Full Day Care*, DfES/0651/2003. London: DfES. Available at www.surestart.gov.uk/_doc/0-ACA52E.PDF. Copies can be ordered from DfES Publications, Nottingham, telephone 0845 602 2260.

Dowling, M. (2000) *Young Children's Personal, Social and Emotional Development*. London: Paul Chapman.

Drake, J. (2001) *Planning Children's Play and Learning in the Foundation Stage*. London: David Fulton.

Duffy, B. (1998) *Supporting Creativity and Imagination in the Early Years*. Buckingham: Open University Press.

Early Childhood Education Forum (1998) *Quality in Diversity in Early Learning. A Framework for Early Childhood Practitioners*. London: National Children's Bureau.

Goldschmeid, E. and Jackson, S. (1994) *People Under Three*. London: Routledge.

Hobart, C. and Frankel, J. (1994) *A Practical Guide to Child Observation*. Cheltenham: Stanley Thornes.

Hutchin, V. (2000) *Tracking Significant Achievement in the Early Years*. London: Hodder and Stoughton.

Nutbrown, C. (1994) *Threads of Thinking: Young Children Learning and the Role of Early Education*. London: Paul Chapman.

Pascal, C. and Bertram, T. (1997) *Effective Early Learning: Case Studies in Improvement*. London: Paul Chapman.

Pugh, G. (ed.) (2001) *Contemporary Issues in the Early Years* (3rd edition). London: Paul Chapman.

Qualifications and Curriculum Authority (2000) *Curriculum Guidance for the Foundation Stage*. London: QCA. Available at www.qca.org.uk/ages3-14/downloads/cg_foundation_stage.pdf.

Qualifications and Curriculum Authority (2001) *Planning for Learning in the Foundation Stage*. London: QCA. www.qca.org.uk/ages3-14/downloads/planning_for_learning.pdf.

Qualifications and Curriculum Authority (2003) *Foundation Stage Profile. Handbook.* London: QCA. Available at www.qca.org.uk/ages3-14/downloads/handbook_web.pdf. Copies can be ordered from QCA publications, telephone 01787 844 444.

Roberts, R. (1995) *Self-esteem and Successful Learning.* London: Hodder and Stoughton.

Schaffer, H.R. (1999) *Social Development.* Oxford: Blackwell.

Schweinhart, L. J. and Weikart, D. P. (1997) *Lasting Differences. The High/Scope Pre-school Curriculum Comparison Through Age 23.* Ypsilanti, MI: High/Scope Press.

Siraj-Blatchford, I. (ed.) (1998) *A Curriculum Development Handbook for Early Childhood Educators.* Stoke: Trentham Books.

Sylva, K. (2000) 'Early childhood education to ensure a "fair start" for all'. In Cox, T. (ed.), *Combating Educational Disadvantage: Meeting the Needs of Vulnerable Children*, pp. 121–135. New York: Falmer.

Tassoni, P. (2002) *Planning for the Foundation Stage. Ideas for Themes and Activities.* Oxford: Heinemann.

Tassoni, P. (2003) *Supporting Special Needs. Understanding Inclusion in the Early Years.* Oxford: Heinemann.

Whalley, M. (1994) *Learning to be Strong: Integrating Education and Care in Early Childhood.* London: Hodder and Stoughton.

Whitehead, M. (1996) *The Development of Language and Literacy in the Early Years.* London: Hodder and Stoughton.

Wood, D. (1988) *How Children Think and Learn.* Oxford: Blackwell.

Useful websites

Literacy strategy: www.standards.dfes.gov.uk/literacy.

National curriculum: www.qca.org.uk/ages3-14/5-14/2812.html.

Numeracy strategy: www.standards.dfes.gov.uk/numeracy.

4 Managing the Needs of Children in Early Years Settings

This chapter looks at relationships with children and how these are managed within early years settings (Chapter 5 looks in depth at the value of partnerships with parents and carers, the other set of 'service users'). Children should remain the key focus of every aspect of the setting:

- the planning of suitable, age- and stage-appropriate activities, which encourage and stimulate children to investigate their environment (this is covered in Chapter 3);
- suitable routines, which enable children to feel safe and emotionally secure in their surroundings;
- a warm, welcoming environment, which is also child centred, safe and stimulating.

Research suggests that children develop best in environments where adults are highly responsive (see the section 'Allowing for creativity and free choice' in Chapter 3). The role of the early years practitioner has changed dramatically over the years – partly as a result of legislation, they now have more responsibilities and more paperwork to manage, but this must not be at the cost of the children. Early years managers need to manage their time effectively so that they are able to remain highly responsive to the needs of the children. How the children are managed in the setting has an impact on their development and learning. The role of the early years practitioner is to ensure that the needs of each child are met in order to encourage independence and confidence. Children who feel confident about themselves are more able to have a positive learning experience, which will lay a strong foundation for later learning. The quality of the support children receive from the early years practitioners in the setting will have an effect on how valued they feel. When children feel part of the community within the setting they are able to develop their independence and confidence. By regularly reflecting on and reviewing practice, you will be able to maximise the opportunities for high quality learning and minimise challenging behaviour.

This chapter looks at how early years practitioners manage the needs of children within the setting and thus provide a quality service. It explores the following:

4.1 Creating a welcoming and supportive environment for children.

4.2 Positive behaviour expectations.

4.3 Providing routines.

4.1 Creating a welcoming and supportive environment for children

As an early years manager you will be managing a range of people:

- your team;
- students;
- the children.
- other professionals;
- parents and carers;

It could be argued that the children are the most important on this list. How you and your team manage the children's experiences will affect their learning. The relationship with the children starts from their initial contact with the setting and ends with supporting their transition to the next setting. Between the two there is the important matter of settling the children in and welcoming them each day. This section looks at all these matters.

Initial contact

Children's initial contact with the early years setting comes in a variety of forms, all of which are as important as each other. They are detailed in Table 4.1.

Table 4.1. The different forms of initial contact with children starting in an early years setting

Form of contact	What is involved
Home visiting	Members of the team offer home visits to meet the children and families in their own homes. This gives families the opportunity to ask questions and start to develop contact with the setting.
Visits to the setting	Visits before the children start at the setting help the children, parents and carers to become familiar with its staff, routines and the organisational structure.
Letters home	Letters to the children, parents and carers before the children start help them to feel valued and included. A colourful card or decorative letter addressed to the child can be very welcoming.

Settling in

The routines and processes in place that support the smooth transition from home to the setting must be flexible and take into account the needs of individual children and their families. The settling-in process allows children to become familiar with their new surroundings at their own pace, with the support of the early years practitioners caring for them. For some children this will be gradual and require consistent support while for others it will be a much shorter process with less support.

For many children, leaving parents and carers for the first time can be a stressful experience. The sensitive support and reassurance received from the early years practitioners caring for them will contribute to their emotional well-being. For some children it will be the first time they have been left by their parent or carer and others may have had a poorly managed previous experience of separation. One of the essential elements for working in partnership with parents (Herts Quality Standards, 2000) is encouraging parents or carers to stay with their child while he or she settles in. It is good practice to encourage them to stay for as long as it takes for their child to settle. This could be a few minutes each day or for the whole of the session. It can take up to half a term to settle children, especially those who have not spent any time away from home before.

In order to ensure a successful settling process the early years practitioner needs to be sensitive to the needs of both children and parents. The majority of parents are willing to support their child by gradually introducing them to the setting and staying with them if required; however, there are those who feel leaving promptly is a better strategy for their own child. Explaining the benefits of parental involvement here may encourage more parents to participate. These include:

- it lessens distress for the child;
- it facilitates the development of a trusting relationship between the child and the early years practitioner;
- the child is likely to settle much more quickly.

However, early years practitioners need to respect the wishes of those families who prefer the setting to be solely responsible.

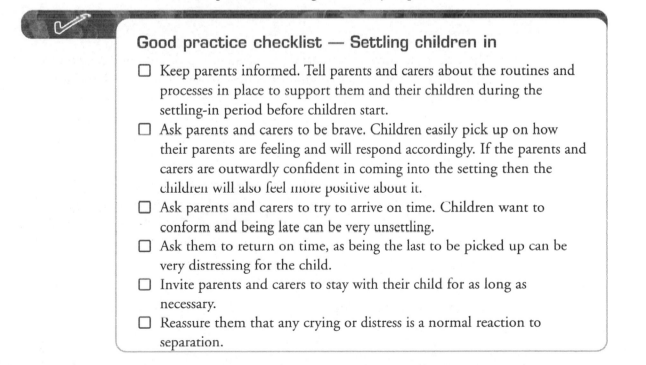

Good practice checklist — Settling children in

- ☐ Keep parents informed. Tell parents and carers about the routines and processes in place to support them and their children during the settling-in period before children start.
- ☐ Ask parents and carers to be brave. Children easily pick up on how their parents are feeling and will respond accordingly. If the parents and carers are outwardly confident in coming into the setting then the children will also feel more positive about it.
- ☐ Ask parents and carers to try to arrive on time. Children want to conform and being late can be very unsettling.
- ☐ Ask them to return on time, as being the last to be picked up can be very distressing for the child.
- ☐ Invite parents and carers to stay with their child for as long as necessary.
- ☐ Reassure them that any crying or distress is a normal reaction to separation.

Welcoming children each day

Children need to feel the setting welcomes them.

In order to cope with such a momentous experience as starting nursery, children need to feel the setting they are entering welcomes and values them. Unfortunately this is not always given the thought and planning it deserves. The aim is to create a warm and welcoming first experience and thereafter every day. If this point of the day is not treated with sensitivity it is possible to damage the newly established relationship between the setting, the parents and carers and the children.

Different welcoming strategies

Welcoming strategies include the following:

- *Whole-group welcome time.* As children arrive they sit in either small groups or all together and are greeted by an adult as a group rather than individually.
- *Singing a welcome song.* Once the children have started their chosen activity at the start of the session a welcome song is sung.
- *Individual contact at some point during the early part of the session.* Adults make a conscious effort to speak to each child individually during the first part of the session.

These strategies are not personal or immediate, and they do not meet the children's need for emotional support as they arrive. Research has shown that whole-group activities can be stressful, especially for new children. These children found it less threatening to be involved in self-directed activity for the first part of the session. Therefore there is a strong argument for individual and personal greetings.

However, a few children may not wish to be acknowledged as they arrive, and prefer to arrive discreetly and just get on with an activity without any fuss. You need to recognise this and respect the unsaid wishes of individual children. This does not mean that you ignore the child but replace a greeting with a more subtle form of acknowledgement.

Consider the arrival routine in your setting.

- How are the children greeted as they arrive?
- Is this done in a well organised manner?
- Is there anything that prevents you from greeting each individually?
- List the advantages and disadvantages of various greeting strategies.

Elements of a warm welcome

Individual greetings provide the ideal basis for the development of good relationships. In order to promote children's self-esteem, Dowling (2000) suggests that early years practitioners use the following:

- eye contact;
- a genuine smile;
- a warm, friendly, approachable manner.

Although Dowling meant for these strategies to be used when interacting with the children throughout the day, they are also elements of a warm welcome. In addition to these, making physical contact (such as holding a hand), using the child's name, making a personal comment and if possible sustaining a conversation are also valuable.

It is also helpful to ensure that each child has a peg for a coat and a named drawer, as this will reinforce the feeling of belonging. These should be ready on the child's first day.

A practical approach to personal greetings

It is not always possible to greet every child every day. For example, a setting may have only two members of staff, you may be in an informal meeting with parents, or a particular child may need extra support. However, it is possible to plan effectively so that these events have minimum effect.

Arrange to visit an early years setting that is similar to your own and observe the arrival routine. Take note of how the team manages this part of the session, including contact with parents and carers, room preparation and welcoming the children.

Good practice checklist — Early morning routines

- ☐ Ensure that all the necessary preparations are complete before the children arrive. This will mean you are free to greet the children and their parents and carers.
- ☐ Ensure that the initial activities do not require large amounts of adult support. Other activities will be more inclusive for the children and will allow you to be available for them.
- ☐ Ensure that the parents are familiar with the arrival routine and know what they can expect from the setting.
- ☐ Have a system for parents to leave messages for you. However, it is important that this is not a substitute for your personal availability. Remember that not all parents are comfortable with written communication.
- ☐ If there is a child who gets distressed at being left and needs extra support on arrival, ask the parents to arrive a little later. This will enable you to give the necessary support to both the child and parent, as well as to reduce the stress in the room as the other children arrive.
- ☐ Take time to observe the children as they arrive. You are aiming for an atmosphere that is relaxed, happy and productive.
- ☐ New problems are inevitable as group dynamics change. Involve the whole team in resolving any new problems as they arise.

Why welcome each child?

Greeting the children provides the early years practitioner with the opportunity to assess how each child is feeling and to respond with appropriate support. Young children especially benefit from having routines in their lives (see section 4.3). They thrive on the regularity of familiar events and gain an immense sense of security from them. Greeting children as part of the regular routine enhances their feelings of security and belonging. This in turn has a positive effect on their emotional development and their success as learners.

Supporting transitions

Transitions are the move from one environment to another. Adults have numerous strategies to cope with transitions such as starting a new job, moving to a different part of the country, getting married or becoming parents. However, young children have not had the opportunity to develop these strategies. They can experience a range of reactions to transitions, including feeling vulnerable and frightened, which in turn has an effect on their ability to integrate and learn. For these reasons it is important to support children during times of transition. It is the role of the early years practitioner to be sympathetic to any anxieties and to be sensitively supportive.

Transitions are not only the move to a new phase of life but can also be:

- the daily move from one environment to another;
- a new experience;
- a sudden change in routine;
- an unexpected event.

The most common form of early transition is the daily separation from a parent or carer when children attend day care or nursery school.

All forms of transition can be stressful for young children and the levels of stress can be influenced by many factors. For example, children may be less able to deal with transitions at times when they are dealing with other events (see below). Children's reactions to transitions can therefore change over time, as can their need for support. In order to provide appropriate support it is helpful to think about the types of events the children in your care may experience. These include:

- the birth of a sibling;
- parents separating;
- a change in daily routine (holidays, special events);
- a change in childcare arrangements;
- a stay in hospital;
- moving house.

Even something adults may consider to be a small or insignificant event can be quite traumatic for children.

Think it over

Think back to the last time you experienced a major transition in your life (e.g. a new job or moving house).

- How did you feel?
- How did you prepare yourself for this new phase in your life?
- How could this transition have been made easier for you?

In order to provide children with effective support it is necessary to understand why transitions need to be incorporated into the setting's daily planning. The transition from home to nursery can be a difficult time for young children, and any negative experience here can have a detrimental effect on the subsequent transition to school (Blatchford *et al.*, 1982). It is the role of the early years practitioner to provide effective support to ensure that transitions are as positive as possible. This can be achieved by:

- knowing the children – try to get to know each child as quickly as possible so that you are aware of individual needs and can act on them;
- actively fostering warm and positive relationships with parents – if children see that their parents are welcome and trust the setting, they will too.

Providing a supportive environment for transitions

Bronfenbrenner (1979) considered the environment in which children develop to be a major influence on their ability to be successful learners. Just as adults do, children apply previous experiences, both negative and positive, to new situations. Children who have been traumatised by poorly managed transitions will naturally presume all transitions to be traumatic, whereas if young children have had positive experiences of being left by their parents or carers they are more likely to be able to make successful transitions. When children enter a new environment they apply previously learned skills and behaviour and continue to use this strategy throughout life (Gelfer and McCarthy, 1994).

Bronfenbrenner (1979) believed that at times of transition a positive partnership between home and setting makes the event less stressful. It is reassuring that something so simple can have such a major impact. However, it is because it is so simple that it can sometimes be overlooked and left to chance. Chapter 5 looks at ways of developing positive partnerships with parents and carers and how they can affect children's early years experience.

Think it over

Think about the transitions made by the children in your setting.

- How were these transitions accommodated?
- What preparations were made for children leaving the setting?
- What strategies were used to involve parents at times of transition?

Compare your answers with someone else's. Are there any notable differences?

Case study — Sideq starts day care

Sideq is 3 years old. He has just started attending day care for four mornings per week. Before he started, the early years manager invited Sideq and his mother to attend two introductory sessions. During these, he was shown around the nursery and given a peg and drawer for his belongings. Sideq started to attend the following week and initially settled well and began to make friends. However, he is now becoming distressed when left by his mother and staff are unable to comfort or distract him. He is unwilling to participate in activities and wants to sit by the door and wait for his mother to return. During the next team meeting staff discuss their concerns about Sideq. A senior practitioner suggests that they ignore his behaviour. Another member of the team suggests that his mother should leave him as quickly as possible, as her 'fussing' is making the situation worse.

- How do you think Sideq and his mother can be best supported at this time?
- What do you think may be the cause of Sideq's change in behaviour?

4.2 Positive behaviour expectations

Some of the more direct ways of managing behaviour are considered below. First, however, two of the prerequisites to good behaviour within a setting are considered: showing that the adults value young children and promote their self-respect; and good communication between adults and children.

Valuing young children and developing self-respect

Experience has shown that the quality of the relationship between the early years practitioner and the children is a crucial element to how well they do both socially and academically. When children see that they are supported and respected it leads to positive attitudes and feelings of being valued, and in turn these help children to develop self-respect. Self-respect is one of the most important qualities needed to be a good learner. Children who do not feel valued or respected often demonstrate this through inappropriate behaviour.

Positive relationships with carers can have a beneficial effect on behaviour. The child who has a secure relationship initiates positive interactions with others and responds positively. It is not unusual for children who have insecure relationships with their carers to use various negative strategies, such as ignoring instructions given to them.

Communicating with young children

It is the role of the early years practitioner to enable young children to develop effective communication skills. These skills are influenced by the adults around children and how responsive they are. Children who have little experience of enjoyable conversations reflect this in their own communication with others. By providing children with consistent support and opportunities to communicate, they will develop the skills needed to be effective communicators. They will also be much less likely to engage in inappropriate behaviour.

Communication can be both verbal and non-verbal. The latter includes body language, facial expressions and gestures. Early years practitioners need to be sensitive to what message they are giving through their own non-verbal communication. 'Closed' body language – for example folded arms and little eye contact – and negative facial expression give the message that you are unapproachable and not available. Early years practitioners should therefore:

- be aware of both their own non-verbal communication and that of the children;
- be responsive to both the children and other adults in the setting;
- initiate conversation and take time to respond appropriately to conversations children begin;
- extend and encourage children's use of language;
- show a genuine interest in what the children have to say, so that they will be encouraged to communicate;
- encourage curiosity and exploration;
- answer children's questions;
- be an active listener.

You can show children that you are actively listening to them by:

- maintaining eye contact;
- getting on the same physical level as them;
- responding appropriately to what they say to you;
- concentrating on what they are saying.

It is important to show a child that you are actively listening: maintain eye contact, get on the same physical level, and concentrate on and respond appropriately to what is said.

It is not always easy to follow all of these points at busy moments, but you can probably think of a time when you have not paid full attention to what a child is telling you and you have answered with the throw-away comment 'That's nice'. I never made this mistake again when the child replied 'Well, we were very sad that he died'.

Think it over

Think about the daily routine in your setting.

- At what times were the children able to initiate a conversation with an adult or to be listened to by a group of children?
- Which communication skills did the children have the opportunity to develop?

Compare your answers with those of someone from another setting.

Expectations of behaviour

In order to meet the needs of children in the setting and minimise challenging behaviour it is useful to identify what behaviours are unacceptable.

- What do you consider to be challenging behaviour?
- What aspects of challenging behaviour have you experienced professionally?
- What were the expectations in that setting?
- How did the children know what the expectations were?

One of the first steps to managing challenging behaviour within the setting is to look at the expectations and decide whether they are realistic or not. This is not about lowering standards but about giving the children achievable and realistic targets. Children are at risk of behaving badly in response to unrealistic expectations imposed on them by the adults in the setting. Such expectations can often reflect a lack of understanding on the part of the adult about young children's development. Early years practitioners need to bear in mind the social and emotional stages of development, as these will affect how children behave in different situations (see Table 4.2). Linking stages of development to age can be unreliable, however, and therefore only by getting to know each child well can expectations be realistic.

It is important to remember that there is a vast range within the norms indicated in Table 4.2. There are also additional influences on behaviour that need to be taken into account. These could include:

- the birth of a new sibling;
- the death of a family member;
- relationship break-down between parents;
- moving house;
- parental absence (short or long term);
- a change of routine;
- any event that traumatises the child to a lesser or greater extent.

In addition to these social influences, research has also identified the following emotional triggers.

- *The need for attention.* Some children believe that they belong only when they are noticed. The belief is so strong that they do not mind whether it is negative or positive attention they receive. The early years practitioner can respond by giving positive attention and reinforcement at other times, by ignoring inappropriate behaviour if it is safe to do so

Table 4.2. Children's development and the associated social and emotional influences on behaviour

Age of child	Stage of development
0–3 months	Feelings and relationships begin to develop. Children begin to recognise people they know well. They begin to smile and turn towards a familiar voice.
3–6 months	Children can differentiate their mother's voice from others. They like to be held by a familiar person. They may begin to enjoy peek-a-boo games and to be wary of strangers. They learn self-worth from the actions and reactions of others.
6–12 months	Children begin to develop a sense of self-image and become more aware of the feelings of others. They realise that objects and people are separate from them. They show fear of strangers. They understand the word 'no'.
1–2 years	Children begin to have a mind of their own and to develop a sense of identity. They begin to express their needs using words and gestures. Interpersonal relationships are based on taking rather than giving.
2–3 years	Children of this age can imitate others. They enjoy symbolic play. They begin to explain how they feel, to show autonomy, to do things for themselves and to show more patience. They will share and be more affectionate although they can also be inflexible and demanding.
3–4 years	Children begin to be interested in having friends. They are influenced by each other. They can cooperate and negotiate. They can be easily frightened. Routines are less important.
4–8 years	Children establish a stable self-concept and take in and internalise social rules. They respond positively to explanations and reasons for things. They learn to be assertive without being aggressive. They are beginning to sort out real from make believe and truth from untruths.

and by using redirecting and distraction strategies. Distraction strategies require the early years practitioner to be able to pre-empt inappropriate behaviour and subtly intervene by redirecting children away from the situation.

- *The need for power.* Some children believe they belong only when they are in control. The early years practitioner can respond with kind but firm respect, by giving limited choices, setting reasonable boundaries and, again, by using redirecting and distraction strategies.
- *Feelings of inadequacy.* Some children feel the need to show to others through their behaviour that they are inadequate. Early years practitioners can respond by encouraging the child to try new things, focusing on the child's strengths, teaching new skills in small steps and by giving praise and encouragement.

It is also important to remember that the group's dynamics change with each new intake and with each child's departure. You need to be sensitively

Figure 4.1. Attention-seeking behaviour.

aware of all of these influences on behaviour and adjust expectations and goals accordingly.

Finally, there are also physical influences on behaviour. For example, a toddler aged 2–3 years is not yet physically developed to be able to sit still for more than a very short time, and therefore an expectation to do so would be unrealistic.

Case study — Pasta necklaces

Afia is a newly qualified nursery assistant working with 1–2-year-olds in a day care centre. She likes all aspects of her new job but particularly enjoys planning and implementing activities. Today it is raining so the children will not be able to play outside in the garden after snack-time. Afia has been asked to set up a short activity instead. She decides to make pasta necklaces with the children, and sets out all the necessary materials on the table. After snack-time the other nursery staff encourage the children to choose what to play with. Once the children are all busy, Afia encourages four of them to come and do the activity. Once the children are seated at the table it becomes quickly obvious to Afia that the activity is going to be unsuccessful and of no value to the children – it is inappropriate for this age group.

- Think of all the possible causes of the activity being unsuccessful.
- How do you think the children reacted to this activity?
- How does this link to your knowledge and understanding of child development?

Knowing the expectations

Expectations need to be clear, consistent and realistic, and to be supported by all the adults in the setting. But how do the children know what the expectations of their behaviour are? Sometimes this is overlooked and it is assumed that the children 'just know'. Some settings regularly involve the children in drawing up the classroom rules and display a copy in the room as well as sending one home for the parents to reinforce. It is more likely for these rules to have an impact if they are based upon a positive viewpoint. That is, they should focus on actions and behaviour to be encouraged. For example:

- We always try to be kind to others.
- We always try to speak nicely to each other.
- We look after our own and other people's things.
- We take care of our nursery.
- We put things back where they belong.
- We look after living things.

A behaviour policy

If the setting has realistic expectations and each child is known well and understood, the children will be less likely to fail to meet expectations. The key points to remember are:

- consistency;
- forethought;
- respect;
- recognition of children's limits;
- high quality relationships;
- encouragement.

Realistic and consistent targets are likely to foster good behaviour. By creating and implementing a behaviour policy all adults know what is expected of both them and the children. Each setting should create its own behaviour policy, and this should reflect the specific needs of the children. Owing to the frequent change-over of children, parents and staff, it is essential that the policy be regularly reviewed. In order for the policy to be workable it should be created by all those who work with the children, with additional input from parents. It will need to set out realistic and achievable targets that are based on a sound understanding of child development.

Evaluating children's behaviour

When evaluating the children's behaviour it can be helpful to try to decide whom the behaviour is a problem for. Often natural curiosity and the desire to experiment can be mistaken for challenging behaviour.

Case study — The wrong toys

A group of 3- and 4-year-olds are playing in the sand when one of them suggests they make a road. They use the spades and rakes to form paths in the sand. Emily brings a box of cars and some farm animals from the small-world play area and tips them into the sand tray. The children start a game with the cars and animals, playing cooperatively together. They create a road and farm, making up a story as they play. Andrew, a childcare student, intervenes and asks the children to return the cars and farm animals to where they belong. Oliver asks why they can't play with the cars and animals. Andrew explains that they are not sand toys and that they will get spoilt.

- As Andrew's supervisor, how would you deal with this situation?
- What justification would you give Andrew?

Case study — Rukshana and the glue

In the nursery class a group of children aged between 3 and 4 years are sitting at a table doing a craft activity. All the materials needed for the activity have been set up ready for the children to use. Rukshana picks up the glue and begins gently to pour it over the paper in front of her. She uses the glue spreader to spread the glue over the paper. She then presses both hands into the glue repeatedly. Rukshana is clearly enjoying this first experience of glue. Zeena, the early years worker supervising the group, points out Rukshana's action to her colleague, saying 'Look! She's doing it deliberately. She knows we don't allow them to do that. That's so naughty!' Zeena asks Rukshana to go and wash her hands.

- Is Rukshana's behaviour 'naughty'?
- Why do you think Zeena responds in this way?
- How would you deal with this situation?

Encouraging positive behaviour

The most effective strategy in behaviour management is prevention. To this end, the setting should represent an environment which:

- encourages independence;
- builds self-esteem;
- meets the individual needs of children;
- takes into account the likes and dislikes of the children;
- provides the children with a wide range of appropriate, stimulating activities and learning experiences, which encourage exploration and problem-solving;
- caters for the developmental needs of all the children;
- is well organised and stimulating.

The good practice checklists can help you to evaluate your setting in terms of whether it is set up to prevent challenging behaviour.

Good practice checklist — Encouraging good behaviour

- ☐ Ensure that children know and understand the setting's behaviour policy and class rules.
- ☐ Stick to the policy fairly and consistently.
- ☐ Praise good behaviour.
- ☐ Be a positive role model.
- ☐ Discuss right and wrong in appropriate contexts as the opportunity arises.
- ☐ Be well organised and plan effectively. This will help to prevent the children from getting bored.
- ☐ Ensure the routine supports the children's emotional needs.
- ☐ Encourage the children to find their own solutions to problems.
- ☐ Give plenty of opportunities for the children to develop their social skills.
- ☐ Encourage children to understand the consequences of their actions.

Good practice checklist — Discouraging challenging behaviour

- ☐ Provide enough resources and materials so that the children do not have to share too many items and wait too long for their turn.
- ☐ Provide sufficient play materials to allow the children choices.
- ☐ Check that activities are appropriate to the children's age and stage of development.
- ☐ Remove barriers to success, to avoid the children becoming frustrated.
- ☐ Keep waiting times to a minimum.
- ☐ When dealing with challenging behaviour explain why it cannot be tolerated. Remember to remain calm, speak quietly, slowly and firmly, ensuring that you maintain eye contact with the child.
- ☐ Give reasons for your judgements when conflict occurs.
- ☐ Always remember to let the child know that it is the behaviour that is unacceptable, not the child.

Positive reinforcement

Encouragement, smiles and genuine praise for cooperation produce positive results. These strategies lead to the repetition of the desired behaviour, as they build on the children's need for acceptance. Children who are shouted at and scolded do not change their challenging behaviour permanently.

Daily routines

The daily routine within the setting is a central part of the management of children within the setting. All settings are bound by the requirement to meet the physical needs of young children, such as regular nappy changes, sleeping, feeding and snacks. These have an impact on the routine, as activities and experiences are planned around them.

It may be helpful to turn this around and fit nappy checks, for example, around activities, or changing children when needed rather than all together (although snacks and mealtimes are less flexible). Experience has shown that children who are changed when needed receive more individual care and higher quality one-to-one interaction. More time is spent communicating with children and the experience becomes less hurried and more pleasurable. This, however, would require careful record-keeping to ensure no one was forgotten. Children who are engrossed in play can be left until a natural conclusion is reached, rather than be disturbed for a nappy change, causing less disruption and fewer changes.

The daily routine can have an affect on the behaviour of young children. In some cases a child's behaviour will improve if daily routines are simplified. Some young children have difficulty coping with frequent or rapid changes in environments where they are expected to be cooperative, have self-control and be self-sufficient. For these children, a simpler routine with fewer changes can be beneficial.

It is important to create a daily routine that is supportive of children's development. (As explained in the previous section, this will also help to avoid many of the frustrations that lead to challenging behaviour.) A key element here is outdoor play.

Provision for outside play

Consider the decreasing opportunities children now have to play freely outside. Many of the challenges and opportunities that outdoor play used to provide are no longer accessible to children. Outdoor play provides plenty of opportunity for vigorous physical activity, which is essential for using up excess energy (which, again, can otherwise be the cause of challenging behaviour). It is therefore important that children have access to high quality outside play. Settings that do not use their outside provision for a good proportion of each day are not meeting all the children's developmental needs.

The outside play area should not only challenge children physically but also provide them with opportunities for social interaction and exploration.

Children now have decreasing opportunities to play outside, but the outside play area can meet many of their developmental needs.

It should have both natural and manufactured resources, as well as being safe and secure. Children should have the opportunity to explore a variety of physical levels as well as natural habitats.

Gardening is a valuable activity to add to the routine use of the outside play area.

Think it over

List all the learning and developmental opportunities that an outdoor play area can offer. Remember to include social, emotional and intellectual as well as physical aspects of development.

- Work out the percentage of time the children in your setting have to play outside.
- Does the time outside sufficiently reflect the learning and developmental possibilities?

Conclusion

High quality management of the children's needs within the early years setting is central to their all-round development and learning. Positive early educational experiences lay a strong foundation for later learning.

Early years managers need to ensure that they provide a warm, welcoming environment, in order to support positive early educational experiences. They also need to implement a behaviour policy; this in turn will be helped by the establishment of routines for the children.

By implementing and regularly evaluating a range of child-focused strategies, managers can ensure that they are providing the best possible service. Child-focused strategies include:

- home visiting;
- consistent contact with the child's home;
- the settling-in process;
- actively providing a positive and supportive learning environment;
- supporting transitions;
- welcoming children;
- demonstrating that children are valued and respected;
- positive communication with young children;
- expectations of good behaviour;
- appropriate daily routines.

1 What do you understand by the term 'transition'?

2 How can the early years practitioner provide effective support to ensure that transitions are as positive as possible?

3 Individual greetings provide the ideal basis from which positive relationships can develop. What practical steps can be taken in order to greet as many children as possible each day?

4 The environment can affect children's behaviour. Outline the practical steps necessary to ensure the environment encourages good behaviour.

References and further reading

Blatchford, P., Battles, S. and Mays, J. (1982) *The First Transitions*. Slough: Nelson.

Bronfenbrenner, U. (1979) *The Ecology of Human Development*. Cambridge, MA: Harvard University Press.

Dowling, M. (2000) *Young Children's Personal, Social and Emotional Development*. London: Paul Chapman.

Gelfer, A. and McCarthy, J. (1994) 'Planning the transition process'. *Early Years Development and Care*, vol. 104, pp. 79–84.

Herts Quality Standards (2000) *Young in Herts*. Hertford: Hertfordshire Early Years Development and Childcare Partnership.

Lindon, J. (1998) *Working with Young Children*. London: Hodder and Stoughton.

Makins, V. (1997) *Not Just a Nursery*. London: NCB.

Nutbrown, C. (1996) *Children's Rights and Early Education*. London: Paul Chapman.

Pugh, G., De'Ath, E. and Smith, C. (1994) *Confident Parents, Confident Children*. London: NCB.

Riddall Leech, S. (2003) *Managing Children's Behaviour*. Oxford: Heinemann.

Robert, R. (1999) *Self-esteem and Successful Early Learning*. London: Hodder and Stoughton.

Useful website

Hertfordshire Quality Standards: www.hertsdirect.org/hcc/csf/homelife/younginherts/settingupchildcare/standards/hqs.

5 Partnerships with Parents and Carers

This chapter explores the relationship between the setting and the parents and carers of the children who attend. Through sensitive and thoughtful communication with them, the early years practitioner is able to gain an insight into each child's home life. This information will help to meet the children's individual needs.

High quality relationships with the parents and carers of the children in the setting have a positive effect on children and their subsequent learning. Early years practitioners who understand this principle also recognise the importance of encouraging parents and carers to participate in all areas of the setting's work. However, not all early years settings appreciate the full value of high quality relationships between themselves and the parents and carers they work with. Some value the parents and carers as contributors to decision-making and policy-making, while others still permit parents and carers only to supervise snack-time or wash the paint pots. This could be seen as not working in true partnership with parents and carers. There is no doubt that these are necessary tasks, but this approach can give a clear message that parents and carers are valued only for such mundane tasks. Parents and carers have a wealth of knowledge and experience with their own children or from the workplace, in addition to their own personal skills. It is these skills that can be used to the benefit of the setting. For example, those parents and carers who are keen gardeners may like to be responsible for maintaining the garden area. Likewise, those who enjoy cooking may like to have input into the planning and implementing of cooking activities.

This chapter explores why relationships with parents and carers should be valued and the benefits of positive interactions with them. It covers:

5.1   Parents' and carers' ability to contribute.
5.2   The principles and practice of working with parents and carers.
5.3   How strong partnerships can have a positive effect on children and their learning.
5.4   Communicating with parents and carers.

5.1 Parents' and carers' ability to contribute

If parents and carers are going to have a real sense of being valued by the setting they need to contribute their personal skills and see that they are making a difference to the running of the setting. All parents and carers should be encouraged to feel part of the setting and their contributions, no matter how small, need to be appreciated. However, remember that not all parents and carers are able to contribute to life in the setting. You must respect this and not pressure them to do so or criticise them if they feel they cannot.

Today's society requires many parents to work, which does not enable them to spend time in their child's classroom. Nonetheless, firm partnerships can still be built with these parents by involving them in activities which take place out of hours, and by keeping them informed of current issues and their child's progress. Parents' and carers' practical contribution to a setting will greatly depend on their time constraints and other commitments. It will also depend on the type of setting you are working in. Parents with children in day care, for example, are often working and will need to be encouraged to feel part of the setting in other ways. Regular newsletters, information on changes within the setting and invitations to social events are examples. In contrast, parents of children in state-funded pre-school settings may have more opportunity to get involved by volunteering their time and skills.

Parents of children in early years settings may have younger siblings to care for and this needs to be accommodated. In the past, parents and carers with younger children were not always encouraged to help, as it was felt that having younger children in the setting might be disruptive. However, this has generally proved not to be the case. Experience has shown that younger siblings can actually have a positive effect. For instance, children with challenging behaviour can become nurturing and caring towards the younger children, perhaps by showing them around. These are skills that early years practitioners should be encouraging all of the children to develop. Welcoming younger siblings into the setting should be seen as another advantage to working with parents and carers.

Aside from time and opportunity, other factors may inhibit some parents and carers from becoming more involved in the setting. It is important that these are recognised and accommodated so that they can be provided with an equal chance to access a quality service. The factors include:

- the parents' experience of their own school environment;
- their lack of basic skills;
- their having English as a second language.

Think about the parents and carers in your setting.

- Can you think of some who are not involved in any way?
- Other than personal choice, what factors prevent individual parents and carers from contributing regularly?
- How can you support these parents?

Encouraging parents and carers into the setting

Working in partnership is not just about the two very different environments of home and early years setting working together. It is also about people from different cultures learning to work together for the good of the child. However, it can be difficult to persuade some parents and carers to spend time in the setting, as traditionally they have seen school as being completely separate from home and believe that education is the responsibility of the teacher. Their active participation and contributions are valuable because children begin to form attitudes about themselves and others from what they see and hear around them at a very young age. By involving all parents and carers in some way you can give a clear message to children that everyone is welcome, valued and respected.

Case study — Tailoring involvement

Fiona is a new mum at the day care centre and has just recently moved into the area. Before having her two daughters, Sophie and Paige, she worked in a large bookshop. She has expressed an interest in helping at the nursery; however, she is not able to do so regularly during nursery hours because of her work commitments. She is invited to discuss her involvement informally with the nursery staff and comes up with the idea of providing a birthday book for each child. Fiona becomes responsible for the purchasing of suitable books for the nursery children, which are presented to them at their birthday celebration in the setting. She works closely with the fundraising committee in order to support this project financially. Fiona's involvement in the setting has been tailor-made to take into account her skills, interests and her time constraints.

- How have Fiona and the setting benefited from this arrangement?

5.2 The principles and practice of working with parents and carers

The need to develop partnerships with parents and carers was highlighted by Ball (1994):

'Parents are the most important people in their children's lives. It is from parents that children learn most, particularly in the early months and years ... the closer links between parents and nursery the more effective that learning becomes.'

Yet, while the principles of closer working partnerships with parents and carers have been generally accepted within early years settings, practice has often fallen somewhat short. Many settings offer what Wolfendale (1989) describes as 'moderate' involvement. He recognised that early years practitioners work closely with parents and carers but do not always involve them in all aspects of the setting.

Parents are children's first educators. Much has been written about the positive impact close relationships with parents has on children's development and learning, and there are many ways of developing partnerships with parents; the common features to these are shown in the good practice checklist. Table 5.1 summarises three models of parent involvement in early years settings. Aspects of both the transplant and consumer model are being practised widely.

Good practice checklist — Working with parents and carers

- ☐ Parents' fundamental role in their child's education is acknowledged by staff in the setting and a partnership is developed with them, based on shared responsibility, understanding, mutual respect and dialogue.
- ☐ There is recognition of the role parents have already played in the early education of their child and that their continued involvement is crucial to the child's learning.
- ☐ Parents and carers feel welcome and there are opportunities for their collaboration with staff.
- ☐ There is recognition of the expertise of parents and other adults in the family and this expertise is used to support children's learning within the setting (see the case study 'Tailoring involvement').
- ☐ Adults working in the setting give parents and carers access to information about the curriculum in a variety of ways, such as open days, meetings, social events, brochures and video presentations (in a range of languages where appropriate).
- ☐ Parents and carers are fully informed of their child's progress and achievements.
- ☐ The starting times of sessions are flexible, in order to allow for discussion with parents and carers and for children to feel secure in the new setting.
- ☐ Opportunities for learning provided in the setting are sometimes continued at home (e.g. reading and sharing books) and experiences initiated at home are sometimes used as stimuli for learning in the setting.

Table 5.1. Three models of parental involvement in early years settings

Model	What happens	Implications for practice
The expert model	The early years practitioner assumes the 'expert' role, takes overall control and makes all of the decisions. There is little encouragement for parents and carers to become actively involved.	This approach disempowers parents and carers, and makes them dependent on early years practitioners.
The transplant model	The early years practitioner sees parents and carers as a resource, and so hands over some responsibilities but retains control over decision-making.	Parents and carers are involved in a limited range of activities, under the direction of practitioners. Parents' and carers' wealth of knowledge, experience and skills are not fully used.
The consumer model	Parents and carers have the right to decide and select what they believe is appropriate and are fully involved in all decision-making.	The early years practitioner involves the parents and carers in all aspects of the provision; however, this needs to be managed well, as not all parents and carers share the same values and beliefs.

Legislation

The growing recognition of the value and importance of staff and parents and carers working together is reflected in legislation. The Children Act 1989 emphasises the importance of professionals working in partnership with parents and carers to enable them to care for their children to the best of their ability, by enhancing their knowledge and understanding of childcare and development. Similarly, the Education Reform Act 1988 highlighted the need for parents and carers to be given access to information about the curriculum and their child's progress. The Early Years Development and Childcare Partnerships are required to provide children's information services, which enable parents to access information on a range of matters. It is also the responsibility of early years practitioners and teachers to provide support, guidance and encouragement to parents as educators.

Supporting and encouraging parents and carers

The foundation of successful partnership is mutual respect and a sharing of purpose, information, responsibility and decision-making. It is good practice to involve parents and carers in the setting. The more involved parents and carers are in what goes on in the setting, the more guidance and support early years practitioners can provide. This level of interaction increases the availability of the early years practitioner to answer questions on parenting and child development on an informal basis. This can sometimes be more appealing to those parents and carers who have built trusting relationships with the early years practitioners in their child's setting.

Traditionally parents have had limited involvement – home and school were seen as separate. This reflected the attitude that 'schools know best' (the expert model in Table 5.1). However, research has shown that working with parents has a positive effect on the child's early learning. A key function of any early years setting is to help parents to increase their understanding and knowledge of their children's development and education. This in turn will help to build the self-esteem and confidence of parents, and to enable them to support their child's learning at home.

Early years workers need to value and respect all contributions, no matter how big or small. One of the key reasons early years practitioners work so closely with parents and carers is to ensure inclusion opportunities for all families. It is important not to forget about families who may usually choose not to be actively involved with the setting – they can still gain a valuable sense of belonging by feeling included. They do not have to make a practical contribution to be part of the setting. They are part of the setting because their children attend. By ensuring all families feel included and widening participation, more parents and carers can have access to the best possible service available.

Case study — Billy's mother

Billy's mother enjoys cooking and gardening and in the past she has helped with the toddler group doing craft activities under the guidance of the leaders. She has expressed an interest in helping in the nursery but feels embarrassed about her lack of literacy and numeracy skills.

- What are her skills and strengths?
- How could these be used to benefit the nursery?
- How may Billy's mother benefit from helping in the nursery?

The 'working with parents' policy

It is good practice to have in place a 'working with parents' policy. The aim of the policy is to ensure that staff, and the setting more widely:

- respect and value the contribution parents and carers make towards their child's learning;
- support the development of the children;
- provide on-going support and encouragement for parents;

- work in partnership with parents and carers;
- provide opportunities for parents to discuss their child's progress;
- provide guidance, advice and resources to support home learning.

The policy should briefly outline the general principles held by the setting in relation to working with parents, such as:

- the value of working together;
- how the setting works with parents;
- how the setting is able to meet the needs of individual parents;
- all parents are welcome and valued.

The fact that the setting has such a policy will show that work with parents and carers is a key element of the setting's overall ethos. The policy will also allow staff to have a consistent approach to practice with parents and carers, and demonstrate to new families that they are respected and that their contributions are valued.

Value the contribution parents make towards their child's learning.

The policy should be included in an information pack provided to parents and carers before their children start at the setting. In order to raise its profile, it can be referred to during the pre-entry meeting, when the key points can be highlighted.

All staff should also have access to the policy, so that their approach can be consistent. Regular assessment and reviews of the policy as a team helps to maintain its importance and keep it up to date.

A flexible approach

The practice guidelines, policies and procedures in place in your setting aim to ensure a quality service for all families. However, when these procedures are stuck to too firmly they can actually prevent you from delivering a high quality service. It is essential for early years practitioners to be flexible in their approach.

Key principles for working with parents and carers

Hertfordshire Early Years Development and Childcare Partnership has produced a guide to good practice, in consultation with providers of services such as private and voluntary settings, and independent and local authority schools (Herts Quality Standards, 2000). The guide sets out a practical approach to achieving high quality care and education. It is representative of similar initiatives nationwide. The purpose of the initiative is to provide:

- a framework for self-assessment;
- guidance on the registration and inspection processes;
- encouragement to providers to identify good practice;
- an accreditation scheme.

The initiative identifies the following key principles for working with parents and carers:

- Knowledge of the child is shared between parents and the setting before the child starts, through visits to the group and through clear, jargon-free, written information.
- Parents and carers are encouraged to stay until their child has settled.
- Parents and carers are welcome at the end of each session or day.
- If some parents and carers are less able to participate in the setting than others, this is respected and understood by staff.
- Parents and carers are encouraged to discuss concerns, problems, and changes involving the child or family as they occur.
- The child's achievements and milestones are celebrated.
- Experiences and activities are shared through the use of 'open' sessions, parents' and carers' workshops, outings, social events, publicity and fundraising.

- Parents and carers are invited to share skills, hobbies and jobs with children or to join in sessions to support children.
- Themes, routines and 'happenings' are publicised via a notice board or newsletter.

The Early Childhood Education Forum (1998) has also identified some key principles for working in partnership with parents and carers. In the early years setting there should be:

- respect for children as individuals, for their ability/disability, sex/gender, as members of families and as members of ethnic/racial, linguistic, social, cultural and religious groups;
- respect for the different ways that different parents have of loving and caring for their children and preparing them for adult life, according to differences in cultural practices and religious beliefs;
- a willingness to relate to children and their parents and carers in diverse ways and share responsibility;
- respect for parents' decisions about their own lives, in particular for the choices they make about working outside the home;
- a commitment to communicate regularly and in as many ways as possible and in as many languages as possible, as necessary;
- a commitment to listen to parents' views and to take account of their concerns;
- acknowledgement that there are different views of childhood, child-rearing practices and goals of education, different views about the roles of parents and carers and the professionals who look after children, and that these may need to be explored and explained in open and sensitive dialogue;
- clear communication about channels for parents and practitioners to share knowledge of all aspects of children's needs, health, welfare, individual characteristics, progress and successes, in accessible language, free from jargon;
- clear procedures to support parents' involvement in the management and day-to-day life of the setting and in contacting management and parent representatives.

Respect for children as individuals and for the different ways that parents choose to bring up their children is fundamental to good practice. Early years practitioners are responsible for ensuring that children are not discriminated against either by adults or by other children in the setting. They are also responsible for promoting a positive environment for young children, where activities reflect other cultures and religions and resources portray a range of positive images.

The two sets of key principles outlined above aim to improve the quality of service provided, yet have a very different focus. The first set focuses on how early years practitioners can best work with and support families. The second set focuses on the need for practitioners to value and respect the diversity and differences that exist in families and parenting. By involving and valuing the contribution of parents and carers from all cultural and social backgrounds you can enrich the children's experience of society.

Encouraging staff to work with parents and carers

It can be helpful for the early years manager to raise the principles set out above in staff meetings or to use them as the basis for staff training. This would allow you to find out how your team feels about working with parents and carers and what support they will need. By identifying your team's individual skills and preferences you can allocate responsibilities accordingly. This can help your team to be more positive, efficient and productive.

Good practice checklist — Training your team to work with parents and carers

- ☐ Provide staff with extra time to organise, support and train parents and carers, set aside from their contact time with the children.
- ☐ Provide a range of suitable resources that will aid in supporting and training parents and carers.
- ☐ Provide staff with suitable training and support to develop their skills in working with parents and carers.
- ☐ Provide staff with opportunities to observe good practice in other settings.
- ☐ Provide regular opportunities to discuss progress and review practice.

5.3 How strong partnerships can have a positive effect on children and their learning

As parents are the most influential people during a child's formative years it makes sense to involve them in their own child's education as much as possible. 'There is a need to recognize the role parents have already played in the early education of their child and that their continued involvement is crucial to successful learning' (School Curriculum and Assessment Authority, 1996, p. 7). Early years practitioners can learn a lot about an individual child from her or his parents. It is good practice to reflect on information gathered from parents when planning the following:

- the classroom curriculum;
- activities;
- room arrangement and organisation;
- routine and daily structure;
- staffing.

Home visiting: building strong partnerships at the outset

One of the essential elements of parental involvement and partnership (Herts Quality Standards, 2000) is the sharing of knowledge about the child before he or she joins the setting. This can be achieved via visits to the home by the early years practitioners or through visits to the setting by the child and parent. Home visiting has become common practice. It is valued as one of the best ways for early years practitioners and families to get to know each other (see Figure 5.1). Home visiting has several benefits for the child, family and setting:

- It enables the early years practitioner to start to build a relationship with the child and family.
- It provides the child and family with a familiar person to relate to right from the beginning.
- It gives the parents the opportunity to ask questions.
- It enables parents and carers to find out about the setting's policies and procedures.
- It enables parents to find out about the practical things, such as coat pegs, the children's footwear required and mealtimes.

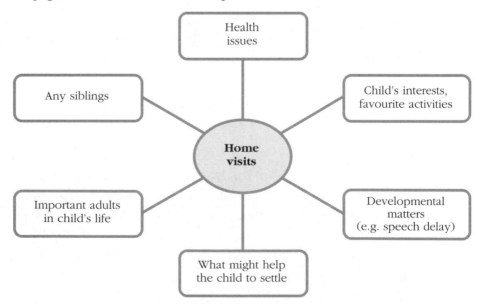

Figure 5.1. The range of information that can be obtained during home visiting.

- It allows parents to express any concerns or anxieties they may have.
- It is an opportunity for personal information to be shared, which can then be used to meet the child's individual needs when an appropriate curriculum is planned (see Chapter 3).

Good practice checklist — Home visits

- ☐ Explain that home visits are offered to all families and that the family can choose to take part or not. Always respect the family's decision not to take part.
- ☐ Explain the benefits of home visits for the family, the child and the setting.
- ☐ Early years practitioners carrying out home visits need to be sensitive to the family's culture and religious and economic background.
- ☐ Ask the family when would be a suitable time to visit and try to be on time. Telephone the family to let them know if you are running late.
- ☐ Accompany a more experienced member of staff before carrying out home visits alone.

Finding time to carry out home visiting can be challenging and there will be time constraints that are particular to your own setting. It may be necessary for you to be resourceful and think creatively about how you are going to manage your time, but the relationships formed at this point are helpful in smoothing the transition from home to the setting.

The effects of partnerships with parents and carers on children and learning

Vygotsky believed that children operated at a higher level when an adult sensitively supported their play. He used the term *zone of proximal development* to describe tasks which children might be unable to perform alone but could do with help (see Chapter 3). Adult support can help children in the following respects:

- extend and introduce new language;
- clarify and develop concepts;
- maintain concentration and interest.

If parents and carers play an active role in the setting and support children this will increase learning opportunities. Both social interaction and communication are essential tools for intellectual development.

Parental involvement increases the child:adult ratio, which is crucial if children are going to be supported at different levels across different activities. It is important that children are offered rich, powerful, first-hand experiences and that they are actively supported by adults to make full use of these experiences and to extend them. Children need access to adults who will behave in ways that will stimulate and encourage language. The adults do not need to be professionally trained – there will be early years practitioners on hand who are. However, research has shown the importance of the adult's own confidence in supporting young children. It is therefore essential that early years practitioners provide parents with the necessary guidance and support in order to enrich children's learning within the setting.

Think it over

- How are parent helpers supported in your setting?
- Compare your findings with someone else's from a different type of setting. What are the similarities and differences?

5.4 Communicating with parents and carers

One of the many essential skills needed in order to work effectively as an early years practitioner is the ability to communicate. This is especially true for the manager. You are required to communicate not only with the children and other professionals, but also with parents and carers. Throughout your career you will be working with parents and carers from a wide range of cultural, social and economic backgrounds, who have varying skills and abilities. It is important that each parent is treated with respect and consideration.

Key principles

When working with parents and carers it can be helpful for all staff to consider the following principles.

- Parents and carers and early years practitioners are equal partners.
- Parents usually know their child best of all.
- It is the role of the early years practitioner to involve parents and carers in the work of the setting.
- Early years practitioners should treat each parent with respect and consideration.
- Parents have a right to be consulted on changes and issues that may affect their children.
- Early years practitioners should recognise the need for confidentiality in dealing with parents and carers.

These principles lay a foundation on which to build firm relationships with parents and carers.

Arrival and departure times

At these times it is especially important that staff are accessible, approachable and welcoming. In most settings this will be when you would have the most contact with parents and carers.

Think about the arrival and departure times in a setting and consider how you may have been perceived by parents and carers.

- Where were you, generally?
- How did you appear?
- Were you always busy?
- Did you engage eye contact with the parents and carers?
- Were you approachable and welcoming?

It can be helpful to ask parents and carers how they feel about these times at the setting, and use the results of the survey to inform staff training.

In order to ensure that staff are accessible, the following are common practice (see also Chapter 4):

- Ensure that all room preparation is complete before the arrival of the children, so that the staff are free to welcome them.
- Have a 15-minute arrival time so that not all of the children arrive at the same time. This also accommodates parents and carers who drop off siblings at other settings.
- Start the session with free play and not an adult-led activity. This allows staff to be available for parents and carers as they arrive.
- Have members of the team stand near the entrance of the room to welcome the children and parents and carers as they arrive.
- Be available to discuss smaller issues with parents and carers (e.g. changes in pick-up arrangements) or to make an appointment for later the same day for issues that need more time.

Staff involvement

It is not appropriate for one member of staff to be solely responsible for liaising with parents and carers. Traditionally this has been seen as the role of either the class teacher or the nursery manager. With accessibility being a key element to building positive relationships with parents and carers, it is no longer practical for one member of staff to take on the role. Parents and carers are individuals and may well relate better to one person than another. To ensure that all parents and carers are reached, staff need to be accessible and approachable. However, it is not always appropriate for students and other parents to deal with confidential matters concerning other families. They should be encouraged to redirect any concerns or queries that are beyond their role to the relevant member of the team. This is not about excluding parents or devaluing helpers but about maintaining confidentiality.

In the case study 'Letters home' Beth, the early years practitioner, is implementing many of the recommendations in this chapter. She is being welcoming, including and valuing the contributions made by this parent without being patronising or judgemental. She is valuing the individual child and family by ensuring that communication is being maintained. But above all she is ensuring that this parent has equal access to written material, as this mother is unable to read. It is not important whether the mother attends the fair or not. What is important is that her needs have been accommodated and she has been sensitively included.

Case study — Letters home

Beth works as an early years practitioner in the nursery class of a school that accommodates children from a variety of backgrounds. Letters are sent home via the children that remind parents and carers of the forthcoming summer fair. Beth gives one of the letters to Pria's mother and says 'This letter is about the fair next Saturday. It starts at 2 p.m. and we are asking the nursery parents and carers if they would like to help with the refreshments. Would you like to help?'

- Why do you think Beth has used this approach with this mother?
- When else would this strategy be helpful?
- How do you ensure that you access all parents and carers in your setting?

Steps should be taken to ensure that all parents and carers know how to contact members of staff and who is the best person to contact about a range of issues. Some methods that will help to ensure you remain in close contact with parents and carers are described in Table 5.2.

Good communication skills

As an early years practitioner you are required to communicate effectively with colleagues, parents and carers and other professionals, as well as the children. You are expected to communicate in a manner which conveys respect and consideration at all times. It is helpful for the early years manager regularly to review the team's communication skills. This can be done as part of a staff development programme (see Chapter 7).

Table 5.2. Methods of contact with parents and carers

Methods of contact	How it works
Open-door policy	An open invitation for parents and carers to meet with staff or access the setting at any time. Parents and carers would be informed of this policy during introduction meetings and in their welcome packs. The practicalities of this policy can be hard to manage, so simple guidelines may need to be issued. For example: ● Small matters can be discussed with an early years practitioner at any time; however, larger issues will need an appointment, which will be made for the same day if mutually convenient. ● Picking children up outside of the normal times is permitted, but parents and carers need to report to reception first.
Meetings with parents and carers	Meeting with parents and carers regularly is a great way to keep in touch and maintain good relationships. Meetings may involve the whole setting, individual groups or individual parents and carers. It is hard to arrange meetings that suit everybody. By being flexible and holding meetings at a variety of times or by giving parents and carers a choice of times you can become more accessible and increase parents' and carers' involvement. Early years teams will hold regular parents' and carers' meetings and conferences. When meeting with parents and carers it is helpful to create a comfortable environment in which they feel free to share information, ask questions and make recommendations. Be careful not to make assumptions about the level of knowledge, understanding or interest parents and carers have. Explain any terminology so that they can develop their understanding of the subject.
Letters home	Regular newsletters home are as important as the daily contact parents and carers have with the setting. They are a means of keeping parents and carers up to date with current events, issues or staff changes which may affect their children. Letters need to be informative and user-friendly if they are going to be read. Small boxes or columns of information, as in a newspaper, can help to achieve this. For more formal occasions and events it can be helpful to follow up any written invitation with personal contact to make parents and carers feel more welcome.
Parents' room	A parents' room provides space for parents and carers to meet with each other or with staff. It can be used to store resources for families to use. It is not always possible to provide a separate room but a shared room or area is a good start. By creating a space to be used by parents and carers you are demonstrating that they are a valued part of the setting.
Staff photograph board	Displays of photographs of members of the team with their name, qualifications, role and any special responsibilities will help parents and carers to find the person they need to talk to. Remember to update this as staff join or leave the team.

Good communication skills include:

- speaking clearly and avoiding or explaining terminology;
- listening carefully;
- clarifying points if necessary;
- positive body language;
- being sensitive to individual needs;
- good eye contact (remember that this is not always suitable, as some cultures regard it as a mark of disrespect to maintain eye contact);
- being sensitive to individual needs.

Good listening skills

Good listening skills go hand in hand with good communication skills. Early years practitioners need to take time to listen to what is being said by everyone they have contact with, not only the children. It is a helpful strategy to paraphrase and repeat what has been said in order to make sure you understand and have heard correctly.

Dealing with concerns

On occasions parents and carers will raise concerns about their child or the running of the setting. No matter how big or small these concerns may seem, they will need to be addressed in a professional manner.

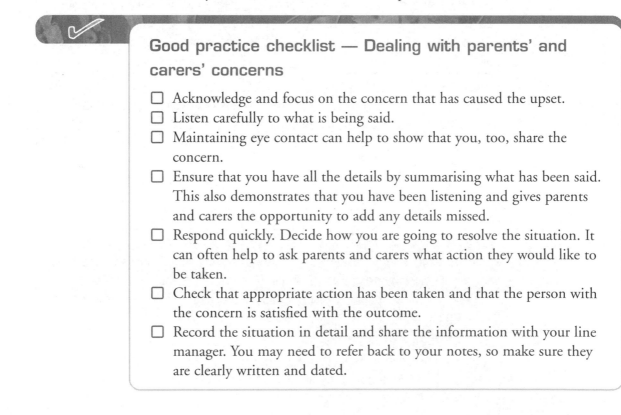

Good practice checklist — Dealing with parents' and carers' concerns

☐ Acknowledge and focus on the concern that has caused the upset.
☐ Listen carefully to what is being said.
☐ Maintaining eye contact can help to show that you, too, share the concern.
☐ Ensure that you have all the details by summarising what has been said. This also demonstrates that you have been listening and gives parents and carers the opportunity to add any details missed.
☐ Respond quickly. Decide how you are going to resolve the situation. It can often help to ask parents and carers what action they would like to be taken.
☐ Check that appropriate action has been taken and that the person with the concern is satisfied with the outcome.
☐ Record the situation in detail and share the information with your line manager. You may need to refer back to your notes, so make sure they are clearly written and dated.

Figure 5.2. Parents' concerns will need to be dealt with in a professional manner.

Although it is impossible to anticipate all potential concerns, one of the best ways of dealing with them is to have strategies in place which help to minimise their occurrence. These include:

- promptly reporting accidents and incidents to parents and carers;
- sharing information with your team, where appropriate;
- keeping your team up to date and well informed of any changes in circumstances that may affect how they work with the children and their families;
- participating in regular training to maintain and update communication skills.

Case study — A parent's concern

Sarah is a newly qualified level 2 early years practitioner. She has been working at the Play Barn nursery for 3 weeks and is still getting to know the children and their families. Sarah has been involved with all aspects of the nursery routine under the supervision of her line manager. Today she is helping six of the older children to bake cakes. One of the children develops an itchy raised rash on his hands and begins to rub his eyes. After being helped to wash his hands he appears to be better and continues as normal. At home time Sarah tells the boy's father what had happened. The father explains to Sarah that his son is allergic to eggs and that the nursery is fully aware of this. He asks to speak to the nursery manager.

- Why is this concern so justified?
- How should this concern be dealt with?
- What strategies need to be in place to ensure this does not happen again?

Conclusion

This chapter has explored why it is so vital to involve parents actively in their child's early education. In the past parents have had limited involvement but with changes in policy and the growing awareness of the value of high quality partnership there has been a shift towards greater involvement. Partnerships between parents and professionals are not only good practice but also the focus of legislation.

Research confirms that young children tend to do better when their parents have a greater understanding of their child's learning. A key function of any early years setting is to share good practice by helping parents to increase their knowledge and understanding of child development and early education. Research has also shown that families who receive frequent, sensitive and positive communication from early years practitioners tend to become more involved in their children's education. It is therefore essential that all parents and carers are welcomed into the setting and their involvement encouraged. The partnership is not just about the two very different environments of home and educational setting working together. It is also about people from different cultures and backgrounds learning to work together for the good of the children. By reflecting the outside community within the setting you can enrich the child's experience of society.

The foundation of a successful partnership is a two-way process. It is one of mutual respect, sharing the same purpose, information and high levels of communication. High quality partnerships with parents and carers can be developed when there is a balance between practical help and active involvement in decision-making.

Good relationships between parents and carers and the setting are too important to be left to chance or to be regarded as an optional extra. They are fundamental to the functioning and success of the setting and should be evaluated and reviewed regularly. As with all areas of provision, it is vital that you reflect on current practice to improve services.

Check your understanding

1   Outline the aims and objectives of a 'working with parents' policy.

2   Why is it important to regularly review and evaluate how you work with parents and carers?

3   As an early years manager you are responsible for training your team to work with parents and carers in a sensitive and thoughtful manner. Outline the key principles to remember when supporting your team.

References and further reading

Ball, C. (1994) *Start Right. The Importance of Early Learning*. London: Royal Society for the Encouragement of Arts, Manufactures and Commerce.

Early Childhood Education Forum (1998) *Quality in Diversity in Early Childhood*. London: NCB.

Herts Quality Standards (2000) *Young in Herts*. Hertford: Hertfordshire Early Years Development and Childcare Partnership.

Moss, P. and Penn, H. (1996) *Transforming Nursery Education*. London: Paul Chapman.

Pugh, G., De'Ath, C. and Smith, C. (1994) *Confident Parents, Confident Children*. London: NCB.

School Curriculum and Assessment Authority (1996) *Desirable Learning Outcomes for Children's Learning*. London: DfEE and SCAA.

Siraj-Blatchford, I. (1994) *The Early Years. Laying the Foundation for Racial Equality*. Stoke: Trentham Books.

Whalley, M. (1997) *Working with Parents*. London: Hodder and Stoughton.

Wolfendale, S. (1989) *Parental Involvement*. London: Cassell.

Useful website

Hertfordshire Quality Standards: www.hertsdirect.org/hcc/csf/homelife/younginherts/settingupchildcare/standards/hqs.

6 Managing the Employment of Staff

Early years establishments are constantly striving for quality provision. Competition is fierce and the success of a setting relies on its 'word of mouth' reputation. This reputation will depend to an extent on the curriculum offered, the experience of the children at the setting and the perceived success of the establishment. Parents and carers are very aware of the pressures faced by their children and rightly expect the best for them. They appreciate the value of play and are keen for their children to have access to high quality experiences that reflect the appropriate curriculum stage.

A key element to the provision of quality, and the patronage of parents and carers, is the staff employed by a setting. The staff are the best asset that a setting has. A well trained, motivated and committed staff team who enjoy their job and work well together will raise the standards and provide quality care and education.

The recruitment of staff can be the most challenging aspect of the manager's job. Well qualified, mature, enthusiastic and caring staff are a tremendous selling point but in today's climate can be very difficult to find. It is necessary to plan the recruitment and retention process carefully and sometimes to provide perks and bonuses to attract suitable staff.

The aim of this chapter is to outline the key elements of managing staff. It considers the following areas:

6.1 Recruitment and selection of staff.

6.2 Retention of staff.

6.3 Communication with staff.

6.4 Stress at work.

6.5 Legal obligations.

6.6 Staff development.

6.1 Recruitment and selection of staff

Before a manager starts the recruitment process, thought must be given to the job that is available. It is necessary to analyse the job requirements and to compile a job description, a person specification and to consider the legal requirement of placing advertisements that avoid discrimination. If time is spent on these aspects, problems such as high staff turnover, absenteeism and disciplinary problems can be avoided. Good recruitment and selection are important, as a more effective, better-motivated workforce can result.

The recruitment process must meet certain legal obligations – for example, individuals must not be discriminated against on the grounds of race, sex or disability, or refused employment on the grounds of membership or non-membership of a trade union. If an applicant feels he or she has been discriminated against, a claim may be made to an employment tribunal. If the tribunal finds in the claimant's favour, it may award compensation or recommend some other course of action to reduce or stop the effect of any discrimination. It is also an offence to employ a person with no immigration authorisation to work in the UK.

The number of people employed by a setting and their qualifications will depend on the current business plan and on the required staff:child ratios determined by the Care Standards Act 2000.

Case study — Diane needs a new assistant

Diane owns a successful day nursery in Norfolk. She has recently decided to expand her pre-school room for the 3–5-year-olds and is currently writing a job description for a new assistant to work with two existing employees. The expansion will take the room from 15 children to a maximum of 24.

- What is the overall purpose of this role?
- Will this be a temporary or permanent job?
- Will it be full time or part time?
- What are the qualifications needed?
- How will Diane determine the nature of the position in order to continue to have a successful team?

The job description

The job description has three main uses:
- to inform potential applicants about the job (prospective candidates can decide whether or not the job is for them);
- to ensure new recruits to the team understand the purpose and functions of the job from the outset;
- to provide information to determine the selection criteria.

When analysing the position to be filled, consider the following points in order to ensure that the job description reflects the true nature of the position:

- the position's overall purpose and objectives;
- whether it is temporary or permanent, full time or part time;
- the level of seniority and qualifications required.

It is always good policy to research the requirements of the position by talking to colleagues within the same sector, to existing employees and to draw on your own experience. If the position already exists then exit interviews can be a useful way to find out more about particular aspects of the job and to provide useful insights for updating the role.

The job description can be used as the basis for the advertisement and application forms, as well as for the questions during the interview (see below). Although job descriptions will vary from setting to setting, a common format is as follows (see Figure 6.1):

- job title;
- overall purpose;
- principal elements of the job;
- description of the establishment;
- reporting arrangements;
- salary;
- location;
- practical requirements.

The person specification

A person specification should briefly describe the ideal person to fill the job. It is a profile of the skills, knowledge, experience and qualifications necessary to perform the role properly. This is useful during the recruitment phase, as it will help you find the ideal person to join your team. It can also be referred to when compiling the advertisement and drawing up a short-list of candidates. At interview it can be useful as a checklist of points to be raised. It is normal practice to divide the elements of a person specification into desirable and essential, and to include:

- education;
- qualifications;
- childcare knowledge;
- skills and abilities;
- personality;
- experience;
- interests and general circumstances.

An example is shown in Figure 6.2 on page 148.

Job title:
Childcare worker

Location:
Nascot Wood College, Harpenden Campus

Responsible to:
Nursery Manager

Nascot Wood College is a large college offering a wide range of courses on three separate sites. The Nursery is situated in pleasant country surroundings on a large rural site that incorporates a working farm (arable, sheep, cows and pigs). Since September the Nursery has been located in the old Manor House, which has been converted sympathetically to ensure an excellent working environment for staff and children. The children are aged from 6 months to 5 years and are divided into small working groups related to their age.

Purpose:
Work as part of the Nursery team to ensure the children and families using the setting receive the highest standards of care and development in early years provision.

Main duties:
1   Act as a key worker to a group of children in your base room.
2   Alongside other staff, plan, develop and carry out a range of age-appropriate activities.
3   Keep up-to-date records of achievement that are shared with parents and used as a basis for planning.
4   Liaise with parents/carers and other staff to ensure all children have equal opportunities and experiences within the setting, while being aware of individual needs.
5   Work with and support children with special educational needs.
6   Undertake certain domestic jobs (e.g. preparation of some meals and snacks, cleaning of equipment and ensuring health and safety requirements are met).
7   Be conversant with developments in childcare practice and use appropriate materials to stimulate education in relation to curriculum requirements such as *Birth to Three Matters* and the foundation stage guidance.
8   Be willing to attend training and development courses.
9   Participate in the training of students on a range of childcare courses.
10 Assist the staff team in promoting the Nursery's positive image and maintaining its reputation in the sector.
11 Assist and support fundraising activities.
12 Attend regular staff meetings.
13 Operate within College policies, including Quality, Equal Opportunities and Health and Safety.

This job description is current but liable to variation to reflect or anticipate changes in the requirements in the post. While you will be allocated a room base associated with a specific age range of children, you may on occasion be asked to cover other base rooms and age ranges.

Figure 6.1. Example of a job description for a childcare worker. (Based on a job description supplied by Oaklands College Nursery, St Albans.)

Essential:

- NNEB/DCE NVQ 3 Childcare or equivalent.
- Recent and relevant experience of working with children between the ages of 6 months and 5 years.
- Knowledge of the foundation stage/*Birth to Three Matters*.
- Experience of implementing a wide range of activities for babies and young children.
- Knowledge of child development, to ensure records and observations are up to date.
- Knowledge of National Standards/Ofsted requirements.
- Knowledge of health and safety requirements relevant to childcare settings.
- Good written and verbal skills with adults and children.
- Ability to work as a team.
- Willingness to undertake further training and development.
- Willingness to attend staff meetings outside normal hours.

Desirable:

- Current first aid certificate.
- Food hygiene certificate.
- Experience of supervising students.
- Car driver.

Figure 6.2. Example of a person specification for the job description from Figure 6.1.

The job advertisement

It is necessary to target a range of potential applicants, but at the least expense. This can be done by recruiting among existing staff, by contacting local schools and colleges and by advertising in local newspapers and Jobcentres of the Employment Service. Online recruitment is also an option, as are commercial employment agencies and job fairs. Sector journals such as *Nursery World* and the *Early Years Educator* can be used.

A job advertisement should be based on the job description and person specification so that readers of the advertisement know what is involved and precisely what is wanted. It needs to be eye-catching, brief, straightforward and non-discriminatory. Remember that the advertisement is a visual representation of your setting and so it is important to consider carefully the image projected.

The contents of the advertisement could include:

- the business logo;
- the job title and location;
- tasks and responsibilities;
- salary and fringe benefits;

- where and how to apply (e.g. an application form) or gain further information;
- when to apply by.

An example is shown in Figure 6.3.

The Jack and Jill Day Nursery
Nascot Wood College
Harpenden, Herts

We are a group of happy, professionally trained and qualified people working in a well resourced, caring nursery. We are looking for a full-time, enthusiastic DCE (or equivalent) trained person to join our team.

We offer:

     39 hour week
     Salary £13,872–£16,710
     4 weeks' paid holiday
     Uniform

If you would like further information, to arrange a visit or an application form, please contact Pauline or Jamie on 01582 333 551.

Closing date for applications March 4th.

Figure 6.3. Example of an advertisement for the job described in Figure 6.1.

Case study — Diane's job advertisement

Diane has decided that she needs a person who has a level 2 qualification, such as the CACHE Certificate in Childcare and Education, to fill her post in the pre-school room. Diane's day nursery is in a pleasant area of Norfolk, near the coast, and has good relationships with the local school. At present the nursery cares for children aged 6 months to 5 years and has 30 children, although Diane is looking to expand the provision to accommodate an extra 8 or 9 places in the pre-school room. The salary is £6.50 an hour, and membership of the local hotel leisure centre is a fringe benefit. The position is temporary at present but may become permanent for the right candidate. Diane has designed an application form and requires two references.

- How would you present this information in an eye-catching advertisement?
- Where would you advertise?
- What are the personal qualities and skills that this role would require?

Application forms or curriculum vitae?

An application form can help you obtain the information you need and to sift through applications. It can be used as a basis for the interview, but the form should ask only for information relevant to the job. Another method of screening candidates is to ask for a curriculum vitae, in which candidates outline their previous experience and skills, employment and interests. The application form provides a standardised format for the presentation of information and enables candidates to be screened against criteria related to the specific needs of the setting. The curriculum vitae comes in several formats and pertinent questions may not be adequately addressed by the applicant. The lack of standardisation may hinder effective comparison of candidates.

The application form and the curriculum vitae should include details of at least two referees. To select the best candidate you will need to take up applicants' references. You may also wish to use a selection test.

Candidates should be short-listed for interview only if they meet the person specification. If no candidate is deemed wholly suitable it is possible either:

- to re-advertise the position with changed specifications;
- to re-advertise at a later stage, and to use temporary staff in the interim.

Interviewing the candidates

An interview can be a stressful experience for the candidate, but it can also be daunting for the manager. There is a lot of pressure to get the choice right and managers are very aware that a wrong decision can affect the success of their business, in both the long and short term. Parents, for example, are quick to withdraw their custom if they find a member of staff abrasive or intolerant of the children. Most managers could tell you a horror story concerning the employment of someone who appeared on paper to be perfect but in reality was inefficient or damaging to the business.

Careful planning of the interview will help to ensure a successful outcome. When the short-list for the interviews has been decided, prepare a letter to be sent to candidates that gives the date, time and venue. Include relevant information such as the setting's brochure, the timetable for the day (e.g. for observations and presentations – see below) and a map for the interview venue.

Prepare the questions beforehand and give thought to the structure, length, time and type of interview. Some employers like to observe the candidates working with the children or giving a presentation on some aspect of the work. A standard list of questions is fairer for the candidates and enables you to compare and contrast the answers. It is important to ask questions that give candidates the opportunity to show their knowledge and to offer their opinions. Questions should be open-ended (those that cannot be answered by a 'yes' or 'no') and should not be discriminatory. It is a good idea to include some scenarios or 'what if…' questions within your list, some examples of which are given below:

- What would you do if a parent failed to collect their child at the allocated time?
- What would you do if you noticed cigarette burns on a child's arm?
- What would you do if a colleague repeatedly turned up late for work?
- What would you do if a parent commented about another child's behaviour?
- What would you do if a child was repeatedly biting others?

Possible areas to discuss are:

- the organisation;
- the job;
- the candidate's education, experience, skills, interests and general circumstances;
- the candidate's aspirations.

Prepare the room to ensure comfort; candidates may not be at their best if sat on an uncomfortable chair faced by a panel of interviewers across a large table. You may prefer a more informal approach, with comfortable chairs and a cup of coffee.

On the day of the interview ensure that visitors or telephone calls will not interrupt you. It may be necessary to have suitable cover arranged for that day to ensure you are free to concentrate, and that the applicants can be welcomed to the setting and put at ease.

At the end of the interview give candidates the opportunity to ask questions, and be clear about when you will contact them with the results. Keep all notes you have made and interview forms so that you can give feedback to unsuccessful candidates.

An informal style of interview.

Selection and job offer

When choosing new staff it is advisable to include existing staff in the process. This improves the chances of the team working well together and can be achieved by including a staff member on the interview panel, or by discussion with staff at appropriate points in the process. However, the final decision belongs to the manager.

Case study — Staff involvement in selection

Nadira runs a Montessori pre-school and is currently in the process of employing a new member of staff. She discussed the job and person specifications with her present staff. She considered the strengths and weaknesses of the team and used this to assess the requirements of the person to be employed. After interviewing prospective candidates, she again consulted the team and took account of their comments in making her decision. The staff felt involved in the process and welcomed the new member of staff.

- What would be the benefits of involving the team in the selection process?
- Can you see any difficulties that could arise?

An offer of a job can be made by letter or telephone. It is advisable to make any offer subject to satisfactory references, health and police checks and proof of relevant qualifications. When the offer has been agreed and the conditions met, the unsuccessful candidates can be rejected.

Staff induction

It is good practice to give each new member of staff an induction period. This will help new staff to settle in and will give you the opportunity to give them information about the setting and how it is organised. A successful induction period can lead to improved performance and better job satisfaction. It can also prevent high staff turnover and reduce absenteeism, resignations or dismissals. If there is more than one member of staff starting at about the same time their joint induction would reduce the demands made on you as manager.

Induction training can be part of wider, long-term staff development training (see below), with the aim of making employees more effective and motivated, and to extend their skills and adaptability in the workplace.

Think it over

A new member of staff is starting in the baby room. She has little experience of working in a day nursery but has worked with babies over the past 10 years as a childminder. Consider how you would plan her induction.

A typical induction programme would last a day and include the following elements:

- welcoming the new members of staff on arrival;
- giving them a tour of the setting, including the toilets, and showing them where to eat their lunch, put their belongings and find the first aid equipment and fire exits;
- an introduction to the team (including the mentor or line manager);
- copies of policies and procedures;
- any outstanding details about terms and conditions of the job and when wages will be paid;
- shadowing an existing member of staff for a couple of days;
- starting job role with lighter duties and some support;
- a chat with the line manager.

The induction programme is a good opportunity to ascertain the training needs for your new (and existing) staff. It is also good practice to ask the new staff to complete an evaluation form of the induction programme to ascertain how effective it has been.

After induction you may wish to set a probationary period of 3–6 months, with a temporary contract and a review at the end. If progress has been successful a permanent contract could then be signed.

Finding recruits

Many managers are, at present, finding there is something of a recruitment crisis. The number of students leaving college with early years qualifications is falling while the demand for childcare and consequently staff is rising. The Chancellor of the Exchequer in December 2003 made clear the government's intention for the number of childcare places to rise from 750,000 in 1997 to 1.5 million in 2006.

Some establishments are tackling this problem by recruiting unqualified staff and training them within the setting. The advantage of this is that the workforce meets their individual requirements, but there are also a number of disadvantages. It is still difficult to find appropriate candidates when there is a lot of competition from better-paid jobs. There is no guarantee that staff will stay with the establishment when training has finished. It is also an expensive and time-consuming exercise, particularly as trainees are not included in the overall staff:child ratio (see Chapter 2). There have been difficulties finding suitable training facilities; some training organisations, for example, do not receive funding for mature trainees, although childcare providers often prefer a range of ages among their staff and actively encourage older people to apply for work.

Managers have found that they can spot potential employees from youngsters involved in work experience. If they show desirable qualities such as enthusiasm, reliability, flexibility, aptitude and a love of children they are worth supporting and encouraging to follow a qualification route that suits them. Some colleges are working in close collaboration with employers to ensure that candidates are finding employment when they complete their course and some employers are funding candidates through college.

There is also greater collaboration with employers and local schools, through the CoVEs (Centres of Vocational Excellence). The CoVE, which is usually based in a college of further education, works with employers to provide appropriate training and to encourage best practice. Through this work people are becoming more aware of the pressures and pleasures of working with children and the qualities and skills that childcare practitioners need. It is particularly important that Jobcentres and careers advisors understand the true nature of a childcare career. In the past there has been too much emphasis on directing people with a low academic ability towards childcare. The childcare sector needs people who enter the career with their hearts, and employers who nurture and help people to develop their talents and fulfil their potential. There is also now a better career structure in place, which allows students to work their way up to the management level – a prospect that is appealing to many in the workforce.

6.2 Retention of staff

Early years managers are naturally keen to maintain a steady workforce with a low turnover of staff. A stable team is able to plan together in the long term and feel secure that they have the mutual support of colleagues. There will be an air of confidence that encourages success. People will be aware of each other's strengths and weaknesses and know their own position in the team. Parents and children prefer a team to be stable and unchanging. A high staff turnover can give the impression that there is something wrong with the establishment and lead to clients losing confidence. The end result will be damaging to the setting's reputation in the local community. The manager nonetheless needs to ensure that a stable team remains motivated and embraces change or the setting can become stale and uninteresting.

It is natural and healthy for people to leave employment from time to time. There seems to be a high rate of pregnancy among early years workers, for example. This does give the opportunity for new members of staff to introduce ideas and freshen the team's approach. However, workers must be retained for a reasonable period otherwise it is very difficult to establish a quality service that is competitive. If labour turnover is excessive it can indicate management problems.

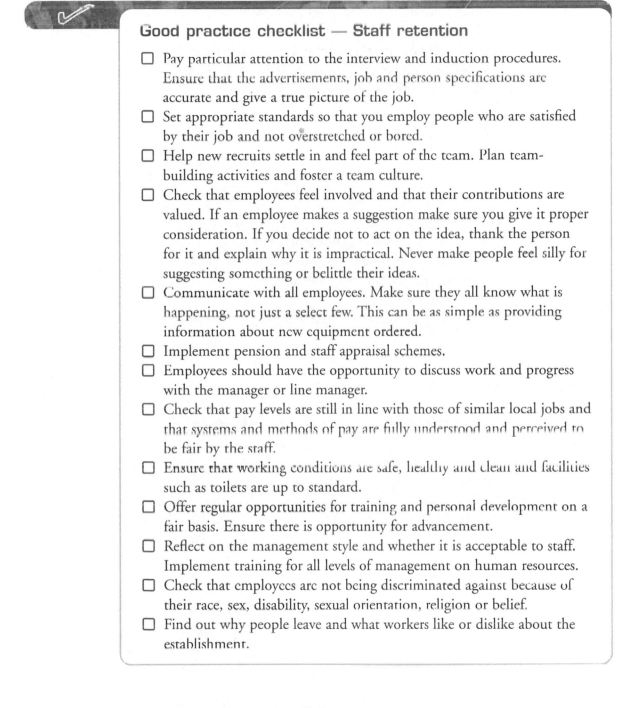

Good practice checklist — Staff retention

☐ Pay particular attention to the interview and induction procedures. Ensure that the advertisements, job and person specifications are accurate and give a true picture of the job.

☐ Set appropriate standards so that you employ people who are satisfied by their job and not overstretched or bored.

☐ Help new recruits settle in and feel part of the team. Plan team-building activities and foster a team culture.

☐ Check that employees feel involved and that their contributions are valued. If an employee makes a suggestion make sure you give it proper consideration. If you decide not to act on the idea, thank the person for it and explain why it is impractical. Never make people feel silly for suggesting something or belittle their ideas.

☐ Communicate with all employees. Make sure they all know what is happening, not just a select few. This can be as simple as providing information about new equipment ordered.

☐ Implement pension and staff appraisal schemes.

☐ Employees should have the opportunity to discuss work and progress with the manager or line manager.

☐ Check that pay levels are still in line with those of similar local jobs and that systems and methods of pay are fully understood and perceived to be fair by the staff.

☐ Ensure that working conditions are safe, healthy and clean and facilities such as toilets are up to standard.

☐ Offer regular opportunities for training and personal development on a fair basis. Ensure there is opportunity for advancement.

☐ Reflect on the management style and whether it is acceptable to staff. Implement training for all levels of management on human resources.

☐ Check that employees are not being discriminated against because of their race, sex, disability, sexual orientation, religion or belief.

☐ Find out why people leave and what workers like or dislike about the establishment.

Harassment and bullying

Employees sometimes leave employment as a result of harassment or bullying. This can be difficult to uncover, as many people prefer to keep silent about bullying and will just find employment elsewhere. It is often difficult to recognise that a person is being bullied; it may not be obvious and may be insidious. Those who suffer it may think it is normal behaviour in the organisation, or be worried that others will think they are weak or not up to the job if they complain. They may be accused of overreacting or think that they will not be believed if they report incidents. There is often fear of retribution too and people are unlikely to take action if they are afraid of the consequences for themselves. Colleagues may even collude with the bully to avoid being bullied.

Harassment and bullying take many different forms. Bullying can be characterised as offensive or intimidating behaviour that may undermine or humiliate the individual. Generally harassment is seen as unwanted conduct that affects the individual's dignity and is unacceptable. Table 6.1 compares the two. Further, harassment can take place on any of the following grounds:

- ethnicity, colour or national origin;
- gender, marital status and family circumstances;
- disabilities and learning difficulties;
- criminal record;
- trade union membership and activity;
- age;
- socio-economic background;

Table 6.1. Characterisations of harassment and bullying

	Harassment	**Bullying**
Definition	Any behaviour that is unwanted, inappropriate, unsolicited and unacceptable to the recipient and that causes stress, distress and a loss of self-esteem	Closely allied to harassment but involves persecution and intimidating, unfair, sarcastic, malicious or angry behaviour that causes the person to feel upset, threatened and beleaguered
Examples/nature	• Telling inappropriate jokes • Making offensive and abusive remarks • Derogatory nicknaming and comments • Cold-shouldering • Making unwanted and deliberate physical contact	• An abuse of power • Deliberately withholding information • Shouting • Setting unrealistic targets • Ridiculing the recipient's work, ideas or opinions • A one-off incident or a series of incidents over a period of time • Committed by an individual or a group

- religious or political beliefs;
- sexual orientation.

It is good practice for employers to give examples of what is considered professional behaviour for staff (Figure 6.4).

Figure 6.4. Professional behaviour.

It is morally offensive for bullying to continue in an establishment and if unchecked it can lead to poor morale and poor employee relations. There may also be a lack of respect for managers, poor performance, absenteeism and resignations.

There is a need for managers to develop and implement policies to protect staff. In practical terms it is a good idea for early years settings to produce a simple policy on bullying and harassment. It should include a statement from management that bullying and harassment will not be tolerated and examples of unacceptable behaviour (see Table 6.1). Staff should be involved in the writing of the policy to give it greater authority.

Setting a good example

Managers must set a good example and encourage a culture where employees are consulted and problems are discussed. For example, there should be a fair, prompt and objective method of dealing with complaints, and a strong commitment to confidentiality. In some cases it may be possible to resolve issues informally, or by using a counselling service. If informal resolution of the problem is not possible the manager may need to investigate disciplinary procedures. Advice on individual cases can be obtained from ACAS at www.acas.org.uk or on its helpline 08457 47 47 47.

Aids to staff retention

Managers are becoming very creative in the methods they employ to encourage retention of staff. The offer of fringe benefits is one from the wider commercial sector. These range from traditional pension schemes to membership of the local golf course or entrance tickets to race courses. Free car parking for employees is a perk that is particularly likely to appeal to staff in a highly populated area where parking charges are high.

Bonus schemes may be offered to reward staff for low absenteeism, and morale-boosting techniques include providing pleasant staff rooms, kitchen facilities and personal lockers. Subsidised childcare has proved to be an effective method of getting people back to work, as has flexible working. Some smaller establishments have introduced Christmas shopping days and bonuses as a reward for staff loyalty.

The wider aspects of retention of staff – for example, that childcare workers must receive realistic wages for the job they do – need to be addressed at government level. However, there are some things that the manager can do, by participating in any forums on staffing problems and by raising the public awareness of the value of childcare.

The use of an appraisal scheme can also encourage retention of staff. This will give managers and staff the opportunity to review overall performance over a period of time and provide useful feedback. It will also facilitate mutual understanding of the objectives and requirements of the employee's job role and give the opportunity to set individual goals and meet aspirations, including future training needs. It is of paramount importance that staff feel that managers care about them and are prepared to invest in their future careers.

6.3 Communication with staff

Why is good communication important?

You will want to create a warm ethos in your establishment, where staff are generally keen to go to work and enjoy the experience each day. Communication is a key element in this. Poor communication can lead to misunderstandings, low morale and substandard performance. In a small business in particular it is easy to assume that everybody knows what is going on. In reality it can be just a select few who are privy to all the necessary information and this can lead to dissatisfaction on the part of uninformed staff. A lack of information can undermine staff in terms of their own feelings of self-worth and in front of the parents when they cannot answer specific questions.

Effective communication can ensure everyone has accurate information and can improve the performance and commitment of staff. It can facilitate the exchange of ideas and views, and reduce misunderstandings. Communication is a two-way process, so you will benefit from the information you receive from employees as well. In turn this may improve your performance and decision-making.

Good communication between staff is beneficial for the children too. The children, for example, may be indirectly affected by a dispute between two colleagues about whose turn it is to supervise outdoor play. The children will be aware of the negative atmosphere and this can make them feel anxious and unsettled.

How can you ensure that communication is effective?

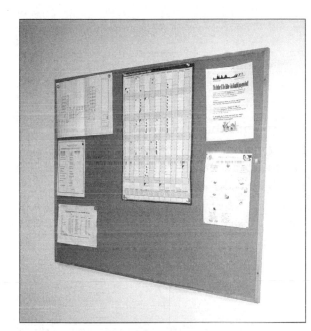

An example of an uncluttered notice board.

Childcare practitioners need to have time in the day to communicate important aspects of the job to each other, such as concerns about the children or noting developmental progress. There needs to be regular opportunities for more formal discussions as well, perhaps in regular staff meetings at a time when all employees can attend. It is also important for you to be available to communicate with your staff regularly. There should be an opportunity, at least weekly, for employees to discuss issues and ask questions. Some managers will arrange for meetings or informal discussions over a cup of tea at the end of the day. It is necessary to make sure that communications include all members of staff, including part-time and absent staff. Notice boards are a useful way to display information but they must be kept up to date and be eye-catching. Most people can walk past a notice for a week and not read it.

It is also useful to include communication skills as part of staff development. People need to be able to communicate with each other in the team, and also with parents and the children in their care.

It is worth remembering that successful communicators are able:

- to listen and observe carefully;
- to understand the other person's viewpoint;
- to be aware of non-verbal as well as verbal communication;
- to recognise that feelings play a part in interpersonal communications;
- to respect other people.

There are times when people try to control others by controlling communications. The spoken message is 'Don't do that' or 'Do this' and the non-verbal message is that the speaker is more important, knowledgeable and powerful than the recipient. These controlling messages are destructive. They can include communications that are disparaging or make the other person feel small. There is very little respect contained in these messages. Examples of controlling communications used in an early years setting include the following statements:

- 'I would never have done it like that. Why didn't you ask me first?'
- 'We never let the children do that....'
- 'Oh, didn't you know the speech therapist was coming to see Nadira? I've known for weeks.'
- 'I told you I needed the prices for those toys. Your problem is that you never listen.'
- 'Didn't you learn anything at your previous job?'
- 'It's so lazy, leaving everything lying around. Always clear up before the children go out.'

In all of these examples the speaker is trying to control, by using language that is designed to hurt, and takes no account of the other person's feelings. A strong message is put across that the speaker disapproves of the recipient. This sort of communication can do a lot of harm to the individual's self-confidence and to the overall ethos of the setting. Communications that are lacking in respect can be destructive between colleagues, staff and students and ultimately between staff and children. They can seriously harm relationships and often the recipient will hear only the part of the comment that is hurtful – important parts may be blocked out and not received. A breakdown in communication can occur.

Think it over

Spend some time observing other people, in real life or on television. See if you notice anyone trying to control another person by using negative communication. Consider the effect controlling communication has on people. Think of ways to change the wording of the comments listed as examples so that the communication is helpful and beneficial to the recipient.

Dealing with criticism

As a manager you may find yourself on the receiving end of criticism, from either a colleague or a parent. In these situations it is important to remain calm. You should be aware that your own feelings could cause you to put up barriers to what is being said. Listen carefully and try to understand the other person's point of view. If you reflect back to them what they say this shows that you are treating them with respect. If there is a misunderstanding, clear it up, and apologise if you have made a mistake. Try to avoid a win/lose situation and use your interpersonal skills to ensure that you both 'win'. Work with the colleague or parent to reach a satisfactory conclusion that you both feel good about.

6.4 Stress at work

Stress can be defined as the adverse reaction people have to excessive pressures or other types of demand placed on them. A colleague once referred to stress as feeling like you are being pecked all over. The pecking is continuous and does not go away.

Stress is a health issue that can affect people in any form of employment and is an issue that is regularly discussed in staffrooms. Childcare and education work is particularly vulnerable to stress and managers will need to be aware of the effects on themselves and on their employees. Working with children has a relentless pace and a high level of responsibility. There are no clear time parameters to the work and issues often spill over into home life. There are also the pressures of maintaining high standards in a close team.

Sometimes the working environment can cause pressures by being unsuitable – for example the playgroup in a church hall where all equipment has to be set out each morning and put away at the end of each session. There can also be pressures from working in a building that is used by other groups.

Some stress is caused by the general public not understanding the nature of the work or by managers putting undue pressure on their staff by setting unachievable targets. Many childcare practitioners work very long hours, often for small financial recompense. They are often people with families to look after. It is not unusual for early years practitioners to work a long shift in a day nursery and then go home to start again with his or her own family responsibilities.

The Ofsted inspection process can cause additional stress on top of the day-to-day work, and it is important to realise that people often have a reaction to this the week after the inspection.

A little stress can be good for people: it can motivate them to achieve targets they have set for themselves and to rise to new challenges. This can bring a sense of well-being and a relief from boredom. Too much stress, though, can affect health negatively and interfere with work and home life. Repeated and severe stress can be weakening and demoralising. However, people will react to potentially stressful situations in different ways: one person's source of stress is another person's source of fun. It is necessary therefore for you to identify the particular sources of stress for your staff and yourself, and try to ensure these are minimised or avoided.

How to recognise when an employee is suffering from stress

Too much change in too short a space of time is a major cause of stress. Most people can cope with a few changes or difficulties in their life but too many demands can affect their ability to cope. Throughout life people experience small and large events, and social changes such as marriage, divorce, pregnancy, change of work, trouble with in-laws or a son or daughter leaving home. Some of these life events are considered to be more likely than others to act as a trigger for stress. For example, the highest stress ratings are for the death of a spouse and moving house. Lower stress ratings are given to Christmas, holidays and changes in work hours or conditions. The more events that happen, the more likelihood there is of a person suffering from a stress response, which can be manifested as physical as well as emotional and cognitive symptoms (e.g. forgetfulness, muddled thinking). The severity of the stress response is usually related to the significance of the events and changes experienced. Stress can be triggered by pleasant events as well as by unpleasant ones.

Events are particularly stressful when they are:

- unpredictable;
- major;
- unavoidable;
- unfamiliar;
- intense;
- inevitable.

The warning signs of stress vary from person to person. They can include headache or an outbreak of eczema. Sometimes the first signs of stress are changes in emotional life or behaviour, and these can be more obvious to others than to the subject. The most important signs to be aware of are increases in tension, irritability and moodiness, and small annoyances seeming unbearable. Some people lose interest in food while others want to eat constantly. The ability to cope at home and work may suffer. It is necessary for a manager to recognise these signs or an employee may develop serious illness and subsequently be absent from work. An employer has a duty of care for his/her employees. Table 6.2 summarises the signs of stress to watch for.

Table 6.2. Physical and mental reactions to stress

Physical reactions to stress	Mental reactions to stress
• Changes in appetite	• Feelings of being under pressure
• 'Butterflies' or feeling sick	• Tense and unable to relax
• Sleep problems	• Feeling mentally drained
• Headaches	• Feeling frightened
• Indigestion	• Irritable, complaining, frustrated and aggressive
• Frequent desire to pass urine	• Restless
• Muscle tension	• Tearful
• Odd aches and pains	• Indecisive
• Constipation or diarrhoea	• Unable to feel pleasure or enjoyment
• Tiredness	• Fearful of failure
• Backache	• Fear of social embarrassment
• Breathlessness	• Lack of concentration
• Rapid heartbeat	
• Dry mouth	
• Panic attacks	
• Persistent minor illnesses	
• Heart problems	
• Increased smoking or drinking	

What can the manager do to help stressed colleagues?

Sharing the problem with family or friends can significantly help individuals to cope with stress. Employers can offer this sort of support or suggest a suitable individual to talk to, such as a doctor or counsellor. A trouble-free environment at work may also be a solution, so look carfully at the relationships between staff and the pressures that are put upon them. Be realistic about the deadlines that are set and do not spring too many surprises. 'Last minute' or 'crisis' management puts a lot of pressure on employees.

You should ensure that the workload is equally divided between staff and that people are not dealing with an excessive amount of work. You must make sure that everyone has the opportunity for a lunch break and that there is suitable cover for illness so that staff do not feel pressured to come into work when they are not fit to do so.

Above all, it is imperative that staff feel they have an element of control over their working lives and that their opinions and needs are valued and respected. Praise, encouragement and reassurance that 'they are doing a good job' are vital elements for helping people to feel relaxed at work and to enjoy their job. If staff enjoy going to work, they are more likely to be able to cope with the pressures. Managers can encourage staff to make a list of the causes of stress in the workplace and the team can work together on strategies to solve them. These might include setting aside a place for staff to be quiet, away from the children or telephones, while eating their lunch. Team-building activities after work could include exercise or relaxation groups. Staff may also enjoy a speaker, such as a life coach, who can discuss diet or achieving a healthy work–life balance.

Case study — Stress at work and home

Jamie works in a day nursery, where he is the deputy in the room for children aged 6 months to 1 year. He qualified last year and although he is delighted to have a position of responsibility he is concerned about his lack of experience. Jamie recently got married and his wife is expecting their first child in November. There are six babies in the room and the parents seem very pleased with the care they are given. The eldest baby is due to move to the next room in 2 weeks and a new baby of 6 months will be starting. At the staff meeting Jamie was told that the staff rota would be changing and that some staff would need to change their pattern of working. There was also a drive to encourage staff to plan their work according to *Birth to Three Matters*. Jamie is very worried about this, as he has not received any training on this and does not really understand how it will work. The manager of the nursery noticed that Jamie was a bit irritable when he was talking to a student from the college and refused to help her with her coursework.

- What are the potential causes of stress for Jamie?
- Think about the ways of minimising stress and the reasons for doing this.

6.5 Legal obligations

Establishments have certain legal obligations. It is necessary to have systems in place, for example, for controlling finances. The business aspects of the running of a childcare setting are covered in Chapter 8. This section looks at the obligations and responsibilities managers have in relation to the care and administration of their team. These are many and varied, and include, for example:

- to ensure that prospective employees fit the legal requirements for working with children;
- to ensure that staff are working in a safe environment;
- to provide contracts of employment for staff;

- to ensure employees are paid;
- to keep appropriate personnel records.

The first two points relate to the National Standards covered in Chapter 2. The more administrative tasks are considered below.

Contracts of employment

A contract is a legally binding agreement between employer and employee formed when the employee agrees to work for pay. A contract is made up of oral as well as written agreements. It can include both express terms (those that are explicitly agreed) and implied terms (those that are too obvious to mention). Some terms in the contract will be determined by law, for example the right not to be discriminated against on the grounds of race, sex or disability.

Changes to a contract should be made only with the agreement of both parties. The employee or employer, after giving the required period of notice, can terminate a contract.

Contracts should include details of:

- salary;
- holiday entitlement;
- sickness and maternity rights associated with the job.

- hours of work;
- notice period;

It is best to ensure that contractual obligations are clear, as any confusion can lead to friction and misunderstandings. In the worst scenario this can lead to claims in civil courts or appeals to employment tribunals for breach of contract. Employees who consider that their contracts have been terminated unfairly may apply to a tribunal claiming they have been unfairly dismissed. If employers fail to give the required notice, the employee can make a claim to the courts or to an employment tribunal for damages for wrongful dismissal. If an employee leaves without giving the required notice, the employer has a similar right to claim damages.

Good practice checklist — The employment contract

- ☐ Agree terms and any subsequent changes with employees.
- ☐ Set out the main terms and conditions of employment within 2 months of an employee starting work.
- ☐ When terminating employment ensure the minimum notice period is given.
- ☐ Put any agreements in writing to avoid confusion.
- ☐ Seek advice from your local Early Years Development and Childcare Partnership, the Pre-school Learning Alliance or the National Child Minding Association.

Paying employees

It is important to develop pay arrangements that are right for your establishment and that reward employees fairly for the work they do. It is a good idea to make sure that your rates of pay are competitive; this will need to be reviewed annually. If you decide to make any changes to pay, consult colleagues to gain their agreement first. Make the payment system as simple to understand as possible and explain to employees how their pay is calculated. The system should be reviewed as often as possible and accountants approached to ensure that everything is kept up to date with legal developments affecting pay.

You may decide to use performance- or skill-based pay systems, where individuals are rewarded for the skills they possess or acquire through training. One day nursery is known to pay employees a fixed sum of £100 bonus on completion of 3 months' work without absence. Other establishments reward staff with additional days' off or even free air-miles. It is also becoming common practice to reward staff with lunch parties or pampering sessions following a successful Ofsted inspection. Performance can be assessed through an appraisal system where managers and staff assess progress, formulate action plans and decide on training needs (see Chapter 7).

Many small businesses use a computerised database system to manage the mechanics of payment of wages, including taxation and National Insurance contributions. A recommended system is available from the Sage software group (www.sage.com). The Inland Revenue's website (www.inlandrevenue.gov.uk) gives precise information regarding all aspects of taxation, National Insurance contributions and PAYE schemes. An advisory booklet entitled *Pay Systems* is available from ACAS (www.acas.org.uk/publications/B02.html) and the Department of Trade and Industry's Employment Relations Directorate website (www.dti.gov.uk/er) has fact sheets available that outline the legal requirements for the payment of wages. For example, it is a legal requirement (see www.dti.gov.uk/er/pay/statement-pl704.htm) to produce an itemised pay statement that gives the following particulars:

- the gross amount of the wages or salary;
- the amounts of any fixed deductions and the purpose for which they are made (e.g. trade union subscriptions) or the total figure for fixed deductions, when a separate standing statement of the details has been provided;
- the amounts of any variable deductions and the purposes for which they are made;
- the net amount of any wages or salary payable;
- the amount and method of each part-payment when different parts of

the net amount are paid in different ways (e.g. the separate figures of a cash payment and a balance credited to a bank account).

The difficulty faced by managers is ensuring that staff are paid competitive wages while continuing to provide affordable childcare in a well stocked and innovative environment. Managers have to balance pay and fees amid difficulties in recruiting appropriate staff. Increases to the national minimum wage and employers' contributions to National Insurance mean that fees have risen in order for settings to maintain a suitable profit margin. It may be necessary to justify the reasons for fee increases and to be able to argue the case for competitive wages within the sector. This can be particularly difficult if the setting is in an area of low average wages, where parents are likely to have difficulty paying the fees (see also Chapter 9).

Personnel records

Under the Data Protection Act 1998 employees are entitled to have access to all the personal details on them that are held on computers or as manual records. Personnel records are needed to fulfil legal requirements, such as for statutory sick pay, tax and National Insurance contributions. Information kept should include:

- personal details – name, date of birth, address, qualifications, previous experience, tax code, National Insurance number, and emergency contact number;
- employment details – date employment started, job title;
- details of terms and conditions – rate of pay, hours of work, holiday entitlement;
- absence details – sickness and lateness;
- details of accidents at work;
- details of disciplinary action;
- training and development courses attended.

Personnel records do not need to be complicated – a card index system can be effective or a computerised system can be used. An effective personnel system will enable you to keep track of staff and monitor individual performance, and to have better control of staff turnover, problems of recruitment and discipline issues. It may also assist in the creation of fair and consistent promotion and help in the development of a successful equal opportunities policy.

6.6 Staff development

As discussed earlier in this chapter, one method for retaining staff is the provision of opportunities for regular personal development through training and updating courses. These courses are available through training providers and recognised awarding bodies such as the Council for Awards in Children's Care and Education (CACHE).

Provision for professional development is also a key factor in providing quality in early years settings. However, the training itself needs to be of a high standard and delivered by knowledgeable and suitably qualified people. The Green Paper *Every Child Matters* (Department for Education and Skills, 2003) highlighted the need for integration of children's services and the establishment of a young people's sector skills council (SSC). The intention is for the SSC to play a key role in providing models of high quality training and in providing a more coherent training 'map'. It could also form the basis of a national strategy to tackle recruitment and retention of staff. The establishment of an SSC will take time and will need interested parties to work together to create a practical working body.

Qualifications and courses available

The government has initiated a programme of business skills training through A4e and has introduced a fast-track qualification, the APEL NVQ level 3, for unqualified early years workers and play-workers already running their own settings or working at level 3.

At present, the Qualifications and Curriculum Authority (QCA) provides a standardised programme for vocational qualifications (see www.qca.org.uk/qualifications/index.html). The programme is outlined in Table 6.3.

Table 6.3. Summary of courses and qualifications for early years practitioners

Jobs	Vocational qualifications	Occupational qualifications
Level 2 Nursery assistant Pre-school/playgroup assistant Crèche assistant Parent/toddler group assistant Toy library worker Home-start worker Mother's help Baby-sitter/au-pair	*CACHE* • Foundation Award for Caring for Children (foundation level) • Certificate in Childcare and Education • Certificate in Pre-school Practice • Certificate in Early Years Practice *C&G* • Progression Award in Early Years Care and Education • Certificate in Contributing to the Early Years Setting	NVQ in Early Years and Education (awarded by C&G, CACHE, Edexcel, Open University)

Jobs	Vocational qualifications	Occupational qualifications
	NCFE • Intermediate Certificate in Developing Skills for Working with Children and Young People *Edexcel* • Btec First Diploma in Early Years	
Level 3 Nursery supervisor Pre-school leader Crèche leader Playgroup leader Toy library leader Special educational needs coordinator Nursery nurse Nanny Childminder	*CACHE* • Diploma in Child Care and Education • Certificate in Childminding Practice • Certificate of Professional Development in Work with Children and Young People • Diploma in Pre-school Practice • Diploma in Early Years Care and Education (Welsh Medium) • Playgroup Practice in Wales • Diploma in Early Years Practice *Edexcel* • Btec National Certificate in Early Years • Btec National Diploma in Early Years • Btec National Award in Early Years • Btec National Certificate in Early Years	NVQ in Early Years Care and Education (awarding bodies as for level 2)
Level 4 Manager Development officer Advanced practitioner	Certificate in Early Years Practice (Open University)	NVQ Early Years Care and Education (awarded by CACHE and C&G)

Awarding bodies

The awarding bodies include City and Guilds (C&G), CACHE and Edexcel. Other courses have been submitted to the QCA and are awaiting accreditation. These include the CACHE level 4 Advanced Diploma in Childcare and Education and the Open University's level 4 certificate course for early years practitioners. The process of accreditation is vigorous, to ensure quality, and the submission of a qualification does not guarantee accreditation.

In addition to the courses mentioned, there are numerous training organisations and national charities that also provide training within the early years sector. These often appear in *Nursery World* magazine (see also www.nurseryworld.co.uk). These courses cover all aspects of childcare and education, from first aid to dealing with difficult behaviour. They are an excellent way to increase and update knowledge and to re-energise staff members.

The Early Years National Training Organisation (NTO), despite its title, does not develop or deliver training but is involved in the development of the National Occupational Standards on which vocational qualifications are based. The NTO also works to increase the number of trained and qualified people working in the early years sector and represents the views of employers and employees to the government. There is a concern within the NTO to ensure that training is of a high standard and it is currently inviting training providers to register with the voluntary Code of Practice scheme to encourage quality.

The barriers to participation in further training

The biggest barrier to taking part in training is time, especially for workers with family responsibilities. Many people participate in courses in their own time, so that settings do not have to pay for cover. Some courses are becoming available through online distance learning, which will help people to study outside working hours.

Payment for courses can also be a barrier, particularly in settings that make little or no profit. Early Years Development and Childcare Partnerships offer a solution, by providing access to free or subsidised courses. There are also concessions available on selected courses and for people on a low income; it is worth checking with the provider of the course or training. The Partnerships also offer their own courses for settings and individuals within their area, and these are generally free.

Another significant barrier for early years workers can be a lack of confidence. Many people have not been involved in education for themselves since leaving school and are daunted by the prospect of sitting in a classroom again. Others found school an unsatisfactory experience and have deep-seated feelings or low self-esteem. A manager will need to identify these barriers and work with the member of staff to overcome them. Simply acknowledging their existence can be sufficient, as can emotional support and encouragement.

Many people find that once they start doing a course they enjoy it so much they continue attending until they have accumulated an impressive number of qualifications.

It is often a good idea to encourage staff to attempt a short course initially so that they can build their confidence with a sympathetic trainer. Many people find that once they start doing courses they enjoy it so much they continue attending until they have accumulated an impressive number of qualifications. This success will be transferred into their approach to work and the establishment will reap the benefits.

One-to-one mentoring can provide the necessary support during training. The Northamptonshire County Council and Early Years Development and Childcare Partnership came first in the Partners in Excellence Awards in 2003 for their guidance and mentoring scheme, which had significantly increased the number of people completing training in the early years, childcare and play-work sector. The scheme aims to match students to the appropriate training and to provide support during the course.

Case study — Vocational training

Claire left school at 16 with four GCSEs at grades C and B. She was encouraged to stay on at school to take an A-level course but had never really enjoyed school and was keen to leave. She worked for a while in a supermarket and as a receptionist at a health centre, but neither of these positions gave her fulfilment. Claire had always enjoyed baby-sitting her younger cousins and helping out at the local Brownies on Monday nights, so she decided to apply for a childcare course at a college of further education. Claire was put on the CACHE Diploma in Childcare and Education and within 2 years had successfully completed the course and gained employment at a day nursery. Over the next 5 years Claire worked her way up the career ladder and, encouraged by her manager, attended several short courses and eventually became deputy manager of the day nursery. She is currently enrolled on the Foundation Degree in Early Childhood Studies course at her old college. Her employers are paying for the course and she has her sights set on a manager's position within the chain of day nurseries. Claire cannot believe how successful she has been and friends and family notice how she is much more confident and self-assured.

- Consider how you would encourage a member of staff to attend training.
- Reflect on the training needs within an early years establishment.

Conclusion

This chapter has looked at the management of staff within the childcare and education setting. It has reviewed strategies for the recruitment and retention of staff. The effect of stress on the workforce has been investigated, as has the motivation of staff through effective personal development and training.

Check your understanding

1 What are common reasons for people leaving employment in the early years sector?
2 How could you encourage staff to stay for the long term?
3 Why is it important for junior members of staff to have access to managers and the opportunity to express their views?
4 How can stress be minimised within an establishment?
5 Consider the opportunities for training within your area. How can you ensure equality of opportunity for staff to access these opportunities?

References and further reading

Bunch, M. (1999) *Creating Confidence. How to Develop Your Personal Power and Presence*. London: Kogan Page.

Department for Education and Skills (2003) *Every Child Matters*, Cm 5860. London: DfES. Available at www.dfes.gov.uk/everychildmatters/downloads.cfm.

Dickson, A. (1982) *A Woman in Your Own Right. Assertiveness and You*. London: Quartet Books.

Honey, P. (1997) *Improve Your People Skills* (2nd edition). London: Institute of Personnel and Development.

Makins, V. (1997) *Not Just a Nursery. Multi-agency Early Years Centres in Action*. London: National Children's Bureau.

Nicolson, P. and Bayne, R. (1990) *Applied Psychology for Social Workers* (2nd edition). London: Macmillan.

Petrie, P. (1989) *Communicating with Children and Adults. Interpersonal Skills for Those Working with Babies and Children*. London: Edward Arnold.

Useful websites

ACAS: www.acas.org.uk.

Council for Awards in Children's Care and Education: www.cache.org.uk.

Department of Trade and Industry Employment Relations Directorate: www.dti.gov.uk/er.

Early Years National Training Organisation: www.early-years-nto.org.uk.

Inland Revenue: www.inlandrevenue.gov.uk.

National Day Nurseries Association: www.ndna.org.uk.

Nationwide Payroll Company: www.nationwidepayroll.co.uk (provides payroll services for pre-school establishments, etc.).

Nursery World magazine: www.nurseryworld.com.

Qualifications and Curriculum Authority: www.qca.org.uk.

SureStart Business Success for Childcare: www.surestart.gov.uk/support4business.

7 Developing a Team

This chapter looks at the issues involved in developing a team. This will involve reflecting on your own ideas and thoughts on how teams can be developed; the chapter also looks at some of the theories surrounding team building and communication. The purpose of this is that you broaden your theoretical knowledge and reflect on your present and future practice. There is as an immense amount of material on the development of teams. Some settings are working towards or have already been awarded the Investors in People standard (mentioned in Chapter 1). More effective teamwork can be one of the benefits of this standard being achieved. Working towards such standards can help an organisation to operate more effectively by clarifying its objectives.

It is important that you understand the part you play in your team in order for you to evaluate how you might improve not only your own performance but also that of the team. The chapter therefore also looks at communication and possible barriers to this, as well as some of the day-to-day things managers can do to build a cohesive team who can work together through the mundane, everyday challenges and responsibilities and keep pace with the changes which are continually taking place in early years work. This chapter looks at the following areas:

7.1 The theory of organisational culture and team roles.

7.2 Effective teams.

7.3 The manager as a communicator.

7.4 The manager as a motivator.

7.5 Training, development and appraisal.

7.1 The theory of organisational culture and team roles

Before the more specific and practical aspects of team development are dealt with below, it is helpful first to consider the wider picture of the sort of organisations in which teams work.

Organisational culture

Different organisations have different atmospheres, ways of doing things, levels of energy and vitality, personalities and cultures. They have different norms, values and beliefs – all of which are reflected in their systems and structures. For early years settings the culture is usually formed by a common goal – to meet the needs of the individual children in the setting. Although a great deal has been written about organisational culture, only a brief overview of some theories is given here. You will need to take note of the suggestions for further reading to deepen your knowledge of this area. This section examines one model, by way of illustration.

Find it out

Look at schools of thought regarding organisational classification and analysis. These include the classical school, the human relations school and the systems approach.

The model considered here is of four types of organisational culture, which are based on ideas about:

- the way in which work is done;
- the degree of control to be exercised;
- how people should be rewarded;
- what loyalty and obedience are expected;
- what hours should be worked;
- how people are expected to dress.

These four cultures are termed:

- power;
- role;
- task;
- person.

Table 7.1 gives a brief explanation and examples of each.

Table 7.1. Characterisation of four organisational cultures

Name	Power culture	Role culture	Task culture	Person culture
Description	Best pictured as a web. It is dependent on a central power source; rays emanate out from this and are connected by functional or specialist 'strings', but the power rings are the hub of activity and influence. The organisation works on precedent and the anticipation of the wishes and decisions of the central power source. Rules and procedures are few; there is little bureaucracy. Control is exercised through key individuals. It is a political organisation, decisions being taken on the outcome of balance of influence rather than logical or procedural grounds. These organisations are proud and strong – they move quickly and react well to threat and danger. Success depends upon the quality of decisions of the person in power. Such organisations are power orientated and politically minded. They take risks, have faith in individuals and are tough and abrasive. Control of resources is a major power source, plus some elements of personal power at the centre. Judgement is by results.	Bureaucracy – thought of as a Greek temple. Logic and rationality are its strengths; its pillars are functions of specialism that are strong in their own right. Work and interaction are controlled by procedures, definition of jobs and tasks, delegation of authority and rules for operation and settlement of disputes. Coordination is by a senior management team. All persons are expected to be loyal and obedient and carry out instructions. Concentration is on the description of the job, not the incumbent. Selection is by satisfactory qualifications and performance, and over-performance is not always encouraged as it can be considered disruptive. Bestowed authority or position is the main power source; personal power is discouraged. Influence is through methods and procedures. The culture is dependent on rationality and success of work allocation and meeting responsibilities rather than individualisation.	Job and project orientated. The organisation can be visualised as a net, a grid or a matrix. Some strands of the net or grid are stronger than others. Much power lies at the interstices of the net or grid. The emphasis is on doing the task – thus appropriate resources are deployed and redeployed to this end. Influence stems from expert power and is more widely dispersed than in other cultures – it is a team culture – individual objectives are obliterated, as are differences in status or style. It is the unifying power of the group that creates efficiency and absorbs the individual into the organisation. It is an adaptable culture – groups or teams are formed for a specific purpose or task, and abandoned once this is fulfilled and resources are re-allocated. Individuals have a high degree of control over their work and relationships are easy and informal. Judgement is by results – respect is for capacity rather than age or status. Control is difficult and is retained by the overall top management in the allocation of resources to tasks/projects. Reporting on progress and justification of team action is the job of the task/team leaders. Resources need to be readily available. It is a culture in tune with modern management style/thinking and with innovation and development. It is appropriate when flexibility and sensitivity to the market are important.	A cluster or galaxy of individual stars. Such organisations are rare. The individual is the focal point. The organisational structure exists only to serve the individual within it.
Examples	Small entrepreneurial organisations, occasionally trade unions, property and finance companies, some trading organisations, family firms and founder organisations.	Civil service, automobile industry, life insurance, banking, retailing.	Product groups of marketing departments, consultancies, take-over ventures, advertising agencies, merchant banks, management service functions.	Barristers' chambers, consultancies, communes and other special groups, as well as academic university departments.
Possible negative aspects	Size is a problem for power cultures as the web can break if too many activities need linking – it can grow only by spawning other web-like organisations. Maximum independence needs to be given to each web-head. Finance binds the web together.	Role cultures are slow to perceive change and slow to react if faced with problems. These organisations need stable environments – monopoly or market stability – as product life cycles are long. They often try a number of alternative measures to redesign their structure. Collapse can ensue. There is insufficient development of individuals, which can be frustrating for the ambitious.	It is hard to achieve 'economies of scale' in this culture, or growth or depth of expertise.	It is difficult to form this culture as organisational goals are subordinate to individual goals. Control can be only by mutual consent. The organisation seldom has power over individuals. The individuals are difficult to manage as it is rarely possible to influence them; only a strong and similarly interesting individual would warrant attention and individuals tend to be 'wrapped up' in themselves.

These organisational cultures are obviously generic and although you may not recognise one of these as being totally descriptive of your setting you should find that there are aspects of each which do apply. Management theorists have said that an effective organisation will demonstrate facets of some or all of these cultures.

Figure 7.1 shows the factors that influence organisations in their adoption of a certain culture.

Size

Large organisations are usually formalised and tend to develop into specialised groups which need procedural control; large size therefore dictates that a role culture will develop.

History and ownership

Centralised ownership (e.g. family firms) tends towards a power culture. New organisations may need to be aggressive in order to survive and therefore may adopt a power culture, although they may also be task concentrated and so adopt a role culture.

People

People who like security will prefer a role culture; those who enjoy creativity and have a need for self-identification will prefer a task culture; and those who have a dynamic personality, talent or skill will prefer a task or power culture.

Organisational culture

Technology

The type of processing or manufacturing undertaken by an organisation affects its culture. For example, routine and programmable operations lend themselves to a role culture, as do high capitalisation of production functions and mass production, whereas a one-off or jobbing industry will be associated with a task culture and technological and development organisations with a task or power culture.

Environment

If the environment (economic, market, competition, geographical or societal) is changing this may require a sensitive, adaptable culture – i.e. task culture. Diversity in the environment requires diversified structure again a task culture. If the environment poses a threat or danger a power culture may be appropriate.

Goals and objectives

A focus on product quality goals may lend itself to a role culture and a focus on growth to a power or task culture.

Figure 7.1. The factors that influence which culture is adopted by an organisation.

Organisations may change their culture and they may even have more than one culture; a somewhat complex organisational pattern can emerge. Having looked at the four-culture model of organisations, you might feel that you can now link at least one of them to a particular early years setting.

Aspects of the early years culture

The four-culture model outlined above applies in principle to any organisation. Within the early years sector specific questions arise that can be directly linked to the issue of organisational culture. These follow the list of ideas on which the four-culture model draws (see above).

Why do things work the way they do?

For new staff joining a setting there can sometimes be confusion about why things work the way they do. There might be historic reasons for the way in which things are done, as some practices may have been passed down from former staff teams or, where there is a long-established team, some of the practices could have stayed the same because 'that is the way we have always done it'. Because of this resistance to change the setting can appear to be solely task-orientated and the staff will lack motivation.

What degree of control has to be exercised?

Early years managers are expected to exercise control within the setting but most of this control will be set around policies and procedures and will have been explained to the staff so that they appreciate the need for it. Many early years managers will not feel the need to exercise control in an aggressive way and will earn the respect of the team by being a good role model. That is not to say that all early years staff are easily controlled and compliant but that, in the main, if they feel they are valued and working towards a common set of goals they will be happy to comply. This will depend very much on how the manager communicates with the staff and handles any conflicts or disputes (see section 7.3).

How are people rewarded?

Obviously there is a monetary award (if small!) but for most people working with children this is not the primary motivator – they work with children because it is a vocation and they find it rewarding in terms of the sense of achievement which is gained from seeing children develop as a result of their care, and being valued for that contribution.

What loyalty and obedience should be expected?

Although you will encounter many different personalities within any team, loyalty should not be an issue if there is a cohesive atmosphere and staff are proud of what is being achieved.

What hours should be worked?

This will of course vary from setting to setting. The hours of work become an issue only when there is lack of understanding, too many changes to routine and too high an expectation of staff.

How are people expected to dress?

Many early years settings have dress codes and this is usually decided by the owner or manager. Some will adopt a uniform and others a code of dress (for example a 'no jeans' policy). It is perfectly acceptable to have these expectations as long as it is explained to staff before they start work and that cost is taken into account.

Team roles

Before assigning a particular team member to a task or responsibility within the setting it is worth investigating the individual's personal qualities and how he or she interacts with the rest of the team. This could be done in a team-building exercise or by a trial period within all areas of the setting. Some people are keen to work in a team and benefit from the associated support and security, whereas some will find the same security stifling and are uncomfortable interacting closely with others.

There is no doubt that teams can be complex and getting a team to work effectively can take time, but the use of teams taps a greater range of experiences and abilities. Teams can produce sound ideas when given the opportunity and being able to work together motivates members to do better and work in unity ('team spirit').

Meredith Belbin identified eight different roles which were found to be present in the most successful teams (see www.belbin.com). They are described in Table 7.2.

Belbin's self-perception test comprises a set of questions with corresponding scores which indicate which role or roles suits the respondent. There are other tests and analyses of team roles, for example the Myers and Briggs Type Indicator (MBTI), built on the work of C. G. Jung (1875–1961). The MBTI looks at ways in which people behave in certain situations. The results depend on whether they are introvert or extrovert, and other factors

Table 7.2. Belbin's eight roles within successful teams

Team type	Features	Qualities	Weaknesses
Shaper	Highly strung, outgoing, dynamic	Drive, energy; challenges apathy	Impatience; a tendency to hurt other's feelings
Plant	Unorthodox, serious minded, individualistic	Imagination, intellect, knowledge; solves difficult problems	Up in the clouds; inclined to disregard practical details or protocols
Resource investigator	Extrovert, enthusiastic, curious, communicative	Knows useful contacts; explores new activities; responds to challenges	Liable to lose interest once the initial fascination has passed. Can be over-optimistic and uncritical
Completer finisher	Painstaking, orderly, conscientious, anxious	Perfectionist	Worrier; reluctant to delegate; can nit-pick
Coordinator	Calm, self-confident, controlled	Welcomes all potential contributors on their merits; clear sense of objectives	Not of outstanding intellectual or creative ability
Implementer	Conservative, dutiful, predictable	Organising ability; practical common sense; hard working; self-disciplined	Lack of flexibility; slow to respond to change
Team worker	Supportive, uncompetitive, mediator	Counterbalances friction and discord	Sometimes soft and indecisive – bit of a 'push-over'
Monitor evaluator	Contribution lies in measured and dispassionate analysis	Objective, serious minded, skills in critical thinking	Can be negative and lack spontaneity

such as thinking and judgement. These role tests primarily indicate personality styles. To do the test the participant answers a series of questions and is given a score. If you are taking part in a real test the team's results will be analysed and the results will be fed back to you and your team. However, such tests are generally run by professional psychology consultancies, and so there is a cost involved. In any case, there is no need to take part in such a test to become a more cohesive team.

Early years managers may or may not have the opportunity for their staff to take part in some form of personality test. The important thing is that the manager is aware of the role each member of staff plays as part of the team (in Table 7.2 you are likely to see some of the traits of people you work with). If you are aware, for example, that someone displays many of the qualities of a resource investigator you will be able to make use of their skills. If that particular member of staff also lacks confidence and has low self-esteem your recognition of those skills will boost that person's self-esteem and make him or her feel valued and appreciated.

Think it over

- Can you recognise any of the eight team roles described by Belbin ?
- Are there any you feel you may fall into personally?
- Do you recognise any as describing your colleagues?
- How could you use this information to help a team become stronger?

Team-building exercises

Team-building exercises can give members of the team the opportunity to stand back and look at their own ways of working so that they can then search for ways of improving them. Many establishments use consultants to run a one-day exercise, when all staff dress casually and leave all hierarchy behind. The day can be memorable and fun and raise awareness among the staff of their personal skills. With a little imagination it is also possible for a manager to raise this awareness in a team-building exercise that is planned as an inset training day. These opportunities can help managers to distinguish different viewpoints and identify people who may work well together. However, it will be after the team-building day that the real work will need to take place; the knowledge gained should be used to form a more cohesive operational team.

Find it out

You might want to research the MBTI to find out more about team-building activities. You can find out more at www.ascent-center.com.

Team development

A manager can use a variety of ways to look at how the team has come to a certain point in their development. A group of people working together can take some time to form a team; some groups never do become cohesive teams, although they may want to be known as one. Tuckman and Jensen

(1977) came up with a five-stage theory on how groups form into teams. This theory is quite well known and demonstrates the process teams have to go through in order to achieve cohesiveness. This is set out in Figure 7.2.

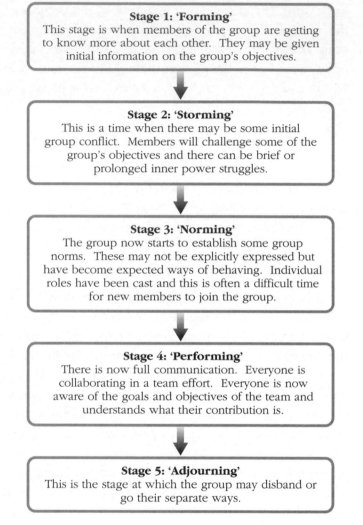

Stage 1: 'Forming'
This stage is when members of the group are getting to know more about each other. They may be given initial information on the group's objectives.

Stage 2: 'Storming'
This is a time when there may be some initial group conflict. Members will challenge some of the group's objectives and there can be brief or prolonged inner power struggles.

Stage 3: 'Norming'
The group now starts to establish some group norms. These may not be explicitly expressed but have become expected ways of behaving. Individual roles have been cast and this is often a difficult time for new members to join the group.

Stage 4: 'Performing'
There is now full communication. Everyone is collaborating in a team effort. Everyone is now aware of the goals and objectives of the team and understands what their contribution is.

Stage 5: 'Adjourning'
This is the stage at which the group may disband or go their separate ways.

Figure 7.2. Tuckman and Jensen's (1977) five-stage theory of team formation.

7.2 Effective teams

A 'team' is a group of people united by a common purpose. Smith and Langston (1999) said that groups are defined as two or more people who work together to achieve a common purpose. 'For many of us they provide the status, security and social relations that make work satisfying, rewarding and in many cases, pleasurable.'

- First, think of a group you have been in that left you feeling good about the group or yourself. It could be a work, social or friendship group. List the things that made the experience a good one.
- Now think about a group you have been in that left you feeling negative about the group or yourself. Again, it could be a work, social or friendship group. List what things made your experience of the group negative.
- When you have done this you will have formed a list of things both positive and negative about working in groups.

Groups can make work satisfying, rewarding and pleasurable.

To make a team more effective, it is necessary to consider what stage of development the team is at (see Figure 7.2). This will of course be influenced by how long the group has been established. Some typical events in the life of a team that might be the stimulus for some sort of team-working activities are when:

- the members of the team are being selected;
- the team begins to work together and needs to establish its purpose and how it will try to achieve this;
- a team has been working together for some time and wants to review its effectiveness;
- team members begin to experience problems working together (this is possible at the earlier stages, when things do not seem to be settling down, or at some later stage, when working relationships deteriorate or if the leadership falters);
- new members join the team and need to be integrated;
- team members also have line management responsibilities and are finding it difficult to reconcile their dual roles;
- a new challenge arises, and the team has to adapt its ways of working to cope with the change.

Alternatively, a team might not wait until a particular need emerges. Instead, the members may regularly devote time to looking at the way in which they work together and see this sort of activity as a means of maintaining cohesion and for preventing small issues from growing into major threats (see below).

The advantages of effective teamwork

Effective teams can lead to greater creativity, improved job satisfaction and increased energy and excitement. Working as part of a cohesive team can make going to work something to look forward to so that you are in fact going to work for more than monetary gain but for the feeling from working in collaboration with a group of like-minded people. But what does working as part of a team mean to early years workers?

Qualitative data from unpublished research has clarified childcare and family day care coordinators' understanding of teamwork in early years settings. The perceived advantages of teamwork were looked at by asking the question 'Why do we work in teams in early childhood services?' The following advantages were consistently recorded (Rodd, 1998, p. 100):

- support and stimulation;
- a sense of belonging and equality;
- opportunity for growth and development;
- stress reduction;
- facilitation of a pleasant working environment;
- opportunity to work through issues;
- the minimisation of conflicts;
- the provision of a role model for children and parents;
- the opportunities for staff members to assume leadership in the short term;
- assistance in the efficient achievement of goals;
- shared workload;
- shared human resources and ideas;
- acknowledgement of staff members' professional capabilities;
- increased motivation and commitment to the task or decision.

What makes an effective team?

There are four key characteristics of an effective team:

- a sense of purpose and clear objective;
- a balance of roles within the team;
- commitment from team members and effective leadership;
- good communication within the team.

A sense of purpose and clear objectives

Working towards a common vision or aim can ensure a team's cohesiveness and cooperation. If the staff share common values and beliefs this makes working together easier. Although it cannot be assumed that everyone holds the same values and beliefs generally, it will be an assumption that most people working in early years settings will be working to the same sets of guidance and principles as set down by the current legislation relating to early years settings (see Chapter 2).

An effective team needs both to consist of members who feel they are working towards the same results and to maintain a sense of purpose. Aims and objectives can be written down in a formal mission statement but this will be tokenistic unless the team can see them evolving in their everyday practice. Early years settings will have the needs of the children at the heart of their practice but they may have quite different ways of achieving this end.

Case study — A family atmosphere

Toad Hall Nursery is a privately run 50-place sessional nursery for children age 2 years 11 months to 4 years 11 months. It has an excellent reputation and always has a waiting list. The nursery manager is also the owner and there is an established, well qualified staff. The nursery has a mission statement based on Christian ethics but religion is not a key feature of the curriculum offered – children are not indoctrinated. The staff are told about the nursery's aims and mission at interview and are very proud of the family atmosphere. As the nursery was formerly a house there is a warm and familiar feel about the place. Children's needs are paramount and it is evident that they take total precedent. The children are courteous and caring and are allowed to move about the nursery fairly freely. The manager is a very professional person who guides prospective parents around but always asks staff members to help explain what goes on at the nursery. Parents are introduced to everyone, including the caretaker and the kitchen staff. The manager does not need to be present for the nursery to run smoothly and has two very efficient deputy managers, who job share. The staff team make cooperative decisions about the running of the nursery but take them to the manager to make the final decision, when her final word is binding. She listens to her staff's ideas and goes away to investigate them before returning to staff with a decision.

- What is the secret of this setting's success?
- What style of management has the manager adopted?
- Would you say the staff were valued?

A balance of roles within the team

A team is not going to operate effectively if all its members wish to be the leader or indeed if no one does. A balance of the roles described in Table

7.2 is necessary. In order to build such a team you also need to take account of the development of teams, as outlined in Figure 7.2. First, the leader needs to create a vision and a set of values within the team (see above), and to generate commitment and involvement from team members.

In building effective teams it is important to note that one person can belong to different teams and adopt different team roles. For example, there are many team-leading roles within the typical early years setting – it is therefore not appropriate for the manager of the setting to be seen as the sole person with any sort of leadership responsibilities. These roles could include:

- team leader – head of room, head of foundation stage, room supervisor (any one person with responsibility for a particular area or stage of development);
- special educational needs coordinator – all settings are required under the Care Standards Act to have a named person who coordinates the management of special needs within the setting;
- coordinator of gifted and talented children;
- head of kitchen (important members of staff who will have the responsibility of providing nutritious meals and snacks for the children and who may be in charge of other employees, depending on the size of the setting);
- training and development coordinators;
- project or fundraising coordinators;
- parent liaison (a person who deals with all parent/carer activities, such as newsletters and parents' evenings);
- key workers – those working with individual children to provide continuity for the child and parents and carers;
- senior members of staff overseeing students in the setting during their training;
- resources manager – required to order stationery, resources and maintain resources already in use;
- outings organiser – the member of staff who will book venues, send out letters for nursery outings, and so on.

Some settings will not allocate so many responsibilities to members of staff and some of these duties will be the part of the deputy manager's duties. The list above does also suggest the ways in which team members can be allocated specific responsibilities.

How can staff be given extra responsibility without causing conflict within the team?

Commitment from team members and effective leadership

Team development requires both strong leadership and commitment from team members. A successful team is made up of individuals who are valued for their contributions and expertise and they will probably have taken part in some of the decision-making about the sort of culture they are involved in. Managers need to analyse how they involve teams in this process and look at ways of motivating them.

Case study — Creating a non-dependent culture

The nursery had its first inspection (these were at the time carried out by social services). The report stated that the nursery was well run and the children appeared happy and their learning needs were being met. However, there was a concern that, should the nursery manager be out of the setting for more than a couple of hours, things would come to a standstill. Staff at the setting were too dependent upon the initiative of the manager – they were unable to function without her. The manager of this setting then had to set about creating a non-dependent culture within the team. The next inspection report stated that this had been turned round and that the nursery could now run effectively without the manager's constant guidance and intervention.

- What strategies do you think the manager might have put in place in order for this change to take place?

In response to the case study 'Creating a non-dependent culture' you may have made suggestions centred around letting the staff become more involved and taking on responsibility. This team did in fact have a meeting when the manager put 'the cards on the table' and explained the situation to the staff. Although anxious at first, the staff did gradually take on more, as part of an action plan and with the guidance and support of the manager. The manager was open to ideas but also looked at the strengths of the individual team members to ascertain who would be best placed to take over certain activities and responsibilities. This process was measured and evaluated regularly.

Chapter 1 looked at the role of leadership and discussed the importance of particular attributes or skills a manager needs in order to lead an effective team. The manager is part of the team and key to ensuring its effectiveness. The manager will need to be good role model for the staff and show respect for team members, while being supportive of their professional development. A good relationship with the staff team will ensure that team members:

- relate positively to other groups – outside agencies, visitors, the wider community;
- form good relationships with children and their parents and carers;
- are enthusiastic about new challenges;
- are willing to take on and train for new responsibilities;
- have confidence to evaluate and look at making improvements to practice when needed.

The level of commitment is important but can be one of the most difficult factors to guarantee. Staff are generally willing to work well as part of a team only if they:

- work for efficient managers;
- are allowed to think for themselves;
- are assigned interesting work;
- are informed;
- see the end result of their work;
- are listened to;
- are respected;
- have their efforts recognised;
- are professionally challenged;
- have opportunities to increase their skills.

Consequently, managers must:

- be efficient and effective;
- give authority to make meaningful decisions;
- listen to employees' comments;
- give positive feedback;
- make group decisions;
- ensure staff have variety in their work, to maintain interest;
- communicate well with staff;
- motivate staff;
- offer guidance and support in times of change.

Good communication

It is essential that there is good communication within a team in order that it can be effective. When recruiting new staff the manager will almost certainly be looking for staff who demonstrate good communication skills. When there is good communication within a team there are opportunities to have an open dialogue between team members which is non-threatening and useful in terms of evaluation and sharing good practice. The following section looks at the subject of communication in more detail.

7.3 The manager as a communicator

Why does communication matter?

Communication is vital to all organisations and is often singled out as one of the greatest challenges for a manager. It is the key to getting things done. It can be intentional or unintentional. Effective communication promotes achievement and success. Employees want to be listened to and informed. Communication is the responsibility not only of the manager but also of each member of the staff team; however, as the manager is the leader of the team it will be her or his ultimate responsibility.

Most (if not all) of the manager's role is about communication. Not only do managers have to communicate information about policies and procedures to their staff, but day to day they also need to communicate more subliminal messages, such as recognition of professionalism, empathy, respect and authority, to name but a few. The staff need to be clear about the manager's expectations in terms of the standard of their work and they need to know that the manager will support and lead them.

Characterising communication

Good communication has the following characteristics:

- it aids decision-making;
- it enhances the setting's reputation;
- it ensures effective and smooth running of the systems, policies and procedures.

In contrast, poor communications result in:

- lack of information;
- misinformation and misunderstandings;
- unclear objectives;
- people being inhibited;
- poor relationships in the workplace;
- values not being shared;
- fear and rumour.

To be effective, workplace communications must be:

- clear, concise and easily understood;
- presented objectively and in a manageable form;
- regular and systematic;
- relevant;
- open to scrutiny;
- a two-way process.

Methods of communication

Communication may be spoken or written, direct or indirect. It does not need to be expensive or sophisticated. The mix of methods will depend on the size of the setting, the size of the team, working times and so on. Table 7.3 shows the advantages and disadvantages of a variety of methods.

Table 7.3. Methods of communication between manager and staff

Method of communication	Advantages	Disadvantages
Face to face (one to one)	Direct and swift, it gives the opportunity to listen to one member of staff informally, and feelings can be communicated	It is an informal method and therefore difficult to record; also, it may cause difficulties with other members of the team if they feel 'they have not been told'
Group meetings	Meetings can be valuable for discussion and feedback and can provide opportunities for team members to contribute ideas and identify challenges	Meetings can drag on too long and often have rigid agendas, which can result in staff feeling that they are pointless
Cascade networks	These are useful for passing on information quickly (especially in larger organisations)	If not clearly defined they are open to misinterpretation
Written communications	Written communication can be especially useful when the need for information is permanent and the topic requires detailed explanation. It is particularly useful for holiday allocation, changes to opening hours and so on	The wording needs to be checked as there may be room for gross misinterpretation and once written there is a tendency for it to remain 'written in stone'
Employee handbooks/ induction bulletins	These are very useful as an 'official' way of informing employees of their job role, possible changes to it, work rotas and so on	As with all written communication, it is very important that they are absolutely correct
Notices on boards	Notices can be very useful for communicating with team members about items of interest such as staff outings or a social get-together	Notices have a habit of 'falling off' boards! And if important but not very popular it is very easy for staff to say they did not see it
Individual letters	People tend to take notice of things in writing	Letters can be misinterpreted and it is sometimes possible for people to say they have not received them

Method of communication	Advantages	Disadvantages
Staff training days	In-house days can be very useful in terms of professional development and as an opportunity to reflect on practice	If not properly organised staff training days can seem like a waste of time; also, not all members of the team may feel involved or feel the day is relevant to them
Informal chats during work time	These can be held anywhere and at any time; they are often the way to get to know staff really well and keep up to date with what is happening	Difficulties arise when there is a need for confidentiality and if some staff have more opportunities for a 'chat' than others this can lead to discord within the team
Electronically (email, fax, telephone)	Electronic means are useful to get information to a person quickly and have a good chance of a speedy reply	They may be open to misinterpretation, are not always available in smaller organisations, and can be time-consuming

Different methods of communication are useful on different occasions. For example, there is little point in holding a whole-team meeting to discuss a resource order when staff can be asked to put in orders for each room to the manager or deputy or the resources coordinator in person. Communication can work only if it meets the needs of the work environment. The ways in which a manager communicates will depend upon:

- how many full-time and part-time staff there are;
- opportunities and time for meetings;
- technology within the setting (e.g. whether there is an internal telephone system);
- the budget available for staff training;
- the size of the staffroom or meeting room.

Styles of communication

Communication will be more effective if behaviour (i.e. what you do, as opposed to what you say) is taken into account. How you behave can help or hinder communication, as people are liable to judge you on the way you behave.

There are three general categories for style of communication:

- aggressive;
- assertive;
- passive (submissive, non-assertive).

Consider the following scenario. You are a busy manager trying to complete some notes you want to circulate to your team today, ahead of your meeting with them tomorrow. These notes are very important as they set out a draft policy for especially gifted and talented children and advice on how such children may be supported within the setting. You also have a stack of paperwork for children due to start next term which you need to complete and the staff rotas need revising. A member of staff from the baby unit calls you on the internal telephone system and says he needs to discuss how the process of informing parents about their child's day can be improved. He has the time to come down now to talk to you, as they have the staff available at present. You would prefer to discuss the topic later, not now. Your response to this request, in terms of the above three styles, might be:

- Aggressive – 'You can't expect me to talk to you right now. I am in the middle of something really important. You'll just have to ring me back.'
- Assertive – 'Fine. I'll be happy to talk with you about these issues but not just now. I am in the middle of a report for the team for tomorrow. I suggest you ring me again after 2.00 p.m.'
- Passive (submissive, non-assertive) – 'Well, I'm really busy just now and a lot of people need to get the piece of work I am doing at the moment but seeing as you have the time now....'

Think it over

What type of response are you likely to make to a request that is difficult to grant – aggressive, assertive or passive?

As a manager it is often easier to be passive, as you may feel this is meeting the needs of the staff, but in the long run this can be destructive and your own work does not get done. If in the above scenario the manager had taken the time to talk to the member of staff, when would the notes be completed for the meeting? Would they be as effective if produced in a rush for the meeting? Would the other team members understand that the baby room member of staff took priority the day before?

The benefits of being assertive

There are many benefits for both individuals and organisations when the people who work within them learn to be more assertive. For individuals they might include the following:

- People are happier in themselves and with the way they handle difficult or tricky situations.
- Individuals get the best from people at work, including themselves.

- People are much more likely to get results and outcomes which are satisfactory for everyone.
- Stress is reduced as people are more likely to manage conflict early and in a competent way.

For the organisation (i.e. the early years setting) they might include the following:

- Staff are more confident and competent.
- People work together better and are more flexible.
- There are fewer 'hidden agendas' and more direct talk.
- Issues are resolved at an early stage, before they become long-term problems.

What assertiveness is

Assertiveness is based on a philosophy of personal responsibility and an awareness of the rights of other people. Being assertive means being honest with yourself and others. It means having the ability to say directly what it is you want, need or feel, but not at the expense of other people. It means having confidence in yourself and being positive, while at the same time understanding other people's points of view. Being assertive means being able to negotiate and reach workable compromises. Above all, being assertive requires you to have self-respect and respect for other people.

What assertiveness is not!

Being assertive is *not:*

- about getting your own way and winning every time;
- a series of techniques to learn parrot fashion and then bring out in a difficult situation;
- a way in which you can manipulate other people so that you can get your own way while looking as though you are considering others.

Techniques for managers

There are various techniques you can use to communicate what you want to people without being rude or appearing self-centred. These are some of them:

- inner dialogues;
- negative feelings assertion;
- broken record;
- saying no;
- fogging;
- body language.

Inner dialogues

All of us talk to ourselves regularly, usually inwardly. If done negatively, it can guarantee a self-fulfilling prophecy of real disaster! For example, a negative inner dialogue before a meeting could go like this:

> 'It's Friday … the meeting is today … it's a difficult enough meeting at the best of times but when I tell them I have to cut back on resources they are not going to like it. They will tell me I haven't done enough forward planning. It's not my fault the cost of things has gone up so much. Especially Jill … she is always so on the ball … I ended up giving in to her the last time….'

All of this of course is very negative and causes a downward spiral, leaving little room for assertive behaviour.

The world of sports discovered a way to use this kind of inner thinking in a positive way quite a few years ago and consequently there are many books about the 'inner game' of tennis, golf, squash and so on. The *positive* inner dialogue technique is very useful before a crisis to coach yourself into doing your best in the given circumstances. It is not a question of thinking rosy thoughts so that you can pretend it will be all right with a false sense of optimism. It is a way of stopping the downward spiral with positive but realistic options:

> 'It's Friday – the meeting is today … it is not going to be an easy meeting but I do have a good case and can present a valid argument. Not everyone will be helpful… but I do know how to be assertive should there be any comebacks … yes I believe my case is a good one. Now, what else is happening today?'

As you can see from the examples, with a positive inner dialogue it is so much easier to move on to the next thing and not to remain trapped in a difficult situation.

Negative feelings assertion

In many cultures and situations it is much easier for people to tell other people what they 'think' about something rather than what they 'feel'. Human beings are not robots, however, and feelings are important. It would be unrealistic to think that feelings were left at home in a box marked 'Personal'. At work it is often the case that feelings are shown reluctantly or as a last resort. While no one wants to be overcome all the time by feelings when at work, it is necessary for people to find a way to say what they feel before they erupt, become angry and lose control. Negative feelings assertion is used to tell someone what is happening and how you feel in a constructive way. It is very useful for people who tend to be either aggressive or passive. Two examples of negative feelings assertion are given below:

> 'When you shout and lose your temper with me it becomes hard to listen to your message. I feel upset when you do it, so I'd like to take it more quietly.'

> 'Each time you arrive at the meeting unprepared it means we have to recap for your benefit only. I feel irritated about this. In future I would like you to prepare in advance.'

Broken record

Children are experts in the use of broken record technique. Sometimes people pay very little attention to what you have to say as they are 'wrapped up' in their own concerns. This technique makes sure that your message gets through *without* nagging, whinging or whining. You simply keep on repeating the same message until it can be no longer ignored or dismissed. For example:

> 'I'm afraid we will not be able to take your child until the 15th. I realise this may cause you problems but we will not have a space before the 15th. However, I can promise that we will take your son from the 15th for as many sessions as you require.'

Saying no

Saying no can be tremendously difficult for some people, for many different reasons. Some people just like to please others and feel that 'No' would be an unwelcome response. Others are afraid of an aggressive reaction a 'No' might provoke. On the other hand, some people are just unthinking or unrealistic about what they are able to deliver. Conversely, some people's natural reaction is to say 'No'. It is interesting that one of the first words many children learn to say is 'No'. They may so much enjoy saying 'No' that sometimes they say it when they mean 'Yes'! If your first reaction is to say 'No', then it is important for you to think about why you do so.

If 'No' is the appropriate response to a request, then you should find a way to say it as directly as possible, without making excuses and beating about the bush, or giving long-winded explanations. The key to an assertive 'No' is to remember that you have the right to say it without guilt. Saying no firmly and reasonably is quite acceptable to most people and much better that letting them down later. It can be helpful to think about the kinds of things you find it hard to say no to and also what kind of people are hard to refuse. Is it doing favours for friends? Turning down staff who need overtime? Saying no becomes easier with practice and saves a lot of worry and lack of self-respect later. It is worth trying!

Fogging

When people behave aggressively they tend to expect disagreement and charge ahead, not listening. Fogging is used to slow them down by an unexpected response. It is a way of side-stepping their issue and still retaining your point of view and integrity by agreeing with some part of what they say. It is called fogging because the effect is very like suddenly being faced with a bank of fog when the way appeared to be clear. Fog is not solid but is hard to get through – it is necessary to hold back a bit and pay attention to what is being encountered.

Saying 'Yes' is one way of fogging, as the word can take an aggressive person by surprise and help to calm matters. For example, if someone said 'Well, that was a pretty stupid way to behave in a meeting!' and you wanted to 'fog' you might say 'Yes. I can see that you think it was a pretty stupid way to behave'. You are not agreeing that you behaved stupidly – only that you can see that the person thinks it.

Fogging gives you time to get things on a more even keel and can calm a potentially explosive situation.

Body language

It has become quite fashionable in recent years to talk about body language as though it were a recently discovered way of communicating. A number of books have been written about this subject by experts who have studied and analysed what each gesture and action means, but children soon manage to learn to tell whether someone is angry or approachable, happy or sad.

Passive style

Assertive style

Aggressive style

Figure 7.3. Assertive, aggressive and passive body language.

Body language is an important aspect of assertiveness. It is no good if you have the right words and then contradict them with your posture and demeanour. Table 7.4 lists the differences between assertive, aggressive and passive body language, and these are illustrated in Figure 7.3.

Table 7.4. Assertive, aggressive and passive body language

	Assertive	**Aggressive**	**Passive**
Posture	Upright/straight	Leaning forward	Shrinking
Head	Firm but not rigid	Chin jutting out	Head down
Eyes	Direct, not staring; good and regular eye contact	Strongly focused, staring; often piercing or glaring eye contact	Glancing away; little eye contact
Face	Expression fits the words	Set/firm	Smiling even when upset
Voice	Well modulated to fit content	Loud/emphatic	Hesitant/soft, trailing off at the ends of words/sentences
Arms/hands	Relaxed/moving easily	Controlled/extreme; sharp gestures, fingers pointing	Aimless/still
Movement/walking	Measured pace suitable to action	Slow and heavy or fast, deliberate, hard	Slow and hesitant or fast and jerky

Dealing with conflict

There will be times when, as a manager, you have to deal with conflict. This can be:

- conflict within the team;
- conflict between individuals;
- conflict between the manager and the team;
- conflict with someone outside the setting.

Conflict is an inevitable part of human interaction and cannot be avoided entirely. Conflict can also be healthy in open and honest relationships, and the outcome can be both creative and rejuvenating. It is possible to cope with conflict but not all conflict is resolvable. If staff become too embroiled in inner conflict and hurtful gossip, it may be worth taking full charge of the situation, even at the risk of becoming unpopular.

There are different responses to conflict:

- avoidance – denial, working round the problem, not being explicit about issues;
- diffusion – smoothing things over, dealing with minor aspects only;

- facing it – admit conflict exists, raise it explicitly and address it as an issue.

Good practice checklist — Dealing with conflict

☐ Be open about what you want and need.
☐ Establish what the team members want and need.
☐ Search for some kind of common ground. This may well be both parties wanting what is best for the setting.
☐ Listen to and understand both cases.
☐ Produce ideas to address differences.
☐ Build on and develop suggestions.
☐ Summarise to check that both sides understand and agree.

What do you do if it all goes wrong?

- Take time out – arrange a date when the matter can be discussed again.
- Reflect on what happened before, during and after. What were the triggers? Is there a history of conflict? What were the consequences of the conflict?
- Review the way the staff communicated – was it assertive, aggressive or passive/submissive?
- Decide how you will move forward – plan how to address the original and any further conflict.

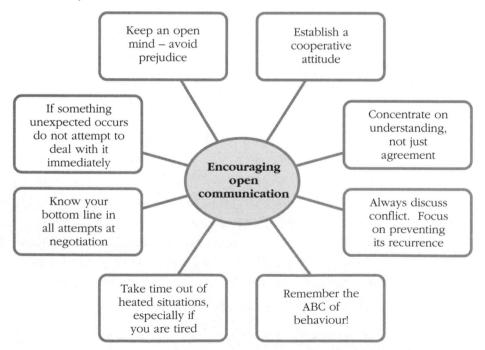

Figure 7.4. Negotiation skills which can be utilised to open communication to resolve a conflict.

There are also certain negotiation skills which can be utilised to open communication after conflict has become entrenched. These are shown in Figure 7.4.

Dealing with children's conflicts

Both the manager and the team should be aware of the ABC of behaviour when dealing with children's conflicts:

A   The antecedent. What happened before the conflict, to set it off?
B   The behaviour. How does the conflict manifest itself? Are there tears? Does someone get emotionally or physically hurt?
C   The consequence. What happens afterwards?

Meetings that succeed

The last point to cover on the subject of communication concerns meetings. Meetings are of course enormously useful when a lot of information has to be communicated to many people; however, there is probably not a professional alive who has not been to a meeting that was long, bureaucratic, boring and seemingly pointless! For this reason it is important to plan each meeting carefully. Before the meeting make sure that:

- a suitable room is booked, where the team will not be disturbed;
- all staff know the date and time well in advance – it is often better to have pre-arranged meeting slots in the week;
- you draft a brief agenda which tells the team members what will be discussed (but if you are going to discuss a particular project or topic such as 'preparation for inspection' it may be better to send out some written information beforehand as briefing notes);
- you arrange for someone to take minutes and to come prepared to do so (e.g. with paper and pen, etc.).

Within meetings there are likely to be opportunities for professional development. For example, different members of the team can take it in turn to lead the meeting (with pre-warning). There will also be opportunities for staff to give progress reports on their particular area, to build their self-esteem and ensure they feel valued. Make sure that you also wait your turn to discuss items, so that staff do not feel that the manager is dominating the agenda.

Meetings may be used to introduce new equipment or resources, and to present current matters of interest on the political agenda and to discuss the effect they may have on the setting. It can be a good idea to invite a speaker from another setting or another agency to come and lead a discussion, and to invite a parent or carer to come along so that staff can keep in touch with parents' changing needs. Meetings can also be an opportunity to encourage sharing of good practice or research and observation work within the setting.

Good practice checklist — Meetings

☐ Have a clear purpose for the meeting and an agenda.

☐ Allow sufficient time for the agenda items and then make sure the meeting starts and finishes on time.

☐ Refer to the last meeting and check through any actions noted to check progress.

☐ Always start by stating the purpose of the meeting and briefly stating what you expect to achieve in the time allocated (this will be an opportunity for you to say that a further meeting can be held to discuss wider issues that could be pending).

☐ Introduce each item in turn and allow time for full and fair discussion before moving on.

☐ Chair the meeting effectively – do not allow anyone to dominate the proceedings, avoid getting side-tracked and attend to time keeping.

☐ Encourage effective listening.

☐ Check understanding intermittently, by summarising.

☐ Outline any agreed actions and give a brief summary.

☐ Thank all the team for their contribution and give a date for the next meeting if possible.

☐ Ensure everyone leaves the meeting with a clear idea of what has been agreed, what is expected of them, what action is required and what follow-up there will be.

☐ After the meeting make sure all team members receive a copy of notes of the meeting and written confirmation of the agreed date of the next meeting.

7.4 The manager as a motivator

What can a manager do to meet the differing motivational needs of the staff? It would seem that managers who want to motivate their staff need to get to know them; they need to have an interest in each team member as a person. In order to do this the manager will need to find out what interests them and get to know their strengths and weaknesses. Good managers will ensure that all team members have the opportunity to utilise their strengths and play to them. They will also ensure that weaknesses are addressed through staff training and appraisal.

The team members will want to increase their skills, so they will need to be provided with training opportunities and challenges in their job. This will entail some delegation of responsibility on the part of the manager, which many find quite difficult, as there is an element of risk involved.

Case study — Moving boxes

Jack is a very busy manager of a large nursery. A large delivery of resources arrives at the reception area and the maintenance person is off-site. The children are beginning to arrive for the afternoon session and the boxes are in the way and causing a health and safety risk. Jack is aware that the staff are not required to lift heavy items but is also aware that some of the team have just finished a meeting along the corridor. He goes into the meeting room and finds four of his staff chatting. At this point he does find it a little difficult to cover his feelings (after all, they are standing chatting and there is bedlam ensuing in the reception area). He interrupts their chatting and says quite loudly: 'There are loads of boxes cluttering up the reception area and the children are arriving. Please come and give me a hand to move them.... Now.' The team members respond by muttering a variety of excuses and reasons for not going down to reception, keeping their backs to the manager: 'Oh, I need to get back' and 'I can't – I have a bad back'. Jack was cross but left the room and went along and piled the boxes as safely as possible until the maintenance person got back.

- How do you think Jack handled the situation?
- Would you say the team had respect for Jack?
- Could you hazard a guess as to some of the underlying problems within this team?
- What do you think Jack should have done?

Look at the case study 'Moving boxes'. You might have thought that this response was indicative of other problems within the team. The way a team is treated in these sorts of situations demonstrates the manager's ability to work as part of the team to make them feel included. If Jack had taken this opportunity to ask the staff to help him in this particular emergency and appeal to them as colleagues, he may have met with a more positive response. For example, Jack could have said:

> 'I apologise for interrupting. I know you are all just finishing your meeting.... Joan don't you come because I know you have a bad back but would everyone else mind giving me a hand to move these boxes out of the children's way? I wouldn't ask ordinarily but the maintenance man is on his break.'

This manager's attitude to the staff could be seen as demotivating. He has given the staff cause to complain about his indecisive behaviour and has not used the opportunity to involve the staff enthusiastically. If the team are unwilling to take part in the smooth running of the setting they are less likely to be enthusiastic about larger challenges. The manager who is positive and responsive motivates and enthuses staff. The case study demonstrates an example of a small opportunity to motivate which was lost and instead the manager only demonstrated his intolerance.

Giving praise and encouragement is vital for motivating staff and does not need to wait until a team member is having an appraisal. This helps to boost self-esteem and show staff that you value their contribution. It is also motivating for staff to involve them as much as possible in the decision-making, to seek their views and to consult them on potential changes. Sharing information about how things are going guarantees staff involvement and encourages them to take ownership of their setting.

Figure 7.5 summarises the things that motivate staff teams. In contrast, what will reduce their motivation is a manager who allows them little or no control over their own jobs. Similarly, supervision that is too close can cause team members to feel stifled and patronised. Allowing team members to take some of the control is not only motivating for the staff but beneficial for the effective running of the setting.

Figure 7.5. Ways in which to motivate staff.

7.5 Training, development and appraisal

A team can become a dynamic learning environment with the right sort of encouragement from a manager. As part of good practice all staff, even those who are more recently qualified, should be encouraged to further and update their skills. Table 7.5 shows the three broad categories of training available to early years practitioners. Chapter 6 looks at training towards formal qualifications; this section examines some of the in-house training that can be undertaken.

Table 7.5. Three broad categories of training for the early years setting

Purpose of training	Types of training and where they might take place	Benefits to the setting
To meet statutory requirements, Ofsted requirements, curriculum guidelines	Training to meet statutory requirements such as: first aid, food hygiene, NVQ training to train staff to correct level. Also specialist training for the special educational needs coordinator. These types of training could take place on or off site and will require training provider input (e.g. St John's Ambulance/Red Cross, local further education college, NVQ assessment centre)	To ensure all staff are trained to required standard. This will benefit the profile of the setting and the care and education of the children
To develop good practice	This part of the training could cover a plethora of subjects such as: anti-discriminatory practice, curriculum development, working with parents, team-building. This could be in-house training or on short courses offered by independent trainers or Early Years Development and Childcare Partnerships	This will improve overall working practice if disseminated to the team. New strategies for working with children and policy development will be promoted
The personal and professional development of individual team members	Individual members of the team could identify specific areas of professional development, such as further courses of a higher level, which could take place off site in the voluntary sector or in higher education	It will reflect in the performance of an individual team member if he or she feels valued by being allowed time to do further training

You will need to ensure that valuable staff time is not wasted taking part in training which is not effective. All training, whether it is internal or external, must be appropriate for the individual learner. Much time is wasted in many establishments putting staff on training courses that they feel are neither relevant nor pitched at their individual learning styles. This leads to staff being demotivated and they may begin to perceive training as a 'chore' and not something which will help and support them as individuals. If staff are given a 'voice' in the selection of the training and are given opportunities to research possible courses, for example, they will be more likely to make a commitment to the training and become actively involved.

Types of training and development

Much of the training and development of staff in early years settings can take place through work done on site. For example, more experienced staff can coach or mentor more junior members of the team, sharing their expertise (mentoring is discussed in more detail below). The more experienced members of staff have a wealth of expertise to share and will also find that the sharing of this knowledge gives them the opportunity to consolidate what they already know.

In-house training can involve an exchange of skills within the team. For example, having identified their individual strengths, members of staff can be encouraged to form teams based around their interests and each team then puts together a learning programme to develop skills and exchange ideas.

It can be useful to develop a team learning plan, which gives members of the team the opportunity to work on things such as a staff newsletter, a bulletin for parents and carers, or a yearly outing for parents, staff and children. This can develop staff skills. It is important that the staff are aware at the outset of both the learning and organisational objectives.

Delegating duties to team members not only builds their self-esteem but can also increase their knowledge and experience. For instance, they may be given the opportunity to register and introduce a new child to the setting, coordinate with the parents and carers and get feedback from the staff on the child's progress. Other opportunities for staff to train and develop their knowledge and skills include the following:

- *External development teams or networks.* This involves networking with other professionals.
- *Project-based work.* There may be an area within the nursery, such as use of information technology, which needs improvement; a team can set about researching the present provision and investigating needs.
- *Specialist training for special needs coordinators.* This may be necessary for them to keep abreast of the latest information and knowledge on the support of children with special needs. This information can then be disseminated to the rest of the team within a staff development session.

Such opportunities will lead to muti-skilling and integrated team work. They also empower staff to make decisions and become involved. The manager will be moving away from the authoritarian image to one of leader, facilitator and coach.

Training and development plan

It is crucial, however, that there is a development plan in place rather than an informal approach, for the following reasons:

- Team members need to know in advance when they will be going on training sessions.
- You will need to arrange cover (allowing for travel, and evaluation and dissemination time).
- If there is no set plan for training some less motivated team members may feel that it is not worth asking to take part in courses, especially if the same (more motivated) people get the opportunities to do training every time.
- If the development plan is in place it can be holistically designed with the staff team to meet the needs of the setting and reinforce good practice.
- A well organised, well thought out training plan will challenge staff, offer encouragement and build the expertise of the staff team.

The first step is to identify the needs for training and development. This can be done in a variety of ways:

- through a SWOT (strengths, weaknesses, opportunities, threats) analysis of present skills (i.e. a 'skills analysis');
- by directives from outside agencies (e.g. Ofsted or curriculum guidance);
- from staff themselves (perhaps in appraisal – see below – or collectively at team meetings);
- as a result of statutory training requirements (e.g. in first aid and food hygiene).

It will then be possible to produce an appropriate plan for the professional development of the staff. This will need to take account of the following factors:

- the budget for training and development;
- staff commitment to further training (such commitment can be initiated at interview and induction of new staff);
- staff time (good quality staff cover will need to be provided, which also has cost implications);
- the availability of suitable facilities for on-site training.

The professional development plan should be linked to the needs of the setting and not to the needs and wants of individual staff, with the proviso noted above that staff should not be sent on courses that they feel are irrelevant.

The three areas of development shown in Table 7.5 can make up the essential components of an effective plan for training and development. You will need to analyse needs through appraisal and team meetings and must link these to statutory requirements. If the plan is well thought through it will be of benefit to the setting in terms of its smooth running and improved practice, and will ensure that team members feel valued. It is good practice for staff to be given the opportunity to share knowledge gained through training by disseminating it to other team members, as this is cost-effective and allows staff to take on another role in mentoring and tutoring.

Mentoring

Mentoring is a largely untapped resource for professional development in the early years sector. Every student who takes one of the new Sector Endorsed Foundation Degrees for Early Childhood Practitioners should have a personal mentor. Mentors are not responsible for the teaching of students but support their learning through regular meetings with them, looking at the assessment work they need to do for their course and verifying their practical skills in the workplace. This role has benefits for both the mentor and the person being mentored, as both can learn from the experience: the mentor has skills and experience to pass on but can also learn from the student's course material (if he or she is doing a qualification) and discuss new ideas. Both people can only benefit. If the mentoring does not work with one pairing, the student should switch to a different mentor, rather than deciding that mentoring itself is unsuccessful.

Evaluation of training and development

After the training or staff development has taken place, it is really important that:

- it is evaluated;
- information is disseminated (particularly after 'development of good practice' training).

The two may be combined on a single form, such as that shown in Figure 7.6. This type of evaluation provides the team member with the opportunity to feedback first to the manager. If the information would be useful to disseminate to the team, the manager will need to provide time in either a team meeting or an internal staff development session to do this. Alternatively, the manager may feel that it would be useful to copy handouts for other staff to use as a reference. Such forms could also be used in appraisal, to consider how the individual team member is able to make use of training. As part of a team-building exercise, the results pooled from evaluation forms can be discussed in order to put together future training

	Information for manager to disseminate
Name: .... **Title of training**: .... **Provider:**	
Please list briefly the key points of the training:	
How do you think the training will be of benefit to you in your role?	
List some aspects which you feel would be useful to disseminate to the rest of the team:	
Were you given any handouts or resources on your training? If so, please can you list them.	

Figure 7.6. A form for the evaluation of training and to record the action required of the manager to disseminate information.

plans. The evaluation form is only one suggestion for a way in which training can be made to benefit the whole team. Teams themselves are likely to suggest a variety of ways to evaluate training and disseminate information.

Appraisal

All contracted staff should receive some sort of appraisal with their line manager. This will vary from setting to setting in terms of time allowed and its exact nature.

When new members of staff start work they are usually given a probation period, during which their employment is still of a temporary nature (see Chapter 6). They should go through an induction at the setting and possibly be allocated a mentor to guide them through their probationary period. When the probation time is up, the line manager will meet with them to discuss their progress and at that point confirm their full employment status. It is at this point that the new employee becomes one of the team, and this will be recorded in a staff file at the setting. After that initial meeting there should then be regular appraisal meetings between the member of staff and line manager.

How often appraisal meetings take place will vary from setting to setting, but there should be at least two a year. These meetings are special because they are:

- confidential;
- one to one;
- for the purpose of discussing that person's progress only.

The appraisal meeting is not an opportunity to discuss other members of staff, children or resources, unless it has a direct effect on that member of staff's development. Together the member of staff and the line manager will discuss:

- successes so far;
- progress made since the last meeting;
- strengths and weaknesses of the member of staff;
- present role and how it can be best developed;
- working relationships with other staff and children;
- objectives for the next period (whatever that may be);
- improvements to be made and support for those improvements identified;
- training needs and how they will be met.

People being appraised should go to the meeting prepared and ready: this will mean having objectives in mind and ideas for training. The appraisal meeting is a time set aside for them exclusively and should be an opportunity for them to discuss any personal or professional issues that might have affected their performance. The line manager will note these details on a confidential appraisal form. If something is written on the appraisal form then it will need to be actioned by the manager as agreed at the meeting in support of the member of staff. Both persons will sign the appraisal form. At the next appraisal meeting the objectives will be reviewed once more. If the member of staff has not met the objectives they can be revised or the line manager may express concerns at this point. It is important that the appraisal scheme is taken seriously, and neither the member of staff nor the line manager should make false promises at this meeting. It is far better that the manager encourages the member of staff to have realistic objectives, and is realistic about the amount of support that can be offered to the member of staff to meet those objectives.

Advantages of appraisal to the setting

- Staff who are listened to feel valued and their performance will consequently improve.
- Procedures such as appraisal demonstrate a professional approach to other practitioners and service users.

- In appraisal there are opportunities for the manager and the team member to discuss any issues and resolve any conflicts.
- Targets can be set for the team member which will have a direct, positive effect on the practice in the setting.

Advantages of appraisal to the individual team member

- Staff who have an opportunity to discuss their personal and professional progress confidentially are less likely to harbour grievances.
- The team member will have this allotted time to have the complete attention of the line manager; this should make them feel valued and listened to, which will result in them being stronger members of the team.
- Appraisal is an opportunity for the manager to praise the team member 'officially' and put it in writing.
- If there are any concerns an appraisal session is a good time for these to be addressed and the manager and member of staff can negotiate targets for improvement; without appraisal there is a risk that poor performance will be discussed in front of other members of the team.

Conclusion

This chapter has covered quite a lot of information. It has briefly looked at some of the theories surrounding organisations and you may want to do further research to investigate this area further. It has also looked at team roles and clarified the importance of individuals as team members. It is clear that if a team is to be effective and its members are to work well together they must have a common aim or mission, as well as a clear understanding of the underlying principles and values that drive that aim. It is also apparent that good communication and motivation are key to a team's cohesiveness and success. A manager will need to be aware of the methods of communication that are most effective. The manager will also need to be careful that the employees' needs are being met and that they are being challenged and valued, and given regular praise and encouragement. There must be opportunities for training and development both internally and externally and confidential opportunity for appraisal. A variety of strategies have been suggested and there will be many more which have not. It is clear that managing is not something which can be taught specifically but there are ways in which managers can develop their teams to become cohesive and effective, which also in turn make them better and more effective managers.

Check your understanding

1 Would an early years setting be likely to be a task, role, person or power culture?
2 What stages might a team go through to form a cohesive group?
3 Can you say which team roles exist in your team?
4 Name three of the characteristics of an effective team.
5 What is the MBTI?
6 Name three methods of communication.
7 Can you give examples of assertive, aggressive and passive behaviour?
8 Name some strategies for communication (e.g. 'fogging').
9 What are the best ways of dealing with conflict?
10 How should you prepare for a meeting?
11 What should be discussed at appraisal?

References and further reading

Cava, R. (1991) *Dealing with Difficult People.* London: Judy Piatkus.

Handy, C. and Aitken, R. (1986) *Understanding Schools as Organisations.* London: Penguin.

Penn, H. (ed.) (2000) *Early Childhood Services. Theory, Policy and Practice.* Buckingham: Open University Press.

Rodd, J. (1998) *Leadership in Early Childhood* (2nd edition). Buckingham: Open University Press.

Smith, A. and Langston, A. (1999) *Managing Staff in Early Years Settings.* London: Routledge.

Tuckman, B. W. and Jensen, M. A. C. (1977) 'Stages of small group development revisited'. *Group and Organization Studies*, vol. 2, pp. 419–427.

Useful websites

Ascent: www.ascent-center.com (a US centre for professional training and development).

Belbin website: www.belbin.com ('Home to the Team Building work of Dr R. Meredith Belbin').

8 Administration of the Early Years Setting

In recent years the administration of early years settings has become increasingly complicated. Managers are required to understand how to run their establishment as a business and to compete in a competitive market. The need for good quality childcare is paramount. Parents and carers are seeking well run settings that are able to meet their diverse needs and those of their children. The number of women in paid work has risen over the past decade, as has the number achieving educational qualifications. With smaller and wider-spread families, the increased workforce must rely on childcare that is flexible, affordable and reliable.

This chapter outlines the important aspects of the administration of childcare settings, under the following headings:

8.1 The National Childcare Strategy.

8.2 The business aspects of managing an early years setting.

8.3 Legislation.

8.4 Policies and procedures.

8.1 The National Childcare Strategy

In May 1998, the government launched its National Childcare Strategy in the Green Paper *Meeting the Childcare Challenge* (Department for Education and Employment, 1998). The strategy is relevant across the whole of the UK, but deals specifically with England. The Secretaries of State for Wales, Scotland and Northern Ireland issued their own documentation in relation to childcare.

The aim of the strategy is to support families and to ensure they have access to the childcare that meets their needs. The background to the strategy lies in the recognition that there were not enough childcare places and the cost of childcare put it out of the reach of many families. It was also difficult for parents to access information about childcare in their area. The general feeling was that childcare provision had failed to keep pace with the needs of families, employers and society as a whole. It was also noted that the quality of provision was variable.

In terms of the administration of childcare settings, the National Childcare Strategy is an important document and managers need to be aware of its elements. Its principal aim is to ensure that good quality childcare for children aged 0 to 14 is available in every neighbourhood. This includes formal childcare, such as playgroups, out-of-school clubs and childminders, as well as informal childcare, for example relatives or friends looking after children. More specific objectives are:

- to improve the quality of childcare;
- to make childcare affordable for more families;
- to increase the number of places;
- to improve information about available childcare.

The National Childcare Strategy is government led; however, the role of parents in making choices for their children is recognised and reiterated. The vision is for the government to provide for the standardisation of services, to enable all parents to make informed choices about the type of childcare that suits their needs and their child's. The child's needs are at the heart of the Strategy. The day-to-day administration of the Strategy is down to the Early Years Development and Childcare Partnership in each area.

Quality

The Strategy seeks to ensure that all childcare settings offer a good quality experience for the children attending. There are numerous ways of doing this: through highly trained staff, sharing of good practice, leading by example, examining settings against nationally agreed standards and through quality assurance schemes.

A key element of the Strategy is the establishment of Early Excellence Centres across the country (the target was 100 Centres by 2004) to encourage the dissemination of good practice. The Centres provide models of good quality integrated education and childcare for local providers. They typically offer: integrated childcare and education, including for children with particular needs; parent and toddler sessions for parents; and other education and training programmes to develop parenting, employment and other skills. Besides spreading good practice they offer support and training to providers in their area. They work in close contact with the Early Years Development and Childcare Partnerships in each county and with a range of providers. The Early Excellence Centre in St Albans, Hertfordshire, for example, houses a day care centre, a state-funded nursery school and an opportunity group under the same roof, as well as paediatricians and therapists. Conferences and training sessions regularly take place and practitioners and parents are encouraged to visit the Centre and witness good practice. There is an ethos of sharing quality.

Find it out

Research your nearest Early Excellence Centre, perhaps by visiting it and recording examples of good practice that are taking place. Similarly, research the work of your local Early Years Development and Childcare Partnership.

Quality assurance schemes

The National Childcare Strategy recognised the importance of quality assurance systems and as a result the Early Years Development and Childcare Partnerships are encouraging settings to attain accreditation through various schemes. Schemes may be developed locally by a Partnership but there are also nationally recognised schemes, such as 'Aiming for Quality' from the Pre-School Learning Alliance. Partnership schemes generally provide a portfolio of criteria to be met by the setting in order to achieve accreditation. The portfolio will include agreed standards by which each setting is judged. This forms a guide to good practice for all those providing care, early years education and out-of-school care and will be applicable to all providers, whether childminders, day nurseries, pre-schools, 'wrap-around care' (i.e. breakfast and lunch clubs), after-school clubs or holiday play schemes. The standards will have been agreed after extensive consultation with providers of services, including private and voluntary settings as well as independent and maintained schools, and will represent a broad consensus of views. Early Years Development and Childcare Partnerships are committed to encouraging and supporting higher standards for the benefit of all children and their families. Each

Partnership is responsible for producing its own scheme of accreditation or 'kite mark', although communication and discussion have taken place between counties.

A mentoring system is provided to assist the achievement of accreditation, with one-to-one assistance or group workshops. Settings are encouraged to build bonds with other providers in similar circumstances in order to create a feeling of camaraderie and an ethos of quality. Cluster groups are established to form a support system. It is generally believed that staff can learn from sharing good practice.

When a setting feels that it is ready for accreditation, and that all the criteria have been met, a verifier will visit to assess the quality of its work and if he or she is satisfied will recommend accreditation. A report is then sent to the Early Years Development and Childcare Partnership, which has the power to grant accreditation if it is satisfied with the evidence. Verifiers are chosen for their early years experience. They must have sound knowledge of what makes an appropriate environment and of child development. They must be committed to parental involvement, equality of opportunity and anti-racism. They will also have the ability to communicate effectively, verbally and in writing. The verifier will want to meet the manager and to talk to representatives of the staff and parents, as well as some children, if appropriate. She or he will also want to see evidence of where the setting considers it has met the criteria.

Training

The National Childcare Strategy recognises that it can be hard for workers within the sector to add to their qualifications and progress in their careers. It was noted that there were a large number of disparate qualifications that did not relate clearly to each other and were not always recognised by employers on a national basis. For this reason it was decided to instigate a framework of training and qualifications that would be recognised by employers and that would enable workers to progress in their careers, moving freely around the country and from employer to employer.

As a result, the training of childcare workers has been scrutinised and attempts made to ensure that courses meet the criteria outlined by the Qualifications and Curriculum Authority (QCA). All courses are rigorously compiled and assessed to ensure continuity in the standard of the qualification. The government has introduced New Deal to generate up to 50,000 new childcare workers and is encouraging people to achieve qualifications from levels 1 to 4.

As a manager you will need to ensure that you have good understanding of the qualifications available (see Chapter 6) and the level of training they provide, in order to ensure that you are employing appropriately qualified staff (see Chapter 2). As a general rule it is useful to remember that workers need a level 3 qualification to be in charge of a setting.

Regulation and inspection

Parents need to feel comfortable with the childcare that they choose and much of this confidence is based on the registration procedures. Before the National Childcare Strategy there had been anomalies, and the nature of the inspection and regulations varied according to the nature of the provider rather than the needs of the children. As a result of the Strategy, improvements have been made to the way early years education and day care providers are regulated and inspected. Ofsted is now responsible for the registration and inspection of settings, and providers are assessed against the National Standards (Department for Education and Skills, 2003). The National Standards represent a baseline of quality, below which no provider may fall (see Chapter 2 for details). Ofsted has issued guidance on how the standards can be achieved for the five different types of provision. Guides to registration are available from the www.ofsted.gov.uk website. You will need to be familiar with these standards in relation to the childcare you provide.

Ofsted is also responsible for investigating complaints. It has the power to impose conditions of registration or to cancel registration. There is also an advisory capacity to the Secretary of State for Education and Skills and local authorities on childcare issues. All these initiatives are aimed at maintaining and increasing the quality of the provision on offer.

Affordability of care and numbers of places

As well as encouraging quality in settings, the National Childcare Strategy also aims to increase the number of families who are able to afford childcare. One of the ways in which this has been done is through financial assistance. This may have a direct effect on your provision, in that you may wish to consider some form of expansion. There are also increasing opportunities for after-school facilities and many settings are providing wrap around care, where they collect children from school and care for them until they are collected later in the day.

Tax credits

Financial assistance has been increased through Childcare Tax Credit. This is payable to many working families on low or middle incomes to help them with childcare costs. The aim is to enable pre-school settings to set realistic fees and to make childcare more affordable for working families on lower incomes. The consequent demand for more childcare places should encourage the provision of new places.

The Childcare Tax Credit is part of the Working Families Tax Credit (WFTC), which has been introduced as a top-up to earnings of working families to ensure that work pays. In effect, tax begins to be paid only on income over £220 per week. Childcare Tax Credit will be worth up to 70% of eligible childcare costs, subject to certain maximums. It is tapered so that the less a family earns the more it will receive in tax credit.

The Children's Tax Credit is a tax reduction for parents with at least one child under 16. It replaces the Married Couple's Allowance and the Additional Personal Allowance and is not the same thing as the Childcare Tax Credit. More information is available from the helpline 0845 300 3900.

Other financial assistance

Further money has been made available to develop new out-of-school childcare, especially for families from ethnic minorities and those whose children have special needs.

Employers are also being encouraged to play an important part, for example through childcare partnerships. In addition they are being encouraged to adopt 'family-friendly' policies. There is an emphasis on helping employees balance work and family life.

Effects of the drive to increase the number of places

Partly as a result of the above arrangements for financial assistance there has been an increase in demand for childcare places. This has put some pressure on current providers to expand their businesses and has encouraged new providers to establish settings. There are difficulties in finding appropriate staff to fill vacancies and some providers fear a flooding of the market. There are avenues of funding available for expansion and setting up a new business and these are discussed below. The Early Years Development and Childcare Partnerships have improved the availability of information for existing settings and also have staff available to give advice on business and financial matters.

It is interesting to note that out-of-school care is burgeoning – there was an 86% increase in the number of providers between 1998 and 2001. Parents are more aware of out-of-school care and many plan their own careers around it. It is becoming easier to find trained staff following the investment by Early Years Development and Childcare Partnerships in play-work training.

What the National Childcare Strategy means to parents

The intention is that the strategy will eventually assist parents in their choices for childcare and that:

- parents will be able to go to work knowing that their children are being well looked after;
- all those looking after children will be able to get the help they need to do a good job;
- parents who are working or studying will be able to afford the childcare which meets their needs;
- more childcare places will be available for younger children;
- more out-of-school childcare places will be available for older children;
- parents will know where to go to get information and advice about childcare.

In relation to the last point, as part of the Strategy the local authority must provide information for parents through its Early Years Development and Childcare Partnership. Previously there had been no consistency in the provision of information about childcare. It was available at a number of different sources and was not immediately accessible to parents and carers. The Early Years Development and Childcare Partnerships are encouraged to establish a Childcare Information Service (CIS) for their area that provides data about a range of local childcare services. The implication for managers of settings is to ensure all information regarding their setting is up to date.

8.2 The business aspects of managing an early years setting

Running a childcare setting, whether it is a day nursery or an after-school club, can be a costly business. There are a number of start-up costs that need to be accounted for and continuous running costs that need to be considered for sustainability. Initially you will require funding for premises, conversion, equipment, recruitment, marketing and working capital to cover early trading losses. In the longer term, funds will be needed for administration costs, telephone, postage, service charges, rent, insurance and staffing. In addition you will regularly need to replace play equipment and supplies such as paper and pens.

This section looks at starting up an early years setting, sources of funding and the expansion of a setting. The matter of planning permission will arise in connection with both setting up and expanding. Finding a market for your provision and marketing the setting are crucial aspects of management, and these are also covered.

The business plan

To analyse the cost of starting up a business, and to define your aims, you should draw up a business plan. It is also a helpful way for raising financial backing and demonstrating the viability of your ideas.

The business plan should be easy to read and understand. It should be based on accurate research and assessment of the market. It could include the following elements:

- *Executive summary*, with the key objectives and level of funding needed. This will include the timescale for development and the amount of finance required.
- *Sector analysis*, with a brief explanation of the marketplace and developments that may affect demand.
- *Market analysis*, to include your market research on potential customers, the competition and its strengths and weaknesses. You could also include a SWOT (strengths, weaknesses, opportunities, threats) analysis of your business.
- *Operational plan*, with business objectives and means of achieving them. This should include the legal structure of your business – whether you are a sole trader, partnership or limited company. It should also state the features of the childcare provision, such as the curriculum, the hours of opening and the nature of the care.
- *Management team*, giving clear details of everyone involved in the business, including their relevant experience and qualifications. This should also outline details of the staff to be recruited.
- *Implementation plan*, to explain how your targets will be met.
- *Financial information*, with predictions about how your business will develop and indications of the cash flow forecast, profit and loss and balance sheet.
- *Appendices*, including your financial data, the curriculum vitae for each of the management staff, proof of registration, and copies of policies and procedures.

Find it out

Contact your local bank or building society and ask for information regarding starting up a business.

Funding

Both existing early years settings and proposed ventures may wish to apply for funding. For the latter, family and friends are the easiest and quickest source of funding and banks may consider funding if you have capital or assets of your own. Banks will supply information on the setting up and sustenance of small businesses. They will also provide information and advice on the help available for those starting a business, such as the government loan guarantee scheme.

Funding is available from a variety of sources and it is advisable to research all possible avenues. Many applications are turned down for funding because the applicant has not completed sufficient research. It is important to ensure that the interests of potential funders match the aims of your setting. The following may be sources of funding or sources of further information on funding:

- Early Years Development and Childcare Partnerships;
- town, borough, parish councils;
- the Community Fund (www.community-fund.org.uk);
- local trusts and charities;
- the Learning and Skills Council (www.lsc.gov.uk);
- the Pre-school Learning Alliance (www.pre-school.org.uk);
- the local education authority;
- your own fundraising committee.

Other useful websites include www.funderfinder.org.uk and www.charitynet.org.uk. Potential sources of funds will depend on the type and status of the organisation that applies as well as the nature of the proposed spending.

Current government funding initiatives include the Neighbourhood Nurseries Initiative (NNI), the Childcare Fund allocated to Early Years Development and Childcare Partnerships and the annual nursery education grant. The £330 million NNI aims to create 45,000 full-time day care places in the bottom 20% of the most deprived areas in England.

For information contact your local Early Years Development and Childcare Partnership. There should be a business development officer and/or a childcare marketing officer available to help you.

The Pre-school Learning Alliance has produced a fundraising pack for pre-school settings. It is full of information and practical ideas and can be obtained from the Alliance's Marketing Department.

Case study — Equipment award

Caroline runs a pre-school group in Hertfordshire. She has 15 members of staff and 56 children spread between two groups, over the week, of 3–5-year-olds and 2–3-year-olds. The group uses a church building in the mornings and has recently opened a lunchtime session for the older age range to prepare them for school. The group is similar to many others in that funds are always in short supply and the staff have a wish-list of expensive equipment that they want to purchase. In 2002 Caroline applied to British Telecom for an Education Award. Many companies are keen to give money to educational causes and arrange competitions or awards to do this. Caroline was sceptical that a 'small pre-school in a church hall' would qualify for any award, but she completed the detailed application form. She was delighted that her establishment was chosen to receive an award; she was given £5,000 to spend on equipment to encourage the use of information and communication technology (ICT). Caroline's group became the proud owners of a projector, two laptop computers, a digital camcorder and camera, printers and training for the staff. This gave Caroline the opportunity to enhance the learning experience of the children and to train her staff to help the children with their development and knowledge of ICT.

- Research companies in your area and nationally to find out about any similar opportunities.

Expanding an early years setting

Many settings have found that expansion is a good way to achieve sustainability. By offering more services they increase income and become a vital resource in the community. They are also responding to the changing needs of families and children. There are many ways of expanding an existing service, such as after-school clubs, breakfast clubs and holiday schemes, and advice is available from local Early Years Development and Childcare Partnerships or from the Pre-school Learning Alliance, which has experienced local development workers (see website).

To be in a position to expand, your existing provision must be in a strong financial position, well managed and well resourced. As with starting a new business (see above), demand must be assessed and a business plan drawn up for the expansion. It is essential to have good management procedures in place in order to keep everything running smoothly. It is all too easy to spread yourself too thinly. It is also necessary to consider the drawbacks to expansion as well as the benefits. It may not, for example, be as easy to be hands-on in the day-to-day management of two or more settings, or even of one larger one. You may find that you miss the intimate knowledge of children and families. Although funding is available for expansion (see above), the future is uncertain and many feel that increased access to funds will create unsustainable competition in a market already faced with recruitment difficulties.

Good practice checklist — Expanding the setting

☐ Ensure your current setting is well financed and managed, and has a good structure.

☐ Recognise that you may need managerial assistance, particularly if you are considering opening another setting.

☐ Seek advice from professional organisations and high street banks.

☐ If you are building on a new site do not compromise on position. Location is important.

☐ Make sure your property is big enough for the financial viability of expansion.

☐ Be realistic about availability of staff and training costs.

☐ Research government funding to see if you are eligible, but remember it will run out eventually.

☐ Be realistic about competition and threats to your future business, and plan accordingly.

☐ Do not overestimate profits.

Planning permission

Planning permission is usually required for the expansion of existing premises or to convert a property for the purpose of establishing an early years setting. It is essential that you check with planning departments before purchasing or leasing premises. Planning permission will be required if you intend:

- to erect a new building;
- to change the use of a building;
- to undertake external work, including extending existing buildings;
- to carry out works around the building, such as installing a children's playground.

Car parking is often an issue that leads to planning permission being refused, so it is worth spending time researching the area and assessing the views of local residents. The nearest neighbours to your proposal will be informed of your plans and invited to comment or object. They may also object to an increase in the level of noise generated by children at play. Access to the area will also be considered, as will the number of similar businesses in the locality. The conversion of a residential property into a business such as a day nursery may also be disallowed if the local authority wishes to keep the area for residential use.

Conditions are invariably applied to any planning application and these may limit the number of children catered for or the hours of opening.

These will need to be taken into account when considering the financial viability of your project.

Finding your market

Whether you are considering starting up a setting for the care and education of children or expanding existing provision, you must first consider the needs of the local community and the nature and extent of the competition (for example, you should establish whether the local nurseries are full and what childcare services they offer). You will need to establish these in a systematic way. Good sources of information about your area include:

- the recent Early Years Development and Childcare Partnership childcare audit;
- the local Children's Information Service;
- the local library;
- the economic development unit/research and information unit of your local authority;
- local directories of childcare services;
- major employers (there may be a need to provide childcare for their employees);
- local parents.

You may find it useful to conduct a survey to determine the exact nature of childcare needs in your area. The methods for gathering information include the following:

- street surveys;
- telephone surveys;
- door-to-door surveys;
- postal surveys;
- open meetings.

Whichever method you choose you should try to contact as wide a selection of relevant people as possible. For any of these methods, you are likely to want to use questionnaires of some sort, and these are considered below.

Street survey

This can be done in an informal way by simply asking people questions and recording their responses. You could use a questionnaire as a basis for your questions, notes or a checklist. This method enables you to obtain information quickly and to clear up any misunderstandings immediately. The response rate is high and you can ask supplementary questions, although it is a time-consuming method of gaining information. You may also need permission from the local council.

Street surveys are one method of gathering information about childcare needs in your area.

Telephone survey

This is a quick way to access information and reaches more people than postal surveys but may be considered intrusive by respondents. Inaccurate responses may be given, as respondents may feel pressured by time.

Door-to-door survey

It is important to get the timing right for this method – for example, avoid mealtimes and peak television viewing times.

Postal survey

In this method respondents have time to think and may express their true feelings. The response rate is low and you should bear this in mind when choosing this – an average response rate is 10%, even when stamped addressed envelopes are provided for the return of questionnaires.

Open meeting

This is a good opportunity to raise awareness about your plans and to establish local needs.

Questionnaires

Questionnaires are a good way to collect information in the types of survey outlined above. However, it is harder to write a questionnaire than many people think. An example is given in Figure 8.1. Much thought needs to be given to its layout and the precise nature of the information sought. It is important to stick rigidly to the task in hand and not to include any superfluous questions. You will also need to consider the piloting, distribution and return of questionnaires.

It is important to ensure that the questionnaire is typed and that instructions are clear. Spaces between the questions will help the reader, and later make it easier for you to analyse the results. Take care over the order of the questions and think carefully about the impression you are giving – to potential clients. Ask a friend or colleague to check the questionnaire, and to pay particular attention to the wording of the questions. Do they fit your purpose? Is there any ambiguity or assumption?

Dear parent,

The Wise Old Owl Pre-school in Bury Lane is considering expanding the service it offers. We are currently open on Tuesday and Thursday mornings from 9.30 a.m. to 12.00 noon. We would welcome your views on expansion and would like to establish what you would find most useful. Please complete the form below and return it to us in the envelope provided by June 21st. We will be using your comments to guide our plans but all answers will be strictly confidential.

Thank you for your help.

1. Please give the postcode for your area..

2. Please give the ages of all your children..

3. Please identify whether you are currently using our provision by circling the appropriate answer.

| Yes | | No |

4. How likely would you be to use new provision at this pre-school?

| Very likely | | Quite likely | | Not likely |

5. If you have circled 'Not likely' please explain briefly why and return the form to us.

6. If you circled 'Very likely' or 'Quite likely' please tick the box(es) for the provision you would use:

	Extra morning sessions on Monday/Tuesday/Wednesday
	Afternoon sessions 12–4 p.m. (with lunch)
	After-school sessions 4–7 p.m. (with tea)
	A lunch club 12–2 p.m.
	A breakfast club (with breakfast) 8–9 a.m.
	A holiday club

7. Would you be interested in attending an 'open evening' to discuss the findings of this questionnaire?

| Yes | | No |

If you would like to be advised if/when these services start, please complete your name and address.

NAME:

ADDRESS:

Figure 8.1. Sample questionnaire. Based on information supplied by the Pre-school Learning Alliance.

Are you asking for knowledge respondents may not have? Are the questions misleading or offensive?

It is a good idea to pilot a questionnaire by sending copies to a similar group of people to your target group. It will then be possible to see if the questionnaire has been worded correctly to give you the information you are seeking.

Make sure you add a date for the questionnaires to be returned by and consider how you will distribute them and get them returned. You can also use local organisations to translate your questionnaire into different languages. It may be possible to ask the local school to distribute your questionnaire to all their parents or to place copies in the doctor's surgery and health clinics. Community groups may also help with distribution. In such circumstances it is a good idea to place a box somewhere accessible for the return of the completed questionnaires, to increase the response rate.

Case study — Market research

Linda is a pre school worker in the south-east of England. She has worked for various employers since leaving the local college in 1990 with an NNEB qualification. Her experience of different settings is wide and she has knowledge and understanding of the needs of pre-school children and their families. Recently she participated in the successful award of accreditation at her place of employment and completed the CACHE Advanced Diploma in Childcare and Education in 2001.

Linda has always had the dream of owning her own nursery and with a colleague as her partner this is a dream that should soon be realised. They have found suitable premises in the centre of their town, near a church and local playing field. Having lived in the town for 11 years, Linda has a good understanding of the provision in the area and now needs to identify gaps in the market on which to base a successful business.

- What research will Linda and her partner need to conduct?

- Suggest sources of support for their plans.

Marketing

It is essential continually to research your market and to satisfy the needs of your customers. This is a component of staying in business. As a manager you will need to continue to offer a service to your customers that is set at a marketable yet profitable price. In order to market your early years setting you will need to establish a package that identifies clearly what you are able to offer prospective clients and the individual qualities that your setting has. Think carefully about product, place, price and promotion.

Product

- What are the benefits to the children and parents?
- What quality is offered?
- What training and qualifications do the staff have?

Place

- Is your establishment in a convenient setting?
- Do young families populate the location?
- Is it welcoming?
- Do you have good facilities?
- Are you near local bus services?
- Is parking available?

Price

- Set your fees carefully – too cheap and clients will not value you, too expensive and they will go elsewhere.
- Bear in mind the going rate for your type of setting and find out what the local competition is charging.
- Consider your costs.

Promotion

- How are you going to tell potential clients about your provision?
- In what areas can you sell your setting?
- Regularly review your marketing methods.

The marketing plan

It may be possible to formulate the above points as a marketing plan. This should involve the whole staff team. It can be decided who does what, how and by when; it will give you an overview of your marketing strategy. The plan could include a timetable, marketing objectives and budget.

Think it over

Consider the different tactics you could use in marketing an early years setting. These could include:

- brochures;
- open days;
- leaflets;
- networking;
- the Internet;
- local press.

What are the benefits and practical implications of each strategy?

A brochure is a good way of marketing your establishment and could set out the philosophy of your setting. This is a chance to establish your views on education and how these will be applied. The organisation, opening times and management of the setting can be included, as can staff experience and policies and procedures. Prospective clients will also be interested in your approach to behaviour and discipline.

Many settings are also marketed by 'word of mouth'. The location of new settings and their quality soon get around, via the playground communication system. Clients are very knowledgeable and discerning. By organising an open day and producing leaflets to accompany this you will be able to kick-start the process. It is always a good idea to get parents involved from the beginning, and to show the achievements of the children by organising events. This will also give you the opportunity to understand the needs of the local community better, as well as to market your setting.

The local press can be a good means of advertising your service, so cultivate positive relationships there. They will appreciate any new activity you are doing, particularly if it is of interest to the general public.

8.3 Legislation

Managers of childcare settings need to keep themselves up to date with regard to legislation in order to ensure that they are meeting requirements for registration and inspection. Legislation takes the form of primary legislation (Acts of Parliament) and secondary legislation (regulations and the like). The single most important legislation for managers currently is the Care Standards Act 2000.

It is essential to keep abreast of current practice and most managers do this by attending training, reading literature and discussion with colleagues. Training, advice and support are available through the local Early Years Development and Childcare Partnership and national associations such as the Pre-school Learning Alliance and the National Day Nurseries Association.

Care Standards Act 2000

Since the Care Standards Act 2000 there has been a single set of standards in relation to the care and education of children. These are enforced by Ofsted's Early Years Directorate. The Act stipulates a set of requirements relating to, for example, space per child and staff ratios, and these requirements are laid down in the National Standards (see Chapter 2). The National Standards must be met in order for a setting to be registered. There are four aspects to the regulation of settings for children under 8 years of age:

- registration;
- inspection;
- investigation;
- enforcement.

These are explained below, and inspection is considered in greater depth in Chapter 9.

Registration

The registration process assesses the suitability of the personnel and premises to provide care and education for children under 8 years of age. This is to ensure that all providers:

- meet the National Standards for their area of provision;
- protect children;
- ensure that all children are safe, well cared for and participate in activities that contribute to their development and learning;
- promote high quality in the provision of care and learning;
- can reassure parents that the setting is providing suitable care and education for their children, and that all staff are suitably qualified and police checked.

There is a process of application in order to be registered and Figure 8.2 outlines this.

Inspection

An Ofsted childcare inspector will visit your setting to provide a regular check, on the basis of at least one visit in every two years, to ensure that it meets the National Standards and other standards. During this visit the inspector's role is:

- to check your identity by looking at personal documents;
- to sign your Criminal Records Bureau forms, and those of your staff;
- to assess how many children you may be registered to care for;
- to view the equipment you intend to use;
- to assess your suitability through an interview.

An Ofsted inspector is also permitted to enter your premises and withdraw documentation if circumstances require it, such as in the case of a serious complaint.

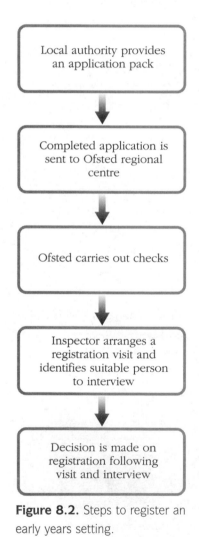

Figure 8.2. Steps to register an early years setting.

The National Standards (see Chapter 2) and the guidance to the National Standards (Ofsted, 2001) will help you and your team prepare for this visit. Chapter 9 looks in more detail at the Ofsted inspection process.

It will be necessary to provide certain documentation such as proof of identity, certificates of qualifications, insurance for any vehicles used to transport children and examples of written records kept on the children and of communication with parents.

After the inspection you will be informed of the outcome of the visit. This could include further checks or further action that is required. The inspector may impose conditions on your registration, for example on the number of children you care for. If all checks are complete and the inspector is satisfied, you will be told that your setting is being recommended for registration.

After the registration visit you will receive one of the following:

- *Action letter.* This details any work that you need to do if the inspector is not satisfied that you are meeting the standards. A timescale will be included and you must complete the action before you can be registered. An additional visit from an inspector may take place to check that the action has been carried out.
- *Checks.* Registration will not take place until checks on you, the premises and staff are completed.
- *Registration.* If registration has been recommended, you will be sent a letter recommending registration with certain conditions, for example the number of children permitted. You are able to discuss any conditions imposed by Ofsted. The letter will also ask for payment of the registration fee at this point. Failure to pay the fee promptly will result in delay of certification.
- *Intent to refuse registration.* If Ofsted intends to refuse registration, a 'notice of intention' will be issued. This is a legal document that outlines the reasons for refusal.

You have the opportunity to object to Ofsted's decision to refuse registration within 14 days of the issue of the 'note of intention'. If notice of appeal is not received within this period a 'note of decision' is then issued, which confirms the refusal. You are still able to appeal within 28 days to the Care Standards Tribunal, which is an independent body.

The registration certificate is proof of registration and must be displayed publicly. A £5 replacement fee is charged if the certificate is lost or damaged. The certificate is a legal document and gives you the right to provide care and education in your chosen setting unless:

- you have any of the conditions of registration changed, either as a result of a request by you or because Ofsted decides to make changes;

- your registration is cancelled;
- you resign your registration.

You will need to continue to demonstrate your suitability to be a provider throughout the time that you remain registered. Ofsted will monitor this through regular inspections and other visits, and by following up any complaints received about the service you provide. If there are any changes to the conditions of registration, Ofsted will normally work with a setting in order to minimise disruption to the service being offered. However, in some circumstances Ofsted has the power to shut a setting with immediate effect.

Always check the identity of Ofsted inspectors who visit your setting. They all carry identification and authorisation documents. After registration, an Ofsted childcare inspector will visit at least once every two years to ensure that you are still meeting the National Standards and that you still provide suitable care and education.

Investigation

This refers to any action taken following a complaint, an allegation, or when a breach of requirements is suspected. Ofsted inspectors are entitled to carry out investigations to check that you are meeting the National Standards and are a suitable childcare provider.

Enforcement

Ofsted can take action if you do not meet the National Standards. If providers are judged unsatisfactory, enforcement action can include cancellation of registration. You have the right to appeal. In extreme cases prosecution may also take place.

Inspectors can:

- enter premises at all reasonable times;
- inspect and take copies of any records kept;
- seize and remove any document or material that may be used as evidence of failure to comply with the law or the National Standards;
- take measurements, photographs or make recordings;
- interview the manager in private;
- interview another adult in private if that person consents.

Other legislation

The National Standards refer to regulations required for registration under the Children Act 1989 and this is another important piece of legislation that early years managers need to be conversant with. The National Standards are closely linked to the Children Act and this is manifested by the need to have policies and procedures in place, to have staff checked for suitability, to keep records on staff and to notify Ofsted of any changes in the premises. Links to the Children Act are clearly outlined in the guidance to the National Standards (Ofsted, 2001). Records will need to be kept in accordance with the National Standards, some of which fall within the scope of the Children Act 1989:

- registers;
- accident records;
- medication records.

These must be kept for a minimum of 2 years from the date of the last entry. You must also keep records of the children's details such as addresses and contact telephone numbers.

You will need to make your own decision about the length of time other records are kept, although also bear in mind that organisations such as the Inland Revenue will have their own requirements. Information may be contained in your records that will be of long-term benefit to the child, particularly records containing details on behavioural or medical matters. You will need to consider which documents should transfer with a child to a new setting (you must ensure that you will have future access to them) and where to store documents when a setting closes. Documents may need to be used for future legal action, as in child protection cases.

Other records that you may wish to keep are a daily diary, attendance records, an introductory leaflet to the setting, a record of achievement for each child, and any compliments, comments, or references the setting has received. Staff details, such as qualifications and rotas, environmental health and fire officer reports will also enable you to show evidence of compliance with regulations.

Records should normally be kept on the registered premises, where authorised people can easily access them. They will need to be kept confidentially, for example in a lockable filing cabinet.

The National Standards also makes reference to the code of practice for the identification and assessment of children with special educational needs. For details of this legislation and further information on the Children Act, see Chapter 9.

Think it over

Research other Acts an early years manager needs to have some knowledge of. This could be through the local Early Years Development and Childcare Partnership or national associations such as the Pre-school Learning Alliance and the National Day Nurseries Association. The legislation could relate to sex or race discrimination, health and safety, fire safety, food safety or employment rights.

8.4 Policies and procedures

In order to conform to the National Standards, and the inspection and registration process, each establishment must ensure certain mechanisms are in place. These include policies and procedures and the organisation of the setting.

As a team it is important to work together to create workable policies and procedures that cover all areas of the National Standards. Policies refer to a course of action agreed by the setting and procedures dictate the way in which the task is to be performed.

A policy is a written document that sets out the rules by which a setting operates. All the members of staff should agree to it so that they feel a part of the process. A policy will need to be reviewed regularly and should be considered a living document that is adapted in pace with changes in your setting. All staff must be given a copy of policies, perhaps in the format of a booklet or portfolio, which must be kept up to date. This must also be accessible for everyone involved in the setting, including students on placement as part of their course or as work experience. This also applies to pre-schools that are run by a committee: policies should be accessible to committee members and to governors of schools that are running after-school provision. Policy documents should always be accessible to parents, too. To this end, many settings find it useful to display policies on the parents' notice board.

Table 8.1 lists the areas that should be covered by the policies.

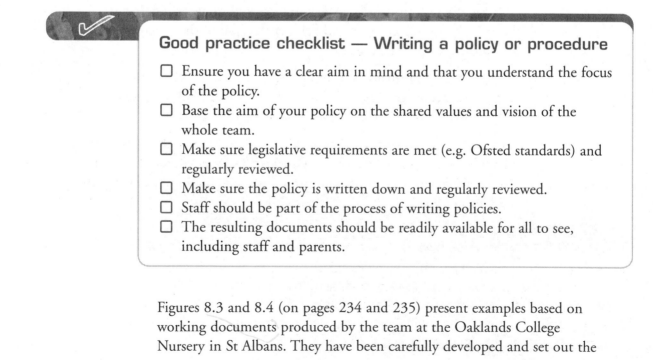

Good practice checklist — Writing a policy or procedure

- ☐ Ensure you have a clear aim in mind and that you understand the focus of the policy.
- ☐ Base the aim of your policy on the shared values and vision of the whole team.
- ☐ Make sure legislative requirements are met (e.g. Ofsted standards) and regularly reviewed.
- ☐ Make sure the policy is written down and regularly reviewed.
- ☐ Staff should be part of the process of writing policies.
- ☐ The resulting documents should be readily available for all to see, including staff and parents.

Figures 8.3 and 8.4 (on pages 234 and 235) present examples based on working documents produced by the team at the Oaklands College Nursery in St Albans. They have been carefully developed and set out the

Table 8.1. Policies and procedures required within an early years setting

Areas to be covered	Policy and procedure documents required
Organisation	Operational plan showing how the setting runs and how the resources are used to meet the needs of the children Procedure for lost or uncollected children Registration system for children and staff
Care, learning and play	Children's activities, to cover physical, intellectual, emotional, social and moral development
Safety	Risk assessment Record of visitors Emergency procedures (e.g. fire) Procedures for outings Vehicle records, including insurance and approved drivers Personal items policy
Health	Administration of medicines Parental consent forms for administration of medicines, sun cream and emergency treatment Accidents and first aid Health and hygiene statement 'Sick children' policy 'No smoking' policy
Nutrition and serving of food	Records of individual children's dietary needs Food management policy
Equal opportunities	Equal opportunities and anti-bias/anti-discriminatory policy
Special needs	Written policy on special needs and code of good practice
Behaviour	Policy on behaviour management Incident record
Child protection	Child protection policy
Working in partnership with parents and carers (see Chapter 5)	Admissions policy and procedure to join waiting list Complaints procedure Activities provided for children Contract with parents Parental consent forms 'Working with parents' policy

rules by which the nursery works. If you use documents from other settings as a guide, make sure that you adapt them with the help of your staff to fit the requirements of your setting and Ofsted.

New staff should be given copies of policies and procedures as part of the induction process and given the opportunity to discuss them with their line

The following behaviour is considered unacceptable in the nursery, whether towards an adult or another child:

- Biting
- Hitting
- Pinching
- Inappropriate language
- Throwing/breaking toys/equipment/furniture

Nursery staff will encourage and support children to develop a sense of right and wrong by helping children to cooperate in the nursery.

Staff will always try to explain, reason with and calm the child.

If the antisocial behaviour continues, the staff will direct the child to more positive activities.

If a child has hurt/upset another child they will be encouraged to apologise to the injured party.

As a last resort the child will be removed from the situation and asked to sit with a member of staff for a few moments to calm down.

Any incident of discipline will be brought to the parents' attention and discussed with them.

Staff will be aware of the age and stage of development of the child and of any cultural, linguistic or particular needs.

Shouting or physical punishment will not be used. Physical intervention, i.e. holding, will be used only to prevent injury to the child, other children or an adult, or serious damage to property.

Figure 8.3. Example of a discipline policy.

manager. As a manager you may wish to compile a staff handbook or pack and ask new staff to sign documentation to say they have read and understood the policies and procedures of the setting. Many establishments do this in the induction period to ensure new members of staff are conversant with the policies and procedures of the setting from the start of their employment.

A framework for writing a policy could be to include:

- the aims of the policy;
- methods of implementing the policy;
- procedures for monitoring and reviewing.

Contain children in a safe area.

Person in charge takes a head count and register of children on the trip. One member of staff to search the immediate area.

Inform the security/information desk if appropriate.

Ring emergency services and give as much detail as possible regarding location and time last seen, description of child, and current location of group and nursery details.

Inform the nursery manager/deputy. They will give instructions (e.g. return to nursery). The police or the nursery will inform the parent.

On return to the nursery, staff will be asked to document the incident.

Figure 8.4. Example of a policy on what to do if a child is lost on an outing.

Think it over

As a manager it is worth regularly reflecting on the nature of the policies that you have in place.

- How could you ensure that all policies are up to date?
- How could you ensure that they cover every area of the care and education of children and meet National Standards?
- How could you ensure that staff and management read, understand and agree to the policies and procedures?
- What kind of consultation process might you implement to review documentation?

Conclusion

This chapter has looked at the administration of the childcare setting and has considered the role of the manager in running a successful establishment that offers quality provision. The emphasis has been on business responsibilities and legal obligations, and ways in which to meet these, for example through the creation of policies and procedures.

Check your understanding

1   In the area where you live or work, what childcare is available? Is there room for expansion? How would you find out this information?
2   Consider how you would market a new nursery in your area.
3   How would you ensure you were providing a quality service?
4   How could you make the childcare you provide accessible and affordable?

References and further reading

Department for Education and Employment (1998) *Meeting the Childcare Challenge*, Cm 3959. London: DfEE. Available at www.surestart.gov.uk/aboutsurestart/challenge.

Department for Education and Skills (2003) *National Standards for Under 8s Day Care and Childminding. Full Day Care*, DfES/0651/2003. London: DfES. Available at www.surestart.gov.uk/_doc/0-ACA52E.PDF. Copies can be ordered from DfES Publications, Nottingham, telephone 0845 602 2260.

Hawksworth, J. (2004) *The Economic Costs and Benefits of Providing Universal Pre-School Childcare in the United Kingdom*. London: PricewaterhouseCoopers. Available at www.pwcglobal.com/extweb/newcolth.nsf/docid/8E02F97C38F7293785256E6700079E5B.

Ofsted (2001) *Full Day Care: Guidance to the National Standards*. London: DfES. Available at www.ofsted.gov.uk/about/childcare. Copies can be ordered from DfES Publications, Nottingham, telephone 0845 602 2260.

Useful websites

Care Standards Act: www.legislation.hmso.gov.uk/acts/acts2000/20000014.htm.

Childcare links: www.childcarelink.gov.uk (provides links to Children's Information Services).

Daycare Trust: www.daycaretrust.org.uk (promotes affordable childcare for all, and offers advice and information).

Department for Education and Skills: www.dfes.gov.uk (produces circulars and guidance).

Health and Safety Executive: www.hse.gov.uk (gives information on health and safety at work).

Information Commissioner's Office: www.dataprotection.gov.uk.

National Day Nurseries Association: www.ndna.org.uk.

Office for Standards in Education (Ofsted): www.ofsted.gov.uk.

Pre-school Learning Alliance: www.pre-school.org.uk.

9 Political and Social Issues and the Management of Change

At the beginning of the last century, children in the UK were treated very differently to the children of today. We have seen vast changes in the way children and their parents and carers are perceived and treated. In more recent years, children have become the subject of political debate and they are now at the top of the government's agenda. Parents and carers have, through legislation, been given clarity about their responsibilities and a voice in how their children are treated by professionals. Similarly, early years professionals have seen vast changes in the care and education of young people.

Managers in early years settings – in the main day nurseries, nursery schools and pre-school settings, some of which will be in the private and some in the voluntary sector   are at the front line of the implementation of government strategies and guidelines. This has meant that today's nursery manager has had to keep abreast of all that is happening in the early years world. Ground-breaking changes have been made in the last 20 years alone. It is essential that managers keep themselves up to date with current thinking, practice and policy. It is beneficial for them to be involved in networking with other professionals and local authorities, to help keep the channels between the implementers and the policy-makers open. They are the most experienced in dealing with children, parents and carers on a day-to-day basis.

This chapter looks at the wider issues surrounding early years services. Some of these issues may not directly affect what happens in the everyday management of an early years setting but it is vital for the manager to be aware of what is taking place across the sector. Managers who have a wide knowledge base are far more likely to be

respected by their teams and will feel more confident in dealing with outside agencies. Managers will have to implement changes. These changes can be externally enforced or they may need to take place for a variety of reasons internal to the setting. This chapter also looks at how the manager can effectively manage change as part of a process that starts with the identification of need. The following issues are covered:

9.1   Government initiatives.

9.2   Children's rights and legislation.

9.3   Keeping children safe.

9.4   Promoting racial equality.

9.5   Child poverty.

9.6   Managing change.

9.1 Government initiatives

Children are high on the government's agenda. A Minister of State for Children has been appointed. The first-ever governmental National Childcare Strategy was launched in 1998 (see Chapter 8). The Strategy was part of a package of policies designed to tackle child poverty and social exclusion (the aim is to end child poverty by 2020). This section covers a few other important initiatives. Sources of further information on these appear in the list of useful websites at the end of the chapter.

Every Child Matters

On 8 September 2003, the Prime Minister launched the long-awaited Green Paper *Every Child Matters* (Department for Education and Skills, 2003a). As *Every Child Matters* is a Green Paper and so is intended to promote discussion, at present there have been no changes to the law. The present obligations and requirements still stand, of course, but it is certain that there will be changes in legislation in the near future which will restructure the way services for children and their families in the UK are run. This will also have a knock-on effect on the expectations of parents and carers and on the manager's responsibility to widen provision and services to families. Knowledge of the Green Paper is essential for all managers in early years settings – they need to be aware of the direction the government plans to move in and be looking at ways in which any changes may affect the service they are offering.

Every Child Matters begins by listing five key outcomes for children:

- being healthy – having a healthy lifestyle while enjoying good physical and mental health;
- staying safe – being protected from harm and neglect;
- enjoying and achieving – getting the most out of life, while gaining skills for a productive adulthood;
- making a positive contribution – not engaging in antisocial behaviour but making a positive contribution to the community and society;
- economic well-being – achieving their full potential in life and not being held back by socio-economic difficulties.

The Green Paper insists that we need these advantages for all children but the latter part of the report focuses on those children who are most at risk in society, that is, those who are neglected or abused, become involved in antisocial behaviour, who experience failure in the education system or who become pregnant as teenagers. The government also wants to help children who are unaccompanied asylum seekers, as well as young people involved in prostitution.

Chapter 2 of the Green Paper reiterates the government's commitment to the following:

- ensuring children are safe against bullying and homelessness;
- SureStart (see below);
- tackling child poverty;
- raising school standards;
- improving children's access to health services;
- more investment in youth services.

Chapter 3 of the Green Paper outlines the support for families and parenting, such as family learning programmes, a national helpline and school-centred support. The need for specialist support for parents of children with special needs is also highlighted, as is the need for support for young carers and children whose parents might be in prison. It also looks at the improvement of the fostering and adoption services.

So that there can be improved information-sharing (termed identification, referral and tracking) to enable services to work collaboratively, local information 'hubs' will be developed in every authority and will consist of a list of all children living in the area, with details about them, so that it can be quickly ascertained whether they are involved with any of the agencies. This will mean that children can be 'flagged up' if there is any concern about them, which will aid early intervention. There is recognition of the concomitant need to respect the individual's privacy, as these measures do raise questions about when such information can be shared and by whom. The 'identification, referral and tracking' measure promises to be a 'tool' so that children do not fall through the gap and services are made aware of concerns at an early stage. However, there will need to be clear guidelines in line with the Human Rights Act 1998 and the United Nations Convention on the Rights of the Child (discussed below), which has been ratified by the UK.

Think it over

- How might the measures introduced by the Green Paper *Every Child Matters* affect the procedures in early years settings?
- What problems do you think there could be in enforcing identification, referral and tracking?

National Service Framework for Children, Young People and Maternity Services

The National Service Framework (NSF) was announced in February 2001. The aim is to develop standards across the National Health Service and local authority social services for children. The key objectives of the NSF are:

- to modernise the present system;
- to break down professional boundaries;
- to encourage partnership between agencies.

Children's trusts

Children's trusts integrate local education, social care and some health services. Most areas are aiming to have trusts set up by 2006 but there are already many 'pathfinder' trusts. Their core features are:

- clear short- and long-term objectives covering the five Green Paper outcomes (mentioned above);
- a children's services director;
- single planning and community functions, supported by pooled budgets, to facilitate the development of an overall picture of children's needs.

Children's trusts will be responsible for services across health, social care and education. These new services will be run from children's centres and extended schools. Extended schools are intended to provide a range of services and activities beyond the school day to help meet the needs of pupils. 'Pathfinder' schools have been set up to start offering this service.

Foundation degrees

The qualifications framework of those professionals working with children will be reviewed. This will mean new challenges for early years workers and highlights the importance of sharing good practice. Professionals across all the sectors of health, social care and education need to establish forums for discussion and sharing of common goals.

The new 'senior practitioner' status, which is gained by completing a foundation degree in childhood studies, will be a useful and transferable qualification for those practitioners wanting to be involved in the new approaches. Many early years workers who have achieved level 3 qualifications are presently studying for foundation degrees and these have been endorsed by the sector. Funding may come not only from the Department for Education and Skills but also from SureStart and some Early Years Development and Childcare Partnerships. (Information on foundation degrees can be sought from your local further education college or university.)

Integration

Integration is key to the present government's strategy for working with families. Historically, parents and carers developed their own integrated service by drawing on the support of grandparents, relations, pre-schools and school, and even neighbours. This would have been achieved within a strong community network. In the present day, however, this can be difficult, as families are often dispersed and not part of a familiar, close-knit community. Parents and carers are often faced with trying to find suitable childcare if they are working and are not able to depend upon close family or neighbours (as they might have done formerly). In doing so, they will need to take certain factors into consideration:

- Who is to provide the childcare – childminder, nursery, friend, after-school club?
- Are they reliable and dependable?
- Are they trustworthy and suitably qualified?
- Where is childcare to be provided – at work, near work, near home?
- What will it cost?
- Is it worth doing? (Will we be better off?)

Integrated services must be able to provide for a variety of diverse needs (Figure 9.1). The most effective service for families is one which provides

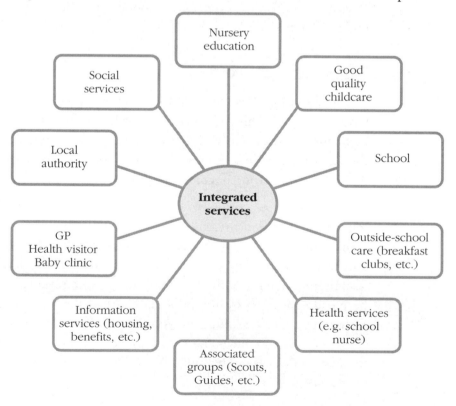

Figure 9.1. An integrated service provides good quality services for all the family.

for all. One example is a 'wrap-around' service (day care, sessional care, nursery, school and after-school). Similarly, integrated health services for families dealing with long-term illness or medical conditions should also offer practical, emotional and financial help.

What action could an early years setting take to work towards becoming part of an integrated service?

SureStart

SureStart is a government-funded programme which began in 1998 and is an integral part of the Children, Young People and Families Directorate. The programme is both far-reaching and innovative and its budget is promised to rise to £1.5 billion by 2005–6. The unit works with all the other agencies, as shown in Figure 9.2.

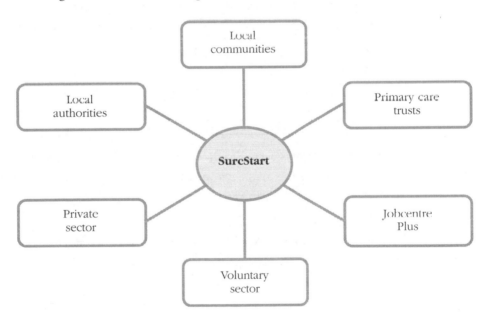

Figure 9.2. SureStart model for integrating services.

The programme is a comprehensive service which will support families, from pregnancy to those with children aged 14 years. The service aims to work with children for the following reasons:

- The earliest years are the most important and young children are particularly vulnerable to environmental influences.
- Multiple disadvantage for young children was becoming a growing problem.

- The quality of services varied for children and their families across the country.
- The under-4 age group needed more concentrated attention of services.
- The cycle of social exclusion can be broken with community-based comprehensive programmes of early intervention and support.

If this early intervention were to take place it would prevent greater costs for government in the future – prevention rather than cure!

SureStart has recognised a need for:

- the involvement of parents as well as children;
- not labelling families as 'problem families';
- the programme to last long enough to make a difference;
- consultation with communities and parents;
- culturally appropriate services.

The SureStart programme was therefore a real endeavour to put 'joined up' thinking' into place and target the very youngest children and their families to prevent rather than cure. It is making a difference to the lives of children. In particular, in disadvantaged areas it ensures the provision of the following:

- free education for 3- and 4-year-olds;
- affordable, high quality childcare;
- after-school care and activities;
- children's centres;
- health and family support.

The programme works with parents and children and includes parents in decision-making about relevant and needed services. It also has its own set of principles:

- services should be for everyone;
- they should be flexible at the point of delivery;
- support should be provided at the earliest stage of development;
- services should be respectful and transparent;
- they should be community driven and professionally coordinated;
- the focus must be on outcomes.

SureStart is an excellent example of working across agencies as part of the 'joined up' approach. It brings together services for children and their families to ensure that all children get the right 'sure start' and are not disadvantaged for any reason. Every SureStart programme provides core services to families:

- home visiting and outreach workers;
- good quality play and learning experiences for children;
- good quality health care and advice (including antenatal advice);
- support for children with special needs.

SureStart works closely with local authorities, primary care trusts, Jobcentre Plus and private and voluntary agencies. Its programmes are concentrated in neighbourhoods where a high proportion of children are living in poverty and where social service providers can help them to succeed. Districts were selected by the government but decisions about catchment areas were made locally. This is to encourage both strong parental and community involvement, and all agencies to work together.

There are over 500 SureStart programmes at present, helping up to 400,000 children living in disadvantaged areas. Children's centres provide all of these services and more, and will have a significant role to play in implementing the government's plans. The centres also serve as examples of excellence in early years practice and are supporting the training of the childcare workforce.

Ofsted and the inspection process

There are different types of inspections, depending upon the setting being visited, and they follow different legal frameworks:

- maintained schools (under section 10 of the Schools Inspection Act 1996);
- funded nursery education (under section 122 of the School Standards and Frameworks Act 1998);
- childcare (under Part XA of the Children Act 1989 and as inserted in the Care Standards Act 2000).

These standards will determine the expectations of the Ofsted inspectors when they inspect any setting under these headings.

In August 2003, Ofsted produced *Early Years: The First National Picture* (a very useful report, which you should obtain as it also contains information about the outcomes of inspections, as well as complaints, investigation and enforcement – see list of references). This gave an overall summary of the make-up of childcare in England. It stated that:

> 'On 31 March 2003, Ofsted had 99,300 registered childcare providers in England on its database. Of these 68,200 were childminders, 9,600 full day care providers, 11,600 sessional day care providers, 8,000 out of school care and 1,900 crèches. Around 1,700 providers were offering more than one type of care.'

The Early Years Directorate of Ofsted has a statutory responsibility to ensure that providers of day care for children are suitable and that they comply with the National Standards. Ofsted has the power:

- to grant, refuse or cancel registration;
- to impose, remove or vary conditions of registration, and grant or refuse requests for variations to the conditions of registration;
- to prosecute providers for specific offences.

As explained in Chapter 8, all day care providers (see definition above) must register with Ofsted and will require a named 'registered person' for inspection and registration purposes. Ofsted guidelines describe a 'suitable person' to be registered to run a setting by their qualification level – level 3 with 2 years' experience of working with children. The setting will need to pay a fee for registration and there is an annual fee once it is registered.

A full programme of combined inspections by Ofsted began in April 2003. Ofsted's combined inspections mean that all settings providing nursery education and receiving government funding for 3–4-year-olds will be inspected and scored on a three-point scale for the quality of nursery education – good, satisfactory and unsatisfactory. In these inspections judgements will be made about the quality of leadership and management and its effect on the progress of children who receive funded nursery education. This is of course very important as the manager will need to demonstrate the following:

- leadership of the setting (covered in Chapter 1);
- the ability of the setting to assess its weaknesses and strengths (Chapter 2);
- how effective the nursery is at monitoring and evaluating the education it provides (Chapter 3);
- commitment to improving care and education for children.

In the past, the Ofsted inspector would make recommendations for improvement, but this is no longer done: the burden is now on the setting to rectify any weaknesses identified by Ofsted. After the initial feedback and as a result of the inspection, the manager or registered person will receive a report on the combined inspection, which will be in three parts:

- characteristics of the setting;
- whether registration will continue and whether any actions or conditions will be imposed for this;
- judgements about the quality of the nursery education, which will include comment on any key issues for further action.

The manager will need to draw up an action plan that states what will be done to meet any requirements. This action plan must be produced within 40 days of receiving the report and made available to parents of all 3–4-year-olds who are state funded.

If you were a manager in an early years setting who was expecting an inspection in the next 6 months.

- How would you prepare yourself?
- What would you do to make your staff ready for the inspection?
- How would you inform parents?

9.2 Children's rights and legislation

The majority of professionals working with children will probably state that most of their work underpins protecting the rights of children. The League of Nations drafted the first Declaration of the Rights of the Child in 1924. In the UK there has long been a concern about how to address the 'needs' of children and there was little emphasis on ensuring their rights. Children are, of course, vulnerable members of society and are dependent, particularly in the early years, on the adult advocating for them. In early years settings it is important that the rights of the child should be considered when making decisions about their future or their developmental progress. Some children are faced with situations where, for reasons beyond their control (family breakdown, abuse, domestic violence or poverty), their rights are being taken away from them. It is important for early years practitioners to ensure that they know the legislation which supports children.

The United Nations Convention on the Rights of the Child

The 1989 United Nations Convention on the Rights of the Child (CRC) is one of the primary resources for anyone who is looking at developing services for children. It was ratified by the UK in 1991. The articles within it cover every aspect of a child's life (children are those under 18 years of age). The CRC highlights the need for countries to work together and 191 countries have now ratified it; only the USA and Somalia have not. All countries that ratify the CRC are required to produce a report after the first 2 years and subsequently every 5 years. The CRC says that the best interests of the child must always be considered and that their views must be taken into account at all times. The CRC contains 54 articles, which address the rights to:

- survival;
- development;
- protection;
- participation.

The UN Committee on the Rights of the Child is responsible for monitoring the implementation of the CRC and in October 2002 it issued a report on the UK. Some of this report praised what was going on in the UK and acknowledged positive moves in areas such as race relations legislation and promotion of children's rights in the UK's international aid policies. The Committee made a recommendation that the UK establish children's commissioners to ensure that the rights of children and young people are being upheld. Wales was the first nation in the UK to implement this and the first children's commissioner began work in March 2001. The Green Paper *Every Child Matters* stated that this will come into force in England as well. The commissioners' role is an independent one and therefore they have the power to review proposed legislation, listen to the views of children and young people, and ensure that children's best interests are being met. This will include investigating the effectiveness of the law, practice and services. The UN Committee also had concerns about the lack of coordination across government departments and the 'piecemeal' approach to putting some aspects of the CRC into law. The government has now put strategies into place to address these concerns.

The Children Act 1989

The Children Act 1989, which came into force on 14 October 1991, was one of the most far-reaching pieces of legislation of its time. It had a major impact on the law relating to children. It repealed 55 statutes and introduced new guidance and regulations on virtually every aspect of private and public childcare. The Act attempted to put the rights of children high on the agenda, as it acknowledged the importance of the wishes of the child. Section 17 of the Act states that is the duty of local authorities to safeguard and promote the welfare of children who are in need. They are required under this statute to provide a range of services appropriate to meet those needs. These are some of the main points of the Act:

- the well-being of the child is paramount;
- statutory services for children in need were introduced;
- parental responsibility is highlighted, as is parents' partnership with the local authority;
- the race, culture, language and religion of the child are to be respected;
- services for children and their families are to be coordinated to ensure holistic provision;
- children are generally best looked after in their families;
- registration and inspection of early years providers were established;
- orders became available to protect children from harm or abuse.

The Act made duties and powers available to enforce a court order in the case of a child needing protection from harm. The Act also introduced the concept of a 'child in need' in Part III, section 17. Part III stresses the importance of family support services, which should safeguard and promote the welfare of the child and offer assistance to parents to bring up their children. Parts IV and V of the Act relate to the local authorities' duty to provide protection for children who have suffered or who are likely to suffer significant harm. Part V provides guidance on the legal steps which may be taken to protect a child. The Act recognises the desirability for children to be brought up by their parents.

A number of reports have looked at various sections of the Act and the results of their implementation. The following suggestions have been made:

- A shift is needed to a more positive partnership between families and services.
- Services should be aimed at preventing family breakdown.
- There is a need for more and better planning of interventions to meet the needs of children.
- Enquiries into whether or not abuse has taken place were alienating parents. It is now seen that assistance and support should be given to maintain a preventive approach.
- There has been an inconsistent response to safeguarding the welfare of children from minority groups and those children with disabilities.
- There has been a lack of attention to parenting issues and skills.

9.3 Keeping children safe

One of the most important responsibilities of anyone working with children is to protect them. The protection of children in their care is an integral part of childcare and education workers' duties and moral code.

The death of Victoria Climbié at the hands of her guardian brought child protection into the limelight once again and highlighted a need for further structural changes to local authorities. The subsequent report by Lord Laming (2003) was (at the time of writing) the latest in a list of 67 inquiries into severe child abuse that have been held in England since 1945. Many of the proposals made in the report into Victoria's death have had a profound effect on policy and have led to early intervention to prevent something similar happening again. The fact that there were 12 opportunities to save Victoria highlighted the need for seamless provision of services for children, and the need to ensure that everyone who comes into contact with children is accountable.

Even though early years practitioners may never come face to face with a child in the same situation as Victoria Climbié, this does not give cause for complacency. Vigilance is required and procedures must be followed. The registered person is responsible for the safety of the children. The manager of the setting (usually the registered person) may be the person the staff or parent or carer will approach with a concern about a child's well-being. All early years settings are required to have a 'designated child protection person' and the manager will need to allocate this role to an experienced team member or take on the role himself or herself. The designated person will need to remain objective and professional. The priority is to pass on all concerns to the relevant agencies. An early call to a fellow professional could save a child's life or at the very least assure the manager that all is well. If there should be any concerns raised, all staff should follow the correct procedures. The manager will need to support staff and let them talk through their anxieties and fears. Staff should be encouraged at appraisal to attend courses in child protection (these are especially useful for non-qualified staff). The manager will need constantly to keep up to date with any changes to the law or local policy.

Case study — Michelle's concerns

Michelle is head of room in a busy day nursery. There is a child whose behaviour has been concerning her for some time. She discusses this with the new manager, Claire, and relates some incidents which have worried her; Michelle also discusses a conversation she has overheard between parents. Claire asks her to make notes so that they have a written record of Michelle's concerns. Michelle carefully records observations of the child, and times and dates when the child was less communicative. Michelle speaks to Claire a second time and gives her the written record. The manager says that she will handle it but offers Michelle no further information or advice. Michelle is very upset by this response and leaves the office feeling indecisive about what to do next.

- What mistake did Claire make?

- How could she have handled this situation differently?

- Would you say Claire works well with her staff team, based on this incident?

The case study 'Michelle's concerns' illustrates a difficult situation for any member of staff, one that can cause a great deal of worry. Childcare professionals need to work together for the good of the child and to ensure that everything observed is documented, in line with local child protection procedures. In the main, the case study relates to a lack of communication within the staff team and reluctance on the part of the manager to share information with the staff member, which causes the latter to feel isolated. It is important that staff teams are aware of the setting's procedures and are aware of whom to contact if there is cause for concern. Each area will have a child protection procedure, which will include contact information for all the professionals working within the child protection team. Area child protection teams are maintained by the Department of Health and it is their role to develop agreed local policies and procedures for inter-agency work to protect children and promote their welfare. Managers should ensure they have a good relationship with the local health visitors, as they are a useful source of advice and guidance, and may also know the children within the setting.

Generally, managers will be dealing with comparatively minor incident within their settings. Staff may be concerned about a parent or carer who seems unusually stressed and impatient with a child, or a situation when a child and family are experiencing temporary difficulties caused by:

- loss of a parent or guardian;
- redundancy;
- financial pressures;
- illness in the family;
- the family moving house;
- new hours of working or promotion for one of the parents;
- a new baby;
- difficulties in dealing with the child in a particular stage of development, such as tantrums, toilet-training or challenging behaviour.

In such cases the manager will need to allow the family (both the child and the parents or carers) individual time. Parents may need to have time to have a friendly chat with the manager and during this time the manager will be able to offer advice or discuss the possibility (if needed) of involving other support, for example the health visitor. It is important that managers have information and contact details on the types of support available.

9.4 Promoting racial equality

Legislation and the Commission for Racial Equality

There is a statutory duty to promote racial equality and specific responsibilities have been laid down for schools. All managers of early years settings need to have read the guidance on the Race Relations Act 1976 and the Race Relations (Amendment) Act 2000, which are designed to eliminate racial discrimination and promote race equality and relations. Local authorities will have produced guidance for childcare settings and the Commission for Racial Equality (2002) has published its own guidance for schools, which supports settings in implementing the requirements of the Race Relations (Amendment) Act 2000.

By May 2002 all settings were advised to have a written statement of policy for promoting racial equality. They were also expected to develop an assessment or action plan to look at the impact of this policy on:

- staff;
- children;
- parents and carers of different racial groups.

Early years settings must evaluate the effects on the above groups of the following aspects of their practice:

- care, learning and play;
- admissions;
- behaviour policies and management;
- the curriculum;
- staff recruitment;
- guidance and support.

If the assessment or action plan is not carried out the Commission for Racial Equality is empowered to issue a notice of compliance.

Ofsted's role

In addition, the ways in which the setting addresses inclusion and valuing cultural diversity will be closely monitored by Ofsted. The registered person in the setting will need to show the strategies that are in place to 'overcome potential barriers to learning'. The staff team will be expected to monitor the children's behaviour to ensure that the setting does not have an adverse effect on the children's learning. Settings must be proactive and take steps to involve parents and carers from ethnic minorities. The setting will also need to collect and keep information on the ethnicity of all children and staff, for the purpose of monitoring equality of opportunity.

Good practice

The 2001 census showed that nearly one in eight pupils comes from a minority background. By 2010, the proportion is expected to be around one in five.

The Department for Education and Skills (2003b) has published the findings of a consultation. Data were gathered from 500 schools. The document identified certain characteristics of successful schools and found that there was a need to spread their good practice in the following areas:

- strong leadership – in implementing an effective strategy;
- high expectations – all pupils encouraged to fulfil their full potential;
- monitoring achievement and identifying areas of under-achievement;
- effective teaching and learning – support for bilingual pupils, cultural identities reflected in the lessons;
- ethos of respect and a clear approach to racism – a focus on prevention of racism, bad behaviour and bullying;

- parental involvement – parents and carers and the wider community involved in the life of the school.

Although the study related to schools, the points of good practice do apply to a great extent to early years settings. It is interesting that leadership and reflective management rate so highly as factors in success! Managers of early years settings can use the school experience as a model for the provision of opportunities for all.

Think it over

- As a manager, what practical things might you do to ensure the setting operates in a non-discriminatory manner?

- What might you have to do to meet the requirements of the Race Relations Act?

9.5 Child poverty

At present it is estimated that some 3.8 million children (one in three) live in poverty in the UK. In 1999, the government made a commitment to reduce child poverty by a quarter by 2004/5, by increasing benefit rates and supporting parents into work by introducing tax credits (see Chapter 8). However, some children, in particular asylum-seeking children, have suffered as a result of political decisions. Moreover, many anti-poverty proposals are long term and for parents living in deprived areas there is not imminently going to be a change in their situation.

Poverty is not caused solely by low income. Factors associated with poverty within a region include:

Poor housing is associated with poverty.

- the unemployment rate;
- the infant mortality rate;
- poor housing;
- numbers of accidents;
- child protection registration rates;
- poor engagement with education.

The emphasis in the present government's strategy is to help parents into paid employment and to continue investing in good quality, affordable childcare. According to the Day Care Trust, the typical cost of a childcare place for a child under 2 years in 2003 was £128 per week. For some parents living on state benefits or a low wage this is unaffordable.

Think it over

- How can 'poverty' be defined?

- If you had a child in your setting who you felt was living in severe poverty what would you do?

- What support could you offer the family?

Some people may find it hard to accept that many children are still living in poverty in the UK, but for some childcare workers and managers this will be readily evident in their setting. Childcare professionals are required to see the child holistically. Some projects and centres of excellence are working to address these needs.

9.6 Managing change

In the current climate, all early years settings must be prepared to implement change. The need for change may arise internally (within the setting) or externally (imposed upon the setting). The types of changes could involve:

- planned changes in strategy as a result of revised mission or goals for the setting;
- legislative changes or other government initiatives;
- the need to improve the practice and quality of services;
- the need to deploy people where they are most effective;
- the need to introduce cultural changes (e.g. to management style).

This can be difficult for the manager to deal with and can cause long-term problems if not handled correctly. Some changes imposed from outside may be more readily accepted by some members of staff if they feel that they are at least necessary. It is easier to make a change or develop an area of the provision if the team has been involved in the decision-making. It is often when the manager acts alone that a problem arises.

If you are going to introduce a new idea or way of working within your setting, it is good practice to consider the following:

- Is it technically feasible?
- Will it work?
- Is it politically acceptable?
- Is it for or against the interests of the people who will be asked to implement it?

- Is it consistent with the practices of the setting or will it mean introducing new administrative ideas, for example?
- Will it make things better – more efficient, easier, better for the children or their parents and carers?

When you have looked at all these factors you can then go about setting up a plan of action, which will involve the staff team from the outset, to engage them in the process. If you have already considered some of the risks, potential pitfalls and challenges, you will be able to pre-empt negative responses. You can do this by making a list of possible negative and positive effects/solutions. For example, see Table 9.1, which shows the hypothetical analysis of a manager who will be asking staff to move around the nursery and not stay with the same age range all the time.

Table 9.1. Example of a plan of action to move staff around the nursery and not stay with the same age range

Questions surrounding your change	Possible negative responses	Possible positive effects/solutions
Will it work?	No. We have expertise in these areas. If we go into another age group we will be out of our depth.	Long term this will ensure sharing of good practice and provide variety for the children. Will allocate time to offer opportunities for sharing information.
Is it politically acceptable?	Some staff who have worked in the same area for a long time will hate the idea.	Will need to discuss as a group, and convince long-serving members of staff that their expertise is needed across the setting.
Will it make things better?	No. The children will find it unsettling. Things work well as they are.	Will need to show evidence things are not working well as they are. Also, explain that change will help meet the needs of the children.

It is very easy to become caught up in your own enthusiasm for an idea and presume that everyone will automatically go along with it! The case study 'Changing drinks time' illustrates this point.

Case study — Changing drinks time

Jan was the manager of a small nursery for 3–5-year-olds. She had been the manager for some years and had a well established, mature and very experienced staff. Jan had been observing that at 'drinks time' some of the staff had grown into the habit of standing at one end of the room drinking their coffee and having a friendly chat while the children were having their drinks and snack. Jan was worried about this, as the staff were not interacting with the children at all and some of the children were becoming a little disruptive and bored at drinks time. Jan decided that she would try to have drinks and snacks throughout the day and not at a set time, and to allow the children to choose when they wanted to have their drink. Jan told the staff enthusiastically about her decision. The team were not supportive of the idea. They complained to Jan about the spilt drinks and the lost opportunity for the children to 'socialise'. Very soon the idea had to be abandoned and drinks time was resumed.

- What were Jan's motives for making the changes?
- Would the changes have been a solution for the problem?
- Why did the staff not support the new idea?
- Can you think of any other ways in which this new idea could have been implemented?

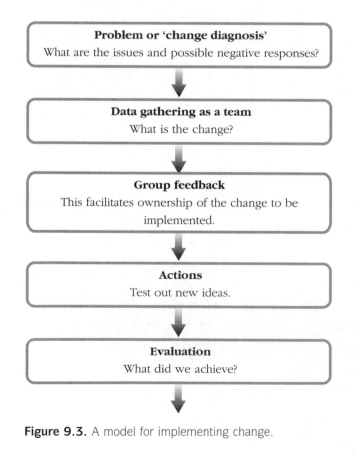

Figure 9.3. A model for implementing change.

Once the manager identifies a need for change and considers the ways in which that idea may be judged, it is time to involve the staff team. If the team are involved at this early stage the change can be implemented through them and they will take ownership. That way they can also feel part of the evaluation stage of the change and can make on-going assessments. This model is outlined in Figure 9.3.

The involvement of staff usually makes the change easier but on occasion it can also weaken the original proposal, which can be frustrating for the manager. However, if the team have been involved in the process of change they are more likely to show commitment and enthusiasm than if they have been instructed or told without prior warning. Even where changes have to be made because of outside influences such as

Ofsted or legislative requirements, it is still far more effective if the team works together to implement the change. Team members will for the most part follow their leader but only if they feel that their leader is willing to listen to their ideas and is initiating the change for the good of all concerned.

Conclusion

This chapter has briefly explored some of the complex issues within the wider world of early years. It has also investigated how the manager would initiate a change within the setting, which is increasingly important in the current climate. It can be all too easy as a manager to develop 'tunnel vision' and become consumed by the day-to-day running of the setting. This is understandable, as the manager's role is a complex one and leading a team requires enthusiasm and drive. However, to become reflective practitioners, managers need to be aware of the wider early years picture. It is a fast changing area of work, growing rapidly and high on the government agenda. What happens to that agenda is of crucial importance to the early years manager. Government policies have an affect on the day-to-day running of the setting, the care and education of the children and the aspirations of the staff. The move towards more 'joined up' thinking will include all sectors of early years and it is important to be aware of what has happened and what might happen. Programmes such as SureStart are a good example of some of the ways in which early years expertise can be utilised to make a difference to children's lives. All early years workers need to be aware of the UN Convention and of the very real challenge of poverty in the UK.

Check your understanding

1   What were the most significant points raised in the Green Paper *Every Child Matters*?
2   What are the main aims of SureStart?
3   What is meant by a 'joint inspection'?
4   Who is responsible for child protection in an early years setting?
5   What would need to be included in a setting's statement of 'Aims and values' for it to be in line with the Race Relations (Amendment) Act 2000?
6   What is the CRC?
7   What might you need to consider if you were to implement a change in your setting?

References and further reading

Commission for Racial Equality (1997) *From Cradle to School. A Practical Guide to Racial Equality in Early Childhood.* London: CRE.

Commission for Racial Equality (2002) *A Guide for Schools.* London: CRE.

Cullen, D. and Lane, M. (2003) *Child Care Law. A Summary of the Law in England and Wales.* London: British Association for Adoption and Fostering.

Department for Education and Skills (2003a) *Every Child Matters*, Cm 5860. London: DfES. Available at www.dfes.gov.uk/everychildmatters/downloads.cfm.

Department for Education and Skills (2003b) *Aiming High: Raising the Achievement of Minority Ethnic Pupils. Consultation Summary.* London: DfES. Available at www.standards.dfes.gov.uk/local/midbins/ema/Aiming_High_Cnslt_Summary.DOC.

Gaine, C. (1995) *Still No Problems Here.* Stoke on Trent: Trentham Books.

Lane, J. (1998) *Action for Racial Equality in the Early Years.* London: National Early Years Network.

Lord Laming (2003) *The Victoria Climbié Inquiry. Report of an Inquiry.* Available at www.victoria-climbie-inquiry.org.uk/finreport/finreport.htm.

Ofsted (2003) *Early Years: The First National Picture.* London: Ofsted. Available at www.ofsted.gov.uk/publications/index.cfm?fuseaction=pubs.summary&id=3372.

Tassoni, P. *Supporting Special Needs: Understanding Inclusion in the Early Years.* Oxford: Heinemann.

Useful websites

Children Act 1989: www.hmso.gov.uk/acts/acts1989/Ukpga_19890041_en_1.htm.

Children's trusts: www.dfes.gov.uk/childrenstrusts/overview.

Commission for Racial Equality: www.cre.gov.uk.

Day Care Trust: www.daycaretrust.org.uk.

Extended schools: www.teachernet.gov.uk/wholeschool/extendedschools.

Foundation degrees: www.foundationdegree.org.uk.

National Service Framework: www.dh.gov.uk/PolicyAndGuidance/
HealthAndSocialCareTopics/ChildrenServices/ChildrenServicesInformation
/fs/en.

Ofsted: www.ofsted.gov.uk/about/childcare.

SureStart: www.surestart.gov.uk.

UN Committee on the Rights of the Child:
www.unhchr.ch/html/menu2/6/crc.

UN Convention on the Rights of the Child: www.unhchr.ch/
html/menu3/b/k2crc.htm.

Index